Snapshot

Snapshot

By

Ryan O'Reilly

Black Oak Press

For further information, please contact:
Angie Pivac
2831 S. Ingram Mill
Springfield, MO 65804

Book design by:
Arbor Books, Inc.
19 Spear Road, Suite 301
Ramsey, NJ 07446
www.arborbooks.com

Printed in the United States

Snapshot
Ryan O'Reilly
1. Title 2. Author 3. Fiction

Library of Congress Control Number: 2007923784

ISBN 10: 0-9794128-0-3
ISBN 13: 978-0-9794128-0-6

This story is dedicated
to the woman who inspired it.

A beautiful Colorado love, who once reminded me
that life is only there for those who want it the most.

Also:
To the people in my life who have made the world
interesting enough to write about.

Like one that on a lonesome road
Doth walk in fear and dread,
And having once turned round walks on,
And turns no more his head;
Because he knows a frightful fiend
Doth close behind him tread.

—Samuel Taylor Coleridge
The Rime of the Ancient Mariner, VI, st. 10

For I am a stranger with thee, and a sojourner,
as all my fathers were.
O spare me, that I may recover strength,
before I go hence, and be no more.

—Psalms 39:12–13

1
═

I met Bryan Hillary on the back byways of the vast Nebraska plains in the early summer of 2006. We had both just experienced strange events in our lives and separately decided to take to the road and travel the dark backwater of the country, the place from where all good stories flow.

For a long time I had forgotten about this part of America, having been lost in the cold processes of her politics, policies and the mechanics of industry and economy. The blind passions of my youth had evaporated and the empty monotony of the beginning of my adult life stared back at me, covering me like the hunched shadow of some feared angel waiting for me across the gulf of my next 50 or so years.

"Life is a snapshot memory," Bryan told me in a recent letter, "and it is strange and beautiful. If you don't remember that then it will all pass you by and you won't even know it was there to miss."

Before meeting Bryan, I didn't understand what that meant, but now I do. I have since seen it: this strange land and these odd people, the greatness of our country measured in the experience of its rippling beauty, and the reserved wanderings of its forgotten people.

Bryan Hillary and I experienced this transcendence together, along the well-worn American highway. However, like anyone else I have experienced or ever will experience, all I have are the fragmented memories of our time together. He's gone now and I will never see him again. I try to remember pieces of him—the conviction of his words, the sound of his voice, the powerful look in his eye. Those fragments are the only heaven I know, the afterlife, and the windowless world of memory.

When we met, it was a pleasant and sweet summer evening, and the air was warm and damp. I could taste the dark aroma of new earth across the twisted winds of the continent, and it gave me the feeling that I was alive. The long, lingering day was beginning to fade and the dark shadow of night stretched its long arms across the sky.

It was an American sort of twilight, under the dome of distant lights with the smell of the rolling farmland in the distance and sense of the open reach of the country beyond, stretching to the great western ocean. We met, then traversed the long road together, traveling in the wake of legions of wayward travelers; for the West has always been the direction of hope for Americans, and a place to seek refuge from the present and the beginning of a new future. Thus we continued on together for a short time, and remained locked in the experience forever.

Those days were part of a strange time in my life, and before Bryan and I parted ways and he slipped into the recesses of the world, we saw the country together in its timeless beauty. We both had left our homes for one grand and marvelous loop through the heart of America—the part that people didn't seem to pay attention to anymore. The two of us began our journeys differently, but came together as the dying day faded over a small town on the Great Plains.

On a night filled with the uncomplicated senses of life, I found a man, a sweet friend, who changed everything about the world in my eyes. The endless meandering roads of the West reminded me that there was always that snapshot memory, and the moments within it; the sights, the smells, the taste, the touch, the love, the hate, the passion and the fear.

—————

At 28 years old, I found myself in the midst of a life which on the surface had seemed like a good idea: sensible, practical and normal. I had gone to college, found a job, met and proposed to a girl named Beth. This always felt like the typical progression of life and it had never occurred to me to question whether or not it was the right path.

My passionate intellectual stage had come and gone in college, and after school I had settled into stationary orbit around the processes of getting older. When I had started my university education, I participated in the normal regimen of college activities. I joined a fraternity, worked at a bar and attended every party and social function I could find. For my major I chose English literature.

This pursuit gave me romantic notions about the nature of the world, and I started to think in what I considered profound leaps, and surrounded myself with other dutiful and intellectual English majors. Practicality won in the end, though, and before long, English was a minor and business became my major. I learned. I tested. I graduated. That was college.

When I returned to my native Kansas City, I began my obligatory post-college, white-collar job. As time ticked away, and my career began to gain priority over my childhood dreams, my life had begun to show signs of added complication. My job became more involved, marriage and a family were on the horizon and I was getting close to ending my 20s and beginning my 30s. Time was moving whether I was ready for it to or not.

As days turned to months, and months to years, the memory of my youthful passions began to finally deflate and fade. As a child, I had dreamed about the limitless possibilities of adulthood, of becoming an astronaut or a doctor, but now all of that was gone. That colorful and sweetly spectacular fire that had driven me so high in my early years had slowly dried up and disappeared, and I was too busy to notice. I willingly allowed the sublime beauty of the world to mask itself behind the surreal, standardized existence of the modern college graduate.

It wasn't long, though, before things began to change. As I drearily began to wake up and realize an underlying resistance to my scripted life, I began to search for a way out of it. Initially, it was boredom that came over me, and my dissent came in the form of ranting blogs and homemade political attack ads, which I plastered all over the Internet, and moderate revulsion to normal social pursuits: dinner parties, fundraising benefits and all of those other seemingly worthwhile activities. These events became games to me as I walked about them with a ridiculous sense of superiority—as if I was the only person who felt trapped in this routine. Everything going on around me simply appeared as an attempt to understand the "great mystery" by people who contend themselves with sleeping through it.

Of course this isn't the case, as I later learned. All of us are either trapped, asleep, or both, and what I was feeling was nothing unique. Yet, that disconnection which I felt was producing negative results, and my boredom eventually eroded into outright contempt.

Like the dutiful legions of graduates before me, I had followed the accepted process of post-college complacency, grounded in the notion of collecting happiness through material acquisition and voluntary subjugation. Although I had a nice house, a job and a fiancée, I would occasionally consider that I was just following the herd through what were supposed be the most fascinating years of my life. I was in my late-20s, at the peak of my physical well-being and my exploratory mental capacity. Yet when I had nearly resigned myself to living out that dull fantasy, something happened. My life shifted just enough to allow me to slide out from under it.

2

One day in late May of 2006, my fiancée and I attended the wedding of a friend. This was to be the last day I would see Beth. It would be the last day of the charade, the last day before I was to take a giant step into places unknown.

At the time, I had a love-hate relationship with weddings. They were fun and good opportunities to see people squirm in overly lavish social settings, which is why I loved them. I hated them because they were reminders of the fate that awaited me. To me, getting married was one of the last doors to close, and it was one that could never reopen. However, I was young, and weddings were a constant part of my summer planning. I had arrived at the age when weddings advanced like avalanches, and it was only a matter of time before you were caught in one.

I tried to get out of going.

"These are *your* friends," I pleaded, "and I've had a terrible week at work."

5

"It will be fun," she said, annoyed, "and anyway, they're just as much your friends as they are mine now."

This was the ultimatum; the last rational exchange before the bell rang and the fight began. Unless, of course, I gave in and accepted defeat.

"Alright," I said, "I'll go and I will have fun with you."

This particular wedding was an unfortunate case of two people who should have done anything *but* marry. That fact didn't matter to Beth, though. To her, weddings were more than just ceremonies; they were social gatherings where she could gossip and show off to all of her friends. She was graceful and socially conscious in all the ways that I was not. It came to her naturally. She did her best to train me and bring me into her world. Naturally, I did my best to resist.

When the ceremony was over, there were a few hours to kill before the reception and we walked to a nearby pub with a group of friends who enjoyed thinking of themselves as happily married. After ordering beer and a bottle of white wine, the conversation turned toward the wedding the same way that people usually talked about death after a funeral.

After a while, I left the table for the men's room, and on my way back, saw my lovely bride-to-be standing at the bar, talking to a friend. I walked to the counter behind her to get the attention of the bartender. She didn't notice me as I stood there, leaning against the smooth counter. In the soft, muffled quiet of a bar on a Saturday afternoon, I heard the last part of a conversation that I was not supposed to hear. She leaned in close to her friend and I heard her sweet voice say, "Oh, it was the best weekend ever. That guy was amazing, we didn't sleep the entire night! I can't wait to go back to New York!"

To me, in that heartbreaking pause, the world stopped spinning. I had never been to New York with Beth. She had been there recently on a girls' weekend, and I had gone fishing with the guys.

As far as I had known, we had been in a truthful, honest relationship. I had shared many beautiful moments with this woman. I had laughed with her, fought with her and cried with her. I had let her into my family and into my complete trust, and I loved her. I had also always had a nagging thought that no matter how much I shared with her, I never really knew her. I dismissed this as good, old-fashioned paranoia, or at least late-20s male fear of commitment, but perhaps I should have listened to it.

My plastic life had just given me an out, and I intended to take advantage of it. I put my heavy hand unobtrusively on her shoulder and spoke her name in a low, dull tone. She shuddered, spun around and we looked at each other. I saw deception in her eyes, then her glance shifted from me to the floor. The truth about her conversation was evident.

I turned away from her and started back to the table that was filled with all of our friends, but stopped a few feet away. I saw only strangers and drifted instead toward the door. In the doorway I stopped, and my eyes met those of my friends. My mind told me to walk away, but my heart told me to say *something, anything.* I walked back to the table and they all watched me. A single tear dripped from my eye.

"Sometimes there are different paths to take," I said prophetically, "and this is where I have to leave you all. Good*bye.*"

The room was silent only to me, and I stopped to judge their reactions, then turned to the door. As I walked I felt their faces following me out of the corner of my eye, not saying a word. I went to the parking lot, put my hands on the hood of my car, and began to cry. I cried for Beth, for her being so cold, shallow and deceptive. I cried for myself because I was so naïve. I cried for humanity, because it no longer cared for me. My sadness quickly turned to anger and I left the parking lot and drove home.

I pulled into my driveway and parked in the garage, got out of the car and stood in the musty room, which was illuminated only by the light of the door opener. Looking around the grim interior, I saw the tools and domestic agricultural implements hanging limply from the wall, my set of golf clubs and a few other reminders of my sad life scattered about.

Then, something in the distant corner caught my eye. In the shadow, under a dirty cloth cover, was my old Harley-Davidson motorcycle. It was as if it had been strategically placed for me to see at that moment. I pulled the cover off the front, exposing the tire, the handlebars and part of the dark blue gas tank.

This bike had been for sale in an empty lot next to the bar where I worked during college, and I'd bought it without hesitation. It had always been my escape. On difficult days, I would hop on, disappear on the back roads for a few hours, and return feeling cleansed.

I sat on the dusty seat and grabbed the handlebars, dreaming of a chance to get away. In a split second, a throbbing pain washed over my body, and everything that had happened clouded over me. What came to my mind were pictures of loneliness and the thought of a world that didn't seem to need me. I thought about Beth. I thought about my job as a corporate hireling, and the fact that I sat in an office for eight hours a day devising clever marketing schemes to snare the unwary consumer. That was not the kind of career I had envisioned as a young boy. It wasn't that I hated the job, but I didn't love it either. It was a lifeless career. What I did hate was that while I pursued those passionate experiences in college I ultimately chose to return home and work for my father. I loved my father, but I had yet to create anything for myself, which was a depressing notion. In a split second, a vision crept into my mind and I knew what I was going to do.

The house sat dark through the dusty garage window, and I got off the bike and went inside. I paced around the first floor for a while, weighing my options, then pulled my phone out of my pocket and made two calls. The first was to my brother, to ask him if he would come over the next day and pick up my dog and take care of him for a while. The next was to Jim, a man who did some handiwork for me on occasion. I asked him to stop by when he had the chance and close up my house. I explained that I wanted him to prepare the old place to be vacant for a long time.

I hung up, dropped my cell phone into the garbage disposal, and flipped the switch on the wall next to the sink. The sound of shredding electronics filled the room to the top of the vaulted ceiling and I ran upstairs to my bedroom. I changed clothes, discarding my wedding suit into a heap on the floor and put on a pair of jeans, a black t-shirt and black boots. In the back of my closet sat my saddlebags, and I grabbed them and started packing. I pulled a leather jacket out of my closet and gathered some clothes, an atlas, a few personal items, three books, a sleeping bag and about $5,000 in cash that I had tucked under my mattress, and then I ran back down the stairs.

My aging black lab, Gunny, was in the backyard, and I went to say goodbye to him. He knew something was going on and he sat down and nuzzled my knees as I stroked the back of his neck. He had been my friend and constant companion through some strange and difficult times, and I felt a flash of guilt knowing that his reward for fidelity was abandonment.

"I'm sorry, old man," I said, running my fingers through his soft hair. "I'll be back for you in a while."

I went back into the garage, pulled the cover off my Harley and threw it into the corner in a dark, dusty pile. I tossed the saddlebags onto the back of the bike and secured them, then straddled the leather seat. I felt a renewed sense of life as I scrolled through my recent past and noticed how decidedly bland things had become.

My memory was of days filled with sitting in an office dreaming for the end of the day and the end of the week. When the weekends came I filled the hours with trips to the lake, golf games, dinner parties and other easily attended social obligations. As a younger man, I had seen my future life as being filled with passion, poetry and a long, lusty thirst for truth. Instead, I felt surrounded by the same auto-pilot people, whiling away the hours between work and sleep with activities that would quickly turn days to weeks, weeks to months and months to years. In the end, years would become decades and decades would become a lifetime, with little to show for it.

I turned the ignition switch on, pulled the choke and hit the start button. The old engine started right away-a good sign-and I wiggled it out of the garage and into the driveway. I used the remote control to close the door, then tossed it into the weeds by the side of the house.

There was a hesitation in my mind as I sat in the driveway and revved the engine, trying to build the courage to leave. I had no destination, just the sudden and unshakable desire to get as far away as

I possibly could. After one last look back, I popped the Harley into first gear, gripped the handlebars, and shot out of the driveway.

A short distance down the street, as I hit second gear, I saw a pair of headlights coming toward me. As the car passed, I caught the eye of my former fiancée sitting, flushed, in the passenger seat. She looked in my direction and our eyes met for a split second. I shifted to third gear and pulled hard on the throttle. I saw the flare of brake lights out of the corner of my eye and I punched two more gears and was off over the crest of a hill, and out of sight.

———

My first stop came at a gas station 25 miles outside of the city, sure that I was far enough away from the hell waiting for me back at home. A dirty, dented pay phone sat under the tall arc of a streetlight in the corner of the parking lot, and I stopped to call my father. I explained to his voicemail, not caring what his reaction would be, that I would be taking an extended leave of absence from work. I put the phone on the cradle and leaned back against a light pole that stood next to the phone booth.

My father and I had never talked much, and when we did, it was usually about business. I knew that he would understand what I was doing, and somewhere in my mind I could even picture him doing the same thing if he were young and in my situation. He would be angry, and most likely I would be unemployed upon my return, but I figured that I could just pick up the pieces later. As I thought about this, I began to notice the activity going on around the dusty parking lot with a clarity that felt foreign.

There was a young woman standing between her car and one of the gas pumps, struggling to hold a small child in one arm and fumbling for her gas cap with the other. At the other end of the lot, a truck full of young kids stood parked, two of them attempting to buy beer inside. Having fooled the apathetic clerk, they burst from the door like two young horses filled with energy over the explosion of spring, arms filled with brown bags. They jumped in the cab with their friends and the truck left the parking lot in a cloud of dust and exhaust. It was as if my sudden departure had broken open some sort of barrier that I had built around myself and for the first time in a long time, I began to notice life again. I felt the pulsing electricity of the world.

The future lurched, showing itself to me as it was right then. I had been on a road leading to marriage, and a life of obscurity, ending my days with youth unspent. There was something different about that path then. Now, though, it branched off and led to a place that I could not see. If I didn't take it then, it would be gone forever.

There was a chill in the air as dark night descended, and I feared a cold ride ahead. I fished around in my saddlebags for a pair of leather gloves and my leather jacket. I pulled the jacket on and slid the faded black gloves on my hands, pointed the front tire of my Harley toward the setting sun and began to ride west.

3

The first evening took me 150 miles away from what used to be home, riding slowly with a head full of bad memories. I shook loose from the long string of scattered obligations that I had left behind and felt the broad taste of the world around me.

I turned onto the main street of a small town. Except for a pair of braking taillights in the distance, the long, dark street was deserted. The black windows and empty streets showed little of the intentions of the town.

The stoplight turned red, and as I waited for it to cycle again, I raised myself up in the seat and scanned the darkness. Down the street, I could see the lights fading in the distance, into the open expanse of Kansas farmland. The air was cool and I was tired. It was time to stop for the night.

A cheap motel of no real corporate significance stood tucked away on the edge of a grove of stringy trees. The gruff employee at the desk seemed annoyed at having to conduct business at that hour. He gave me the key to a room and I walked out the door of the office to a long line of dark doors and the town beyond.

Seneca, Kansas, was an unforgivably small town. The air carried the dust from the outlying fields and sent it swirling around the corners of the buildings like ghosts spinning down the empty street past the blinking red traffic lights. The smell of a nearby feedlot hung heavy in the air, riding a cool breeze that dropped into town from the darkness in the west.

Thin bands of railroad tracks bent into the town from every direction and blended behind the long line of brick buildings. Beyond them stood a group of grain elevators and conveyers reaching up to the thick, concrete tops. They looked like shadowed monsters dragging themselves through the moonless night. Between the downward reach of one of the conveyers and the tracks sat a small liquor store, and I bought a bottle of cheap whiskey and some cigarettes.

There was an odd smell in the breeze from the grain silos, and it peppered the damp, black air as I walked back to the hotel. The last time I had spent a night alone with bad whiskey and cheap tobacco had been in college after a particularly bad breakup, and it felt like a predictable throwback to those confused days of my youth to be doing it now.

When I was safe within the dark walls of my room, I paced nervously. There was an open spot on the floor between the desk and the bathroom door and I fell back on the thin, coarse carpet. The sounds of two people engaged in the throes of cheap hotel passion echoed through the wall from next door. It was the ultimate representation of what I had come to understand as the world of the modern relationship: cheap sex in a cheap motel.

With my back against the wall, I twirled a heavy pour of whiskey around a semi-clean glass and stared at the darkness. In the soft light of that smoky hotel room, I began to feel a flushed heat on my face, and my temples throbbed. My eyes began to burn; I leaned my head back, and the tears came against my will. I fought them for a while, and then invited them. I threw the glass as hard as I could against the bathroom wall, put my face in my hands and felt my heart ache with the memory of those long years of indenture I had endured.

───────────

The next morning, after a few hours of interrupted sleep I re-emerged into the world. The early morning sun punched me and I stood in the doorway, shielding the bright light with my hand and trying to kill the hangover inside. It was a warm, clear day. I loaded the bike, mounted up, started the engine and coasted to the end of the parking lot.

At the intersection of the lot and the road leading out of town, I stopped and looked right, then left. The notion of returning home tugged at the back of my brain. Right was the way back and left was forward. I still had a chance to return and repair the damage. I had been away less than 24 hours and I could go back home, back to the job, back to Beth if I wanted. I hesitated for only a moment and then turned left to the unknown. The morning was late, and I passed out of town on the only two-lane highway that led west, stopping at a small diner for a quick breakfast.

I spent the morning skirting the small towns on the Kansas plains one after the other, putting as much distance behind me as possible. The farther I went, though, the more my thoughts bent toward the ripple this would cause back in Kansas City. What would Beth tell everyone? What would my parents say? It was Sunday, and they wouldn't miss me at work yet. But what about tomorrow?

I wouldn't worry about it. I wouldn't worry about anything until it was time.

The afternoon found me riding in the open nothingness of northern Kansas, deeper into the Great Plains and the empty farm country of the heartland, watching town after town rise and then fall away. Marysville, Bellsville and Kensington went by—crusty little frontier towns, outlasting their life expectancies as the interstates to the north and south diverted travelers away.

I wanted to stay on the two-lane roads because they seemed to offer a little more spiritual fuel than the sterile, ant-like corridors of Interstate 70. I wanted to go west but not *that* way.

The further I traveled from Seneca the better I felt, and the sickness from the previous night's whiskey began to drift away. There is a certain sense of accomplishment that comes when a person triumphs over a terrible hangover, and I smiled. Somewhere around the town of Norton, I leaned back, unbuckled the strap to my helmet with my free hand, and flung it up into the air. It arced and fell onto the pavement behind me. In my side mirror, I watched it roll and bounce off the highway, and into a ditch. I screamed, and pounded my fist against the gas tank and felt a sudden explosion of exhilaration. It was like nothing I had ever felt. A shot of power exploded through my body as I realized that *something* was finally happening to me.

I can't explain it—there was no reason why I should have felt so free. After all, none of my problems had been solved by my leaving. There was still the overwhelming stagnation of life, career and love that I would have to deal with. Someday I would have to face my choices. Someday I would have to face my family, my friends and Beth. For now, though, there was at least the perception of freedom. I could only assume that in a world where I had no dreams or aspirations the future was always just a mile or two down the road. By evening, McCook, Nebraska, was on the horizon and I decided to stop once again.

It was summer, but the deep of the nights was still cool, so the daytime, I decided, would be my road time and at night, I would stop and experience whatever I could in the small prairie towns dotting that part of the country. By the time I stopped, the blue sky was fading to a deep orange along the western horizon and the cool of the evening had begun to descend on the earth.

At the first hotel I came across on the east side of the town, I got a room. I threw my bags on the floor and jumped in the shower. As the thin towel did its best to dry my body, I noticed a red neon sign reflecting against the mirror above the sink, through the open curtains. It came from across the street, from the inside of an old, weatherworn bar standing, bathed in the final shafts of light from the dying sun.

I pulled on my jeans, boots and t-shirt, then fished a dirty, wrinkled, blue Oxford shirt from my saddlebags. In the interest of looking more like a real biker than a college-educated capitalist in the process of kidnapping himself, I left it untucked and partially unbuttoned. In the mirror, I still looked like a yuppie, but my hair was messy, my face sunburned, and a distinct shadow of facial hair clung to my face. I was well on my way to looking every bit as scraggy as the road I was on.

Why not? I thought as I looked in the mirror. *You deserve a little fun.*

Outside, a deep earthy smell met my nostrils. It was the sweet explosion of summer, and the dark odor of the nearby farmlands. These were smells that, along with the taste of cold beer, always created images for me of a time in the not so distant past when the world wasn't made of plastic and silicone.

I dodged the cars and headed across the street to the dark building, which didn't appear open. It was still partially daylight outside, but it looked like the dead of night inside. The stale odor of beer and old cigarette smoke clung to the air and the red stools stood out against the cavernous gloom of the bar. A green glow came from the jukebox, which was playing a scratchy version of "I Believe in Love" by Don Williams.

There were a few older men in a booth near a pool table, and they stared at me as I stood in the doorway. A bartender looked at me with one eyebrow cocked and a strange smile on her face as I approached the bar. She may have once been a beauty queen but had now changed to fit the atmosphere of the room, the way an animal adapts to its surroundings. Her skin was the color of the smoke-stained walls and her hair dropped to her shoulders like the soft light falling out of the dusty fixtures hanging from the ceiling above the bar.

"Have a seat, sugar," she said, motioning toward the row of barstools. "I ain't gonna bite ya."

I settled onto a stool near the corner of the counter, close to the door. The bartender stuck a rag that she was carrying into her left front pocket and leaned into my space suggestively, resting her elbows on the countertop. Her shirt was hanging open, exposing her once-perky breasts, and I wondered if she was doing it intentionally.

I winced the same way a person winces when they see someone hurt themselves.

"Crown with a Coke back, and a beer," I muttered, trying to look at something other than her.

"How old are ya, baby?" she asked in a slow drawl.

"Twenty-eight, born in 1978," I rattled off, without making eye contact.

"You don't look a day over 18," she said, "but I would have served you anyway. When I get a cutie in here, I gotta keep him in. It's good for business, ya know."

I didn't want to be a cutie; I wanted to be a rough-looking biker, but I guessed I wasn't there yet. At least I knew that she liked me and I assumed that no matter how drunk I got, I wouldn't be asked to leave.

"If you want anything else, just holler," she said as she brought me my drinks, "my name's Tina." Then she walked over and sat with the old men in the booth. Periodically, short bursts of laughter came from the table, but that was the only life in the bar.

4

After a while a pair of young girls came in and sat at the bar opposite me. One of them turned in my direction and whispered something to her friend, then they both looked at me and laughed. It was piercing, girlish laughter, and a juvenile demeanor commonly found in small towns.

A few minutes after they arrived, a young, unassuming couple came in and sat down at a table near the bar. The bartender looked up from her group begrudgingly and went back to the bar to take orders.

Half an hour later a tall and skinny guy, with wrinkles around his eyes and mouth, entered the bar. He was in his early 30s, and had soft eyes and a pleasant face, with prim lines set into his dark skin. He was a good-looking man, strongly built, but with a look of subdued confidence. He sat a few stools down from me, and I studied him with interest. His black t-shirt spilled onto a pair of dark, weather-faded jeans and burgundy cowboy boots. Around his neck hung a scratched medal, strung on a thin strip of leather. He ordered a beer and after a few minutes turned to look at me.

"What's going on, man?" he asked.

"Not a whole lot," I replied, turning to face him.

"You're not from around here, are you?"

"No," I said. "Why do you ask?"

"Well, I've been stuck in this town for a few days and I can tell who's from around here and who isn't, that's all. You see, the people around here have a walk and a talk that says, 'We're stuck here, we know it, and we're just trying to deal with it.' Know what I mean?"

"Yeah, I do," I said, glancing quickly at the two girls.

"Take those girls sitting across the bar for example," he said, motioning with his chin to where the two bubbly girls were sitting.

"I'll bet that they've been making eyes at you or talking about you haven't they?"

"Yeah, actually, they have been," I said.

"Well, they're young right? Too young to be from anywhere other than around here. I mean, there's no college here, and no reason for two girls like that to be here unless they're from here."

"True. I guess I hadn't thought about that."

"Well, they've been giggling at you, I'll bet, because they know you're from out of town. They probably know that you came in on that bike that's parked across the street, and they probably want to leave here themselves. Problem is, they won't ever leave here. I'll bet they both have dreams of running off to big things, but they won't make it. They're townies, and I'm sure they're fun, but the reality is that they ain't going anywhere."

I liked this man instantly. He was pleasant and friendly, with a subtle intelligence and the powers of observation, which I admired. Immediately I felt that our journeys had something in common.

"What's your name, man?" I asked.

"Bryan," he replied. "Bryan Hillary."

He offered me a bony hand and I reached out to shake it. There was an unseen power in his grip.

"I take it you're not from around here either," I said.

"Hell no, I'm from back east. I had to leave, you know. Can't really say why, I just had to. I've been stuck here for almost a week, waiting on parts for my bike. I think I'll finally be back on the road tomorrow so I can get the hell out of here. This town has to be the asshole of the country and I have to keep going west. Where you headin', if you don't mind me asking?"

"I don't know yet," I said as I took a long gulp of lukewarm beer. I made eyes at Tina and she returned to fill my glass under the dull, brass taps. The girls across the bar were taking shots.

"Where you from, then?" asked Bryan.

"Nowhere worth talking about."

"Are you in trouble?"

"No," I replied, "not any more than the average Jack, I suppose. I had to leave because I didn't know why I was there, and I had lost my reason to stay."

"See, man," said Bryan, "that's what makes us different from these folks. We know when it's time to go. You leave what doesn't make you smile, and then you can find your life somewhere out there."

He motioned wide with his hand, bringing into his thought the bar, the town, the country, maybe even the whole world.

"I know," I said. "Did you ever sit back and look at yourself from the outside and wonder where all the fire went? I mean, we all have this youthful passion, this big, broad outlook on life and then one day you realize that it's just…gone."

"Yeah," he said. "That's called growing up."

"That sucks," I replied. "Are we just supposed to go on like a bunch of cattle for the rest of our lives?"

"I guess that's the idea. I think most people just assume they'll be happy inside their little bubbles, and if they stick to that, everything will be uncomplicated and solid."

I thought of the rush of exhilaration I had felt that afternoon upon throwing my helmet to the side of the road. It was a liberating feeling, as if I had discarded some heavy weight. Bryan looked at me, then across the bar.

"I'll be right back," he said with a strange smile.

He hopped up and lazily walked over to where the two girls were sitting and began talking to them; an air of musty dust and body spray traveled in his wake. He spoke to them in a casually disconnected way. He was playing the game that rolls between the sexes in social settings across the country, and playing it well. After a few minutes talking with the giggle twins, all three of them stood up and came over to my side of the bar. Bryan sat in his seat and the girls came over and stood behind us.

"I'm Hope and this is Lydia," said the taller girl, an athletic blonde with a slow drawl similar to that of Tina the bartender.

"Very nice to meet you guys," I said, turning toward them.

Hope was a short and delicate-looking girl with dark hair and a broad smile. They both wore jeans and t-shirts that looked as if they had been sized for infants. Their tight clothes showed every inch of their young bodies, which flexed in the dark shadow of the bar as they climbed onto the stools on either side of us.

Bryan and Lydia sat and talked softly and easily, the words flowing between them impersonally, yet they appeared to exchange an obvious sexual compatibility. Occasionally, she would throw out a loud and annoying laugh and lean close to him and touch him. I sat next to Hope, not knowing what to say, and a bored look crept across her face.

"What's your name?" she asked.

"Bill," I said, not caring if she knew that I was lying.

Guys like Bryan had a never-ending supply of prefabricated bullshit to feed simple girls like these and keep them interested and entertained, but I had never been able to talk to girls in that way. My excuse was always that I tried to avoid the overused art of small talk. I liked to think that I could reach beyond the instinct to take home every girl I met while I was out. The truth was that I had always been scared to talk to beautiful girls I didn't know. The only time this didn't apply was when I was drunk; and since I was well on my way, I knew I would be flirting my ass off with this girl eventually.

I ordered shots for the four of us and when they came, we struck our glasses together hard, then tipped them back. I let the liquor roll down my throat with a cold burning sensation. The girls puckered their faces in reaction to the shot, and Bryan and I smiled at each other.

We ordered several more rounds of shots in the next hour, and soon we were all feeling the effects. I was becoming more adventuresome in both mind and body, and put my arm around Hope's chair while loudly telling her about the time in college when I ran over my neighbor's mailbox with my buddy's truck, and it ended up getting towed and I spent a night in jail.

"You're funny," she said with a giggle. "Where did you go to college?"

"Well, actually, I went to NYU in New York City," I said. This was complete bullshit, but it felt impressive to say.

"Oh, wow," she said, and her smile widened. "Lydia and I are heading to California after graduation. We're getting out of this town and we're gonna be famous!"

Bryan heard this and, remembering our earlier conversation about small-town girls, laughed so hard that a stream of beer shot out of his nose. In the midst of his subsequent fit of coughing he winked at me triumphantly, wiped his face with a cocktail napkin and laid two $100 bills on the bar.

"All right, my little darlings, we best be leaving now," he said. "Is there a river around here anywhere?"

"Hell yeah," said Lydia. "The Republican River is near here and there's a beach where we hang out and drink. Do you guys wanna go?"

"Absolutely. You ladies have a car?" demanded Bryan.

"We have a Jeep."

"Even better," he said with a snap of his fingers, and the four of us stumbled out into the cool Nebraska night. The blue dome above was clear, and a sky full of brilliant stars shone through the fat bulge of orange light that hovered over the town.

The girls sat in the back seat; Bryan drove and I sat shotgun. Lydia's light-blue jeep had no top, and rust holes above the fenders. It was dirty on the inside, strewn with clumps of mud and cd cases. The old truck clunked onto the main street and Bryan burned through the gears, topping out way above the posted speed limit.

We were nearing the edge of town and the buildings were growing further and further apart. Then Bryan slammed on the brakes and turned into a parking lot, the rear tires screaming. We came to a sudden stop in a space in front of Tom's Package Liquor Store.

"We need strong drink for this adventure!" said Bryan wildly.

"YEAH!" yipped the girls in unison from the back seat.

I smiled, and Bryan and I hopped out and went into the store. I grabbed a large bottle of Old Crowe whiskey and a two-liter bottle of Coke. Bryan grabbed two cases of Coors and a bag of ice.

Back outside, we put the beer boxes on the tailgate, tore the tops off and filled them with ice until nothing was visible except the bottle caps. Bryan threw one box in the back seat between the girls and I put the other on the floorboard in front of the passenger seat. One by one, the sound of four beers opening in rapid succession echoed against the painted brick of the liquor store and out into the night. We all took long drinks, then Bryan threw the Jeep in reverse, and we headed onto the dark road. In minutes, the lights of the town were distant flickers behind us, and the highway spilled out in front of the jeep's dim headlights like a long, gray ribbon.

Lydia yelled out directions to Bryan over the blasting wind, which slammed through the open top of the Jeep. We turned down one dirt road after another, power-sliding through the turns and laughing maniacally. Bryan and I leaned into the turns, banging the tops of our bottles together with each successive turn. The radio screamed, "The road goes on forever and the party never ends" as we careened down a hill toward some trees and the river.

"*Stop!*" yelled Lydia. "*You missed the turn!*"

Bryan kicked the brake pedal hard and we slid to a stop, sideways in the middle of the road. Without blinking, he popped the gearshift into reverse and flew backwards until he came to the road that we had missed. He jacked the wheel to the right until the front of the Jeep faced the road leading to the river. Then he punched through first and second gear, spraying gravel across the road, and accelerated down the path. Ahead of us, the road tumbled out onto a large gravel beach and Bryan spun the car around 180 degrees, and came to a stop facing the way we had come.

Far down the road, we could see two pairs of ominous-looking headlights coming toward us. The beach was deserted, and the dust settled over the quiet ripple of the river.

"Oh, shit!" said Bryan.

"Yeah, let's get out of here," I said.

We started slowly toward the road but by the time we got there, two police cars were blocking it. The officers inside had evidently witnessed my new friend's erratic driving and were interested in discussing it with us. Bryan stopped the Jeep, shut off the engine and stared straight ahead, both hands on the wheel. There was complete silence in the cab except for the pissing sound of a beer being poured onto gravel coming from the back seat.

Two sheriff's deputies, in khaki shirts and dark brown pants, got out of one car and a short, heavyset deputy with sergeant's stripes on his shoulders got out of the other. The shorter one walked to the driver's side door of the Jeep, pointing a bright flashlight directly into Bryan's face

"That was some drivin', boy! Now step the fuck out of that car!" he said in a thunderous voice.

Bryan looked at me with a look of fear in his eye, and then slid sullenly out of the door and onto the gravel, where he immediately lost footing and stumbled toward the deputy who grabbed his elbows.

"Goddamn it, boy, you smell like a bar!"

The deputy led Bryan to the front of the two patrol cars. I couldn't hear what was going on, but I knew it was a bad sign when the deputy stuck a pen in front of his face and started moving it back and forth. One of the other two deputies walked around to the back of the Jeep and shined his light into the backseat.

"Lydia, what in the hell are you doing, and who in the hell are these two assholes?" he demanded when he saw the girl.

"They're friends of ours," she snapped, "and just because you're my brother doesn't mean you get to tell me what to do. I'm 19 years old, for Christ's sake."

I didn't dare turn around, but I could feel the burning look she was giving the deputy.

Oh, shit, I thought. *What in the hell am I doing in the middle of nowhere with a 19-year-old girl?*

The heavyset deputy returned, and I could see Bryan sitting on the ground with his hands behind his back.

"That little bastard's drunker than hell. How about you?" he said as he motioned toward me with his flashlight. "Can you drive this car?"

"I'm ok, I guess," I said.

He walked over to my side of the car and held the pen up.

"Follow this with your eyes and your eyes only," He said.

He moved it from side to side and I thought that I was doing well until he looked over toward the other deputies and yelled, "He's worse than the other one."

The three deputies conferred quietly in front of their cars for a minute. Then the heavyset one came back and told us all to get out of the car. He lined us up between the cars behind Bryan, who was still on the ground in handcuffs.

"Here's what's gonna happen. Buchanan here doesn't want his little sister in trouble and frankly, I don't want to handle the paperwork on this deal, so we're taking your alcohol and you're gonna stay here and sober up. If any of us sees this car on the road before morning, you're all goin' to jail. Got it?"

"Yes, sir," we all said in unison, except for Bryan, who just stared at the ground.

They looked into the cab of the Jeep, grabbed the beer, and loaded it into the trunks of their cars. The hefty sergeant drove away and Lydia's brother uncuffed Bryan. The deputies looked at us, shook their heads and disappeared into the night, laughing as they got into their car. Bryan, kicking a wad of gravel toward the retreating patrol car.

"Goddamn it!" he yelled. "I know exactly where that beer is going, and it's not into evidence, that's for sure! It's going in their fucking refrigerators! You Goddamn pigs!"

I walked around to the passenger side of the Jeep and fished around under the seat.

"They didn't get this!" I yelled, and held up the bottle of whiskey, which I had thankfully hidden when I saw the cars coming.

Bryan smiled and the girls yipped. Hope went to the driver's side of the car and flipped on the stereo, then came back to me and gave me a long kiss. She took the bottle from my hand and gave it a longer kiss. The night went on.

5

The next morning I woke up to a heavy rhythmic pounding on my hotel room door. I sat up fast—too fast—and an immense throbbing immediately overtook my head.

The knocking was thankfully coming from the opposite side of the door. When I opened it, there stood Bryan, encased in brilliant sunlight and carrying two steaming plastic cups of coffee, stacked one on top of the other. Our eyes met and the strange smirk on his face brought back bits and pieces of the previous evening.

"You, sir," he declared, "cannot hold your liquor!"

I cringed, wondering what I had done that would make him so righteously state the obvious. It wasn't what he said that made me wonder. He sounded triumphant as he spoke, like a man who had won a pointless wager but was nevertheless glad to be victorious.

"Yeah," I replied. "I don't think I should drink anymore and I damn sure don't want to know what I did last night."

"Well, that's a shame," he said, handing me one of the cups, "because you're missing out on a very funny story."

I grabbed the cup, leaned against the door and took a drink, squinting in the sunlight. The coffee was hot and rejuvenating. It helped me enjoy the prospect that the day could only get better from there.

"Come on inside," I said, turning into the safety of my dark room. "I need a quick shower."

He walked past me, flopped onto the unused bed near the bathroom door, and flipped on the TV. I grabbed a towel and turned on the bathroom light. Bryan began to surf through the stations and stopped on the Weather Channel. I closed the bathroom door and turned on the shower, anticipating its calming effect.

"Good day for riding," he yelled. "Sunny and warm from here all the way to Wyoming. By the way, my bike is done and I'm getting out of town today. I recommend that you do the same."

"Yeah," I said , sticking my head out the bathroom door. "That's probably a good idea, what with the law on the lookout for us and all."

"You have no idea, my friend," said Bryan.

"What does that mean?"

"Forget about it," he said. "You probably don't want to know."

Instantly I knew that Bryan was referring to some part of last night that had fled my dehydrated mind. Whatever, it was important, but only semi-serious, like a sunburn: painful, but nothing that won't go away given enough time. However, at the time, it was more important to disregard the mysterious events and concentrate on getting rid of my hangover.

I stayed in the shower for a while with my face pointed to the hot stream of water, letting it massage my headache away. As I stood there, I gradually became nauseous and I doubled over, sticking my head out of the shower to empty the contents of my stomach into the toilet. It was embarrassing, but it was good for me. I grabbed a little bottle of hotel shampoo, lathered the soap into my hair and massaged my scalp, trying to pull the last of my headache away. The shower was helping my state of mind, but that hangover was a tough little bastard, something only time would drive away. I rinsed my hair and washed my face, then got out of the shower.

As I stepped out onto the cold linoleum floor and the foot that held my body weight gave out on the slippery porcelain bathtub. I crashed onto the floor, pulling the shower curtain down with me. As I fell, the last screw holding the curtain rod released its grip and the whole assembly drifted through the air in slow motion, and landed on top of me in a moldy heap. I lay on the floor, naked and covered with bits of hardware and specks of drywall rained down on me. I thought about how glamorous I must have looked.

"You all right in there?" Bryan yelled with a tone of feigned concern.

"Yeah, sort of," I said as I tried to find my way out of tangled mess.

I dried off and got dressed, putting on the same clothes that I had worn the night before. My shirt smelled like cigarette smoke and the faint scent of Hope's sweet perfume.

"So what exactly happened last night that you aren't telling me?" I asked.

"Which part?" He asked. "When you thought Lydia was Hope and tried to kiss her, or when they went to pee in the woods and you tried to take off in their Jeep?"

"Oh God," I said.

"Yeah," he said, "you pretty much turned into a wild animal last night."

"Great," I said, "sounds like I made a great impression on the girls!"

"Well," said Bryan, "I got laid and you didn't, if that tells you anything. Do you want to know how you got back to the room?"

"No," I said, "I don't want to hear any more. I'm never drinking again!"

There was a long pause as Bryan laughed and I took a long drink of coffee.

"Where are you heading?" I asked.

"I don't know, California I think, but I kind of want to see Wyoming and Yellowstone and all that. Why?"

"Well, I'm heading west too," I said. "I think we should stick together for a while, see where the road takes us."

"Two heads are better than one," he agreed, "especially on the road. Plus, I don't want to end up with some idiot who doesn't have anything worthwhile to say. That would be annoying and I'd really hate to have to kill someone."

I wrapped a towel around my waist and stuck my head out the door. "One thing, though," I said sternly. "I don't ride on the interstates."

"No problem here, man. Let's stick to the byways and see this thing like Kerouac would have. It'll be great. We'll sleep outside and stir up the towns, like cowboys on iron horses. We'll go west and see where the road takes us: Wyoming, Colorado, New Mexico, California... Hell, brother, let's see the ocean!"

I detected a note of excitement in Bryan's voice; it was a raw enthusiasm about life, about the unknown. He had the excitement of a young man in love with the possibilities of life, as if he were someone who had not yet been corrupted by the reality of it.

"All right, here's the plan," he said with determined seriousness. "I'm going to get my bike and then head to the store for some food and a bottle. You get packed and meet me at the Frying Pan in 45 minutes, and we'll eat and then take off down the road."

"Done," I said.

———

Bryan bounded out the door and disappeared around the corner of the building like a man on a mission. I looked around the room, feeling excited but hesitant. I didn't feel reserved about going with Bryan. I knew, though, that if I did go with him it would be nearly impossible to go back. At that point the journey was too new to be of much relevance, and thus I still had the option to return. I also understood that if I took on a partner, especially one like Bryan, it would be easy to lose myself in the adventure and forget that I still had unfinished business.

Yet, I had an uncommon sense of bonding to this man. There was something in his manner and attitude that drew me to him. I wanted to see what he was all about, and the only way to do that would be to go with him. We shared a bond not unlike the kind found on mountaintops or battlefields, except that this one had been formed at a bar.

I really didn't have anything to pack, so instead I unpacked my saddlebags to take inventory. When I did, a small slip of paper fell out of one of the saddlebags. "SAVE ME!" it read.

It was an old note from Beth, my former fiancée. She had given it to me the night we'd met, and I had no clue how in the hell it had made its way into my saddlebag. I hadn't known I even kept it.

We had been at a club in Kansas City. I went to get a drink, and sat down on a stool on the other side of the man who was talking to her. His back had been to me, and he was leaning in close telling her a story. Her shoulders had been tense; she was obviously nervous about talking to him. Around her, there had been a dim glow cast from the lights hanging over the bar. She had looked new, pure, and extremely beautiful.

She had turned and slid a cocktail napkin toward me, looked at me, then glanced quickly at the napkin and tensed her eyebrows. The man, only inches from her ear in the loud music, hadn't noticed. His eyes had been fixated on her, as had mine.

"SAVE ME!!"

The bartender had brought me my drink and I'd made my way from the bar, then turned and walked back.

"There you are, baby," I'd said, as I'd approached and put my hand on the back of her stool. "Aren't you going to introduce me to your new friend?"

She'd looked up at me with flushed blue eyes, and smiled. The guy looked at me with contempt.

"I think me and your girl were having a conversation," he'd said flatly.

"Yeah," I'd replied, looking at Beth. "and I think she wants to dance with me."

"Yes, let's do that," she'd said, standing and grabbing my hand.

"Hold on a second, asshole," the guy had said as he'd nudged her aside by the arm.

I'd seen him shove her aside. He hadn't finished his sentence when I'd twisted his left arm behind his back and pinned his neck and head to the bar.

"Can you call a bouncer over here?" I'd asked the bartender.

The man had been escorted out in his humiliation, and the girl and I had danced, bonding in our shared triumph over the demise of the idiot. We had danced and then we'd kissed, and the rest was coming back to me only in flashes of brief memory-the smell of her hair, the taste of her lips, the sound of her laugh.

In that instant I began to miss her. I could still return to the comfortable simplicity of that life. But I knew that what I was missing was not her but a memory of her, and my mind filled in other memories: the shrillness of her voice when she was angry, the shallow range of her emotion, the depth of her deceit.

I held the worn napkin over the sink and flicked a lighter under it. The paper consumed itself, curling up into flaky ash, which I dropped into the sink. I turned on the water and it broke apart, then swirled down the dark drain, much like our relationship had.

━━━━━━

On the way to meet Bryan I passed the liquor store where we had stopped the night before. A set of skid marks stood out darkly in the morning light, leading out of the parking lot and down the road toward the outskirts of town.

I felt tense as I rode, fearful of the night before and what was waiting for me back home. My job, my family, my fiancée—I had left them all, even the ones who deserved an explanation.

A little ways down the street from the liquor store was an orange and black motorcycle parked in a handicapped space in front of the Frying Pan restaurant. The paint on the fenders had been chipped away in spots, showing the wear of the road. On the fender, over the wide rear tire, was a small bedroll and a duffel bag. I pulled up past the space and backed my old Harley next to the Big Dog, dropped the kickstand and loped up the stairs into the building.

I scanned the meager crowd inside the restaurant. In one corner, a bandana, with a pair of sunglasses propped up on top of a sunburned forehead, stuck out from behind a large map. I sat down in the booth and, without taking his eyes off the map, Bryan began to tell me about his plan for the day, speaking quickly and excitedly.

"I think we could take months to see this part of the country. I mean, look at all this land. There's this great gulf of space between where we are and where we need to be, and we have all these squiggly lines to take us there. The question is, which way do we go? Do we go up, down, left, right? By the way, I ordered you an omelet."

He signaled to someone behind me and a server appeared, hovered over us pouring coffee into my cup.

"Food will be right out, boys," she said with a slightly agitated edge in her voice.

"Thank you," I said to her, but she walked away as if she didn't hear me.

"By the way," said Bryan, "I am all for going to the coast if you want, but I absolutely must, *must* stop in Yellowstone. I have a cousin who works there—real lively kid who's a blast to party with, and I absolutely must see him. He's doing an internship and he would absolutely go crazy if he knew I was out here and didn't stop by and say hello."

"No worries, my friend," I said, smiling blindly. "I'm just along for the ride."

"That's very good to hear," he said. "Most people are too goddamn caught up in making *the* living that they forget about what life is all about. It's about the ride!"

The staff and the clientele of the little diner buzzed around the room like moths around a streetlight while we made plans for our journey west. Bryan traced a route along a series of two-lane roads, which would take us through Wyoming, Montana, Idaho, Nevada and finally California. Part of me was listening to his descriptions of the country we would see, but my own thoughts were louder.

I kept thinking of the mountains of central Colorado, a place I knew well from my youth. Something in the back of my head was telling me to go there and the thought struck me that this was the first time on my journey that I had felt compelled to do more than wander the country aimlessly hoping that something worthwhile would find me.

An old college friend of mine lived in Colorado, an exuberant young man named Lance Hamilton, who had always done me well in troubled times like these. It would be nice to take the slow roads through the mountains, south to where he made his home, in Buena Vista, and see his face again, and the wild light in his eyes.

There was something soothing in the notion of traveling so far away from home on a whim, only to see a familiar face. In the end, I decided that I would stick with Bryan for a while, but would keep my options open to parting ways with him if it seemed like I could find a better place somewhere else on the road. A shallow traveling companion I may have been, but at least I was being honest with myself.

When our food arrived I picked at my omelet, eating little of it, and listened to Bryan talk about his time on the road. He gestured wildly and told stories of strange people, odd towns and sad nights alone. After a few minutes of watching me poke at my breakfast, he stopped talking, smiled and motioned toward the door.

"Wanna get out of here?" he asked.

"Yeah," I said. "What about the girls from last night?"

"Eh, forget it," he said, fishing around in his pocket and avoiding eye contact. "I'm not sure that they'll want to see us again. Besides, I don't do goodbyes."

With that, he laid a fifty on the table and stood up. He pulled his glasses down onto his nose, stood up and headed to the door. I followed.

━━━━━━━

The town of McCook disappeared steadily behind us and we both began to relax. We rode side by side, the long forks of Bryan's cycle pointing the way as he leaned back against his bedroll, his right hand on the handlebars and his left forearm draped over his thigh. I hunched slightly forward, both hands on the grips, my arms straight and my elbows locked. Though I had ridden periodically over the last few years, I had never taken a trip that long. My thighs ached, and my back was sore.

We rode northwest to Ogallala, Nebraska, then along the North Platte River through Scottsbluff and into Wyoming. The land slung low between the horizons, the brown grass and budding trees breaking up the monotonous color of the ground. A haze hung in the air, dust settling on the quiet parts of the country. The landscape was dotted with decaying farmhouses and barns; the last remnants of the great American frontier, which had been closed forever.

Yet, there was a green haze around the outlines of the trees and the rolling hills, as summer was breathing life into the plains. It wasn't the old West, it was a new one, and as the day became brighter, the budding season made it clear that it held just as much promise as the old in its simple desolation.

As we rode into Ogallala, we crossed over Interstate 80 and through downtown. Just outside the business district a knoll rose about twenty feet above the street, and an old cemetery sat at the top. A wrought iron gate opened into a long row of stairs leading to the crest. We dutifully stopped to pay our respects to the pioneers and wanderers who didn't quite pass through.

We slowly climbed the stairs to the top and quietly scanned the old wooden tombstones, preserved in the dry air of the plains. Etched into one of the grave markers at the back of the cemetery were the words, "Here lies Rattlesnake Clive, shot by a .45 and no longer alive—1889." We stared at the hilltop and the strange writing on this simple monument in a long silence.

"It's amazing, you know," said Bryan, with his hands in his pockets and his head bowed.

"What's that?" I asked.

"Well, look around at all these headstones. These were all people who had plans, who had a direction. I'm sure there were some bad people in here, like this Rattlesnake Clive guy, but some of them came west to make better lives, or get rich, or whatever, but what was the point? How many of these people came all the way out here just to die?"

This notion struck me and I began to think about direction, substance and dying without reason. I tried to imagine the reasons why these people might have left their comfortable eastern homes for the uncertainty of the West. Everyone who came out there had a reason to, and part of the risk was that they might not make it all the way. I felt myself getting angry about whatever point Bryan was trying to make. Was he saying that the prospect of not finishing the journey made it less worthwhile?

"That may be true, man," I admonished, "but look around here! Right in front of us are 20 or 30 reminders of the people who came out here only to die, but what about all the roads, the buildings, the people? They are all reminders of the people who made it. They scratched out a living, survived, and had children and created everything else you see around here, including this cemetery. Do you know what kind of balls it takes to just pack your shit and go someplace where you don't know anyone and no one would give a shit if you got hurt or killed?"

"Yeah, I do know how that feels!" he bellowed back and then spit on the ground, turned, and walked down the stairs. I stood motionless for a minute, shaking my head, knowing that we were both filled with unshared emotion, and then turned to follow him.

"Look," I said as I trotted down the stairs after him, "I don't know why you're out here and you don't know why I'm out here. I was being selfish because I had it in my head that I was the only one who left something behind, but I think we're in the same boat here."

I held out my hand. He stopped and turned to me, the anger gone from his face.

"Aw, to hell with it!" he said, and grabbed my hand, then threw his arm around my shoulder in a solid embrace. "Let's get out of here."

We parted, and when Bryan looked at me, I saw fierceness in his eyes. We mounted our bikes and took off on Highway 26, toward the North Platte River. The road wrapped around the south side of Lake McConaughy, then turned and crossed it just west of where the river widens to form the lake. We stopped for a quick lunch in Scottsbluff and proceeded on along the tree-lined banks of the winding river.

6

We crossed into Wyoming near Torrington and the sky began to fill with clouds. It started to rain so we stayed the night in a small hotel in the middle of the town. The next day we spent most of the afternoon exploring the short streets and some of the trails near it. In mid-afternoon we left Torrington and made our way northwest along the thin, concrete line, the two-lane highway leading to the confluence of the prairie and the mountains.

At the town of Wheatland, we left the perceived safety of the pavement for the gravel roads leading into the Medicine Bow National Forest in the Laramie Mountains. The wet gravel stuck to our tires and flung chalky residue over the fronts of the bikes.

We stopped in a remote spot near the top of a ridge, far from the common enterprises of the world, and began to look for a decent place to spend the night. We had agreed earlier in the day to forgo the comfort of another hotel and instead search for the mystical seclusion of the mountains of Wyoming. I hoped that in this eternal beauty

I would find part of what I was looking for: the official end to my dissatisfaction of my old life.

Our two days on the road together had taken us about 400 miles from McCook and the stop was a welcomed relief to our road-weary bodies. During the time, I had grown endearingly comfortable with my new companion, sharing stories and experiences as we traversed the countryside. Now we were to spend the night alone in the wilderness far from the pursuits of humanity, and I sensed that the night would be a revelation of some kind. We stopped on the side of the road, under the canopy of a pine forest.

When we found an open grove amongst the tall trees and thick brush, we made a small fire and gathered our bedrolls and bikes around the circle. The fire was warm against the gradually cooling air, and the smell of pine needles mixed with the descending cold stung my nose. It was an aroma that reminded me of being young, when winter brought the promise of adventure.

Bryan Hillary and I sat around the fire, passing a bottle of red wine between us and eating gas station ham sandwiches we had bought earlier in the day. We were quiet, the two of us reverently admiring the stars overhead.

It was a lonely silence, not only in the absence of words but also in the feeling of loneliness that comes even when there is someone sitting next to you. I had felt a sense of bonding with this man. We were both on the same strange journey, though we hadn't directly talked about it. This connection nurtured a sense of unity between us but what had happened in the cemetery the previous day seemed to cool our friendship in a way that I couldn't explain.

"Why did you leave home, Bryan?" I asked.

He paused, his eyes never leaving the hypnotic bounce of the fire.

"Well," he said, "I left home about a month ago—May first, actually. I used to be a responsible guy, but one day I started to feel like I couldn't compete with everything going on around me."

"You mean like getting the job and having the kids and all that?"

He turned and looked at me with those powerful eyes.

"Exactly," he said. "Yeah, that's the exact kind of shit that had me all fucked up. Anyway, I had all that going on and I had this girl-friend and my parents were giving me shit because I wasn't married, and it really fucked me up. I mean, my whole family—I have two very conservative parents and two older brothers and a sister who are all married with kids, and they're all in this routine and anything that's not in line with that is against the normal order of things to them."

"Yeah," I said, "families can be like that. I think it's just an age difference. They grew up in a different world, you know?"

He looked back at the fire and sighed.

"I guess they're 'powerful' people in the business world and all that, so I think they have pretty big heads about the whole right versus wrong thing. It's ridiculous. People in that position have a responsibility to do their part, I understand that, but you have to know where your right to affect other people starts and stops, and hang out somewhere in between."

It suddenly occurred to me that in the unfathomable vastness of the West, I had met a man who was telling the same story as mine, with different names and people. A bond formed between us that night that I knew would never be broken. Meetings like that don't happen by chance and there was a reason that we were sitting around that fire on that particular night. It was the night when the real adventure began. I didn't feel like I was running away anymore; I felt like I had finally stepped out of the darkness.

"So what happened?" I asked.

"So, one Sunday, I went to church, just me and my parents, and at brunch afterwards, I told them everything. I said that I didn't plan to marry, and if I had my way, I would be out experiencing the world as best I could. I told 'em I didn't want the same cookie cutter life that everyone else had and that I hated the fact that they were all so damn righteous about everything. So my dad asked me how I could be so disrespectful, and we just went to town on each other right there in the middle of the restaurant. My mother was crying. It was awful."

He paused and spit into the fire. "You know what that's like?"

"My old man was always too busy to care *that* much."

"Well," he said, "it ain't no picnic. I told him to go to hell and walked out."

"And now you're here?"

"Not quite," he replied. "The next day, Monday, I went to my parents' house. I was so mad and screwed-up in the head that I didn't know what the fuck I was doing. I wanted to hurt him in the gut, the way he had hurt me, so I went into their house and stole about $200,000 in bonds from the safe. Then I rifled through his drawers to make it look like a robbery. I wanted to hit him where it hurt. I was acting like a damn child who just got his toys taken away."

The cold mountain air drifted around the clearing like the icy hand of a haunted past. There was shame and regret in the trembling of his voice and I knew that there was more to the story than what he was telling me.

"So I took the money back to my apartment in the city and naturally, my old man called the cops."

"Now, does this mean that I'm riding with a wanted felon?" I asked.

I was trying to be funny, but I felt dumb the moment I said it. That was the wrong time to be making jokes, but luckily Bryan wasn't the kind of man to chastise anyone for that kind of thing, and he smiled diplomatically.

"Innocent until proven guilty, my friend," he said. "Anyway, I called him a few days later and told him what happened. I figured that enough time had passed and he had stewed about it long enough. He was surprised that I had done such a stupid thing, but in the end he was more apologetic about what had happened in the restaurant than pissed about what I had done. I have to give him credit for that. Long story short, my dad wanted to clean the slate, so he called the county prosecutor and told him what had happened. I guess they went to law school together or something. But apparently, the prosecutor had been dating my mother back in the day, and my pops kind of stole her from him. I guess he was still sore about it and he told my dad that it didn't matter if he didn't want to press charges, that this wasn't TV and that I had committed a serious crime. So Pops called and told me to get out of town until he could straighten it out. I haven't heard from him since."

I said nothing, but stared into the fire, figuring that silence would be a better consolation than anything else. His story veered off in a way that I could no longer relate to, and out of respect, I didn't try. We talked lightly for a little while longer, and I gave him the short version of my situation. He was obviously tired from the exertion of thinking about his trouble, though, and was soon asleep on his bedroll on the other side of the fire. I stayed awake, lying on the rough wool of my bedroll, reading an old, worn-out copy of *Leaves of Grass* that I had brought along, and drinking the last of the wine.

Again we wander, we love, we separate again.

Was life merely a series of introductions and separations? Surely there had to be more to it than that. There had to be reason somewhere in the world, even as we flit around one another, detached from feeling.

I put down my book and turned my face to the warmth of the fire, and let my mind wander deep into the past; into everything that I had avoided thinking about since I'd left. I began to think about the distance I had traveled, and where I had come from. The thick veil of stars and the shadows of the tall pines hovered above me and I realized soberly how far into the unknown I had come. The notion of "home" was becoming as foreign to me as everything I had begun to question, and it had little to do with how far away from Kansas City I was.

Home was a concept that I hadn't thought about much on the road, or indeed for years before that. As the distance between me and my old standardized life became greater, though, the more I began to think about it. There is something greater than a building or a structure that used to make me feel at home. There was a feeling, a sense of security and a stability in thoroughly knowing a specific set of people.

As I traveled farther into the west I began to realize just how far away from home I was. There were a great number of miles between me and Kansas City, but I had been homeless long before I left. As a child, life was absolute, and a person is home when they are young because they haven't been exposed to the world. Once the world is open, and the natural processes of growing up tempt a young person into it, home is only talked about in past tense. The notion of home, I considered, is really only something that a person can remember rather than experience, and this memory is almost always of childhood. The rest of life is a journey to find it again.

This journey of mine was turning out to be far different from the romantic stories of which I was so fond. There seemed to be nothing noble in my own adventure. I made this trip with myself in mind and no one else. I had found dissatisfaction in an alien life and I had run away from it as a child would, not knowing what there was to look for, and leaving behind a long series of broken obligations and un-kept promises. The old writers always had the search for truth in mind in their long and troublesome journeys. I had something, but it was nowhere near truth.

Now I had fallen into the companionship of a man with similar expectations to mine, but who had been on the road longer than I had. He was my *de facto* hero on this journey, as anyone on a journey such as this was supposed to have. Bryan seemed to know where he was going, or at least why he was going, and I did not. As such he had become the leader of the expedition.

I hadn't found the truth I was seeking, and that night I began to fear that perhaps it didn't exist outside the rhetoric of those old stories. I was in the midst of a journey with no end, or at least an end without reward, and I began to feel a certain sense of emptiness in my head and heart at having abandoned my old life. I fell asleep in the cold air, with the expanse of my uncertainty around me, and did not dream.

In the morning, I awoke to the mist of the rising dawn. The fire had dwindled to a small pile of ashes, which swirled and danced in the cool breeze. I stood up and stretched, holding my arms high in the air and feeling the pops in my back.

Bryan's bedroll was empty, and there was no sign of him in the clearing. I rolled up my blankets and attached them to the back luggage rack on my motorcycle. As I worked, the sun began to lift itself over the trees behind me and the warm light cradled my shoulders, then gradually moved down my body. The sun's beams began to defeat the cold, damp of the night and when Bryan returned, we quickly broke camp. We did not discuss the conversation from the night before, and instead packed quietly and rode down the mountain in silence.

7
===

As early morning changed to late morning, we found our way off the dirt roads of the Medicine Bow and back to the paved civility of the highway. Turning north on the edge of the rolling hills of central Wyoming, we passed through the towns of Medicine Bow, through the Shirley Mountains, to Casper. The day was becoming evermore pleasing as the sun rose high, and the temperature soared. The strange feelings I had experienced the previous night began to disappear within the land itself, which brought peace in its broad, brilliant expanse.

The night had been cold, but it was the price for the beauty of the day. Central Wyoming was indescribable in its infinite reach to the horizon, and it unfolded in front of the highway like the limitless embrace of the ocean. The West, as I had always envisioned it, lay in front of me with the soft, rugged beauty of a million years of terrestrial evolution. Scars left by the hand of man were few or unseen in most places; the road and the row of fence on either side quickly became invisible as they crested the distant hills.

It was desolate, but its rugged beauty brought to my mind images of the spirits left by people in their voyage west, which rose up from the golden grass to the deep blue sky. It was the sweet song of a long-ago American spirit, one that rose with the blending of the continent and fell with the closing of the frontier.

We rode on, and I began to remember my long-discarded past. For a short time, within the unfolding breast of this land of dreams and speculation, I remembered the errant thoughts of a young man uncorrupted by the perceived reality of the world. On this stretch of empty highway, there was no email, no rush hour traffic, no forced submission to the pretentiousness of the corporate hierarchy, and none of the perennial obligations necessary to the enterprises of the modern American. Beyond its rugged beauty, the land offered truth, simplicity, passion and uncertainty—all of the virtues that I had exchanged for the comfortable, uneventful, white-collar American life.

Around mid-day, we stopped for lunch at a small diner in the city of Casper, Wyoming. Casper would be a small town in any other state, but within the context of modern-day Wyoming, it was the second largest city, which to me was an indication that perspective was all that really determined the importance of size.

Because I didn't know how long I would be on the road, I was trying to save as much of my limited cash as possible. I did have a wallet full of credit cards, but vowed not to use them in order to preserve the purity of the adventure, at least unless I really needed them. Whenever we stopped, I ate little, and frequently found that the pain that radiated within the body from lack of food wasn't as bad as I'd assumed it would be, and was almost spiritual in a meditative sort of way. Though I rarely went more than a day or so without eating, I found it to be an experience that solidified the religious nature of the adventure.

Bryan and I sat in a corner booth near the back door and watched the sporadic stream of traffic pour in and out of the tiny restaurant.

"Damn good day," I said.

"Oh man oh man," he replied, "we are on it!"

"You know, there is something pure, almost virgin about being out here like this."

As we ate, the slight pulse of the town swirled around us in lazy reflection of the quiet nature of the place.

Leaving the diner, we climbed onto the bikes and headed west to Snoshoni, stopping on the outskirts of town to pick up a pair of hitchhikers. They had the look of two people who had spent a long time on the road, as if they had been dodging and hitching their way across obscure back roads, racing ahead of whatever dark past was following them.

All of us seemed to be running from the same kind of shadow— me, Bryan, the hitchers, the truck drivers and the families on vacation. Everyone on these roads was traveling ahead of some mysterious beast that followed close behind and threatened to catch us all. We were running from the shadow of time, of obligation, of responsibility, of legal containment, of the slow death of natural cultural identity. The road was the last promise of the beautiful, uncertain freedom that we, one by one, eventually exchange for comfort and stability.

The man rode with Bryan, and the girl rode with me. She was much younger than him, certainly not older than 18, and he appeared to be in his mid-20s. They were together, close in age, but outside the legal context of what love or lust was supposed to be.

Perhaps she was a missing person, a runaway. He was her abductor and we were aiding in their flight. I doubted it. In my own romantic notions, I imagined that they were willing accomplices running and hiding in underground America.

We let them off at a gas station in Snoshoni. Unfortunately, I was never able to get their story, though, and I was left to create it in my own mind. The reality of it was probably much different, but my own utopian version felt much more appealing. To me they remained two young kids, nobly preserving their love by taking to the highways, and we were helping them to achieve some kind of distant freedom.

That was the problem with traveling the country by motorcycle: you could never talk to the people you picked up along the way. Perhaps, eventually, I would be able to trade-in the Harley for a car and listen to the real stories of people on the road, rather than making them up.

Bryan and I turned north toward Thermopolis with the intention of reaching the commercialized wilderness of Yellowstone National Park by the end of the day. There, we would find Bryan's cousin and a place to stay for as long as we wanted. From a central base in Yellowstone, we could explore small parts of Montana and Idaho before continuing west to the coast.

In Thermopolis we stopped at One Eyed Jack's Bar for a break. The bar was rough on the outside, but endearingly inviting on the inside. It had been a winding, tiring road since Casper and it felt right to stop for a few minutes and enjoy one of the few true creature comforts that can be found on the road. We stepped out of the brilliant light of the day and into the seductive darkness of the bar.

"You know," said Bryan, shortly after our tall pint glasses arrived, "having a couple of beers during the day is worth at least a couple hundred miles."

I raised my eyebrows in question, and turned to look at him. He held his glass at eye level and examined it with the air of an inquisitive investigator.

"If you have a couple of these, you kind of forget that pain in your ass you've been thinking about for the last hundred or so miles. A couple glasses of the bitter and you will have 200 extra miles that you wouldn't have had sober."

"Well," I said, "that makes sense in a way, but it also just sounds like a convenient excuse to stop and drink."

"Whatever," he said. "The trick is to know how much is helpful, and how much will bring an end to your day."

He paused and turned to me with a puzzled look.

"Wait a second," he declared, turning to me with sarcastic disgust. "Are you lecturing me? What are you, a fucking cop? You should know that questioning a man about his drinking habits is just goddamn un-American!"

He smiled. I finished my pint and part of another while Bryan finished his first, second and part of a third. He was gesturing and talking loudly and waving his glass around in the air, jerking it with every inflection of his voice.

"Yes, I know that you have this idea about finding some missing piece to the puzzle out here," he said, "but you have to realize that it's like sex: once you stop looking, it will fall right on your goddamn lap. But if you keep looking for it, you'll end up empty-handed, or I guess not so much empty-handed, but definitely not getting any."

He laughed loudly and nudged my ribs with his elbow. The people around us who had heard his tirade looked at him, some of them shaking their heads.

"Well, it's true!" he said, looking at them over his shoulder.

Bryan had drunk only a few pints, but had gone down quickly enough that he briefly exuded the air of a man on a binge. He was not drunk, but was certainly flirting with drunkenness.

"You're halfway to hung over already, my friend," I said. "You'd better back it off!"

"Listen, stranger," he said, loud enough for the whole place to hear him. "I don't know who you are, and maybe I'm a little curious, but I will not sleep with you!"

I rolled my eyes.

"Let's get out of here," I said.

I laid three 20s on the bar to pay for the beer and Hillary's behavior, stood up and hustled him out the door.

"All right," he yelled, "I'll go with you, but it's going to cost you."

"You're a dumbass!" I said, pushing him toward his bike. "Now let's go."

━━━━━

We skirted the edge of the Wind Indian Reservation, north of Thermopolis, into the arid basins between the Bighorn Mountains and the foothills of the Absaroka Range. The land was an expanse of flat scrub brush, reminiscent of Southwestern deserts, which faded into green grasses and pine trees at the base of the mountains to the east and west, and swept sharply up to snowy peaks above the tree line.

The farther northwest we traveled, the less certain the weather became. Between the peaks to the west gathered vast ripples of gray and purple clouds. There was a feeling in the air that we were heading for strange territory, but I dismissed it quickly. I had just left my entire life behind, and strange days were bound to catch up eventually.

In Meeteetse, Wyoming, we stopped for gas. The force of the ride and the necessity of mechanical concentration had weakened the effect of the beer, and Bryan was back to his normal, semi-collected self.

"Wow," he said, swinging his long leg over the seat of his bike. "I think I was a little hammered back there."

"Ya think?" I asked.

A swift breeze swept across the gravel lot of the station, one of the few buildings gathered sparsely along the highway. A cloud of dust spiraled straight up into the wind and blew into the corner of the flaky, white, wooden building. From the edge of the lot Bryan surveyed the darkness reaching across the sky in the west. Thick sheets of rain had already veiled the mountains northwest of the road.

"We're not going to make it to Yellowstone today, buddy," he said over his shoulder.

"Well, we're in the ass of nowhere now," I replied, shaking the last few drops of fuel from the ancient nozzle and into my tank. "I say we try and make it to Cody and find a hotel."

"I'm sorry. I was acting like such a jackass back there," he said. "Sometimes I just get caught up in the moment and the drinks. I know it's not as funny and cool as I like to think it is."

The clouds from the western mountains had overtaken the sun, and the landscape assumed hues of blacks and grays against the backdrop of the open valley and the wooden building. It felt like a scene out of a drifter movie of the '50s, wherein the two heroes inch further from the sanctity of the regular world, to the inevitable hell found on its outskirts. In the east, sunlight still bathed the mountains, but sky in front of us was dark and did not seem to want us.

"It's ok, man," I replied, smiling at the thought of his erratic behavior. "I think we need to settle up and get back on the road!"

"Done," he said. "Let's get the hell out of this place. It's got bad mojo!"

Bryan was right. Although the weather had created a strange atmosphere around the small station, there was also something else about the place that made us both uneasy. It was like the anxiety I had experienced as a child at the moment when the lights were turned off before falling asleep.

I went into the small store to pay for the gas. Its slanted floors created an odd angle as I passed the cold doorway and approached the man behind the counter. He was older, with thick black hair and a fat mustache that curled at the ends. His face held weathered contours wrapped around his thick horn-rimmed sunglasses, and he was much shorter than I was.

He stood straight with his hands palm-down and flat on the counter next to the register, and the light over his head flickered with my heavy footsteps on the old floor. The tops of his hands were tattooed. One read, "The darkness will soon be brought to the light," and the other read, "Cast aside all who liken godliness." The air in the building chilled with the passing wind as I approached him, and I shuddered.

"I just want to pay for the gas," I said, laying the 20 on the counter.

He looked at me for a long second with a half smile and narrow eyes, then picked up the bill and stuck it in the register. I shuddered in hesitation as I waited for him to count my change, and the feeling quickly gave way to a twinge of fear. All I wanted to do was to turn and walk away from him, but at the same time, I felt compelled to stay. He handed me the change.

"You ought not go that way," he said in a scratchy voice, handing me a small stack of wrinkled bills and pointing his chin in the direction we were to take to Cody. "You'll only find trouble up there."

I said nothing, but turned away from his eerie smile. Outside, Bryan had disappeared, and the bikes stood alone near the pumps. I scanned the lot but could not see him. I walked quickly toward the pumps, looking over my shoulder at the station. The old man was standing in the open door, leaning against the post, eating a peach. Bryan approached from the side of the building, where he had gone to take a piss.

"Let's get the hell out of here," I said. "That guy is freaking me out."

Bryan hopped on his cycle, started it and looked over at the man in the doorway.

"You know who that is, don't you?" he asked.

"No," I yelled over the sound of his engine, "who is it?"

"That's the devil," he said loudly, a crooked smile on his face with a strange sort of half-laugh. "The devil runs a gas station in Wyoming!"

Bryan shot out of the lot, onto the highway, and I followed quickly behind him. Cruising fast down the road, we tried to beat the rain to Cody, with the devil behind us and bad weather ahead.

I was still shaken by the strangeness of that place, but tried to dismiss it as just one of a string of excuses to turn around. Though my faith was flat, I knew that I couldn't go home. I hadn't worked it out, but there was some reason that I kept going despite being continually pulled back by my own uncertainty, visits from the devil, or close encounters with law enforcement. The difficulties of life expose its goodness, and fearing the devil carries the responsibility of believing in divine providence.

The landscape unfolded slowly as we rode, then sped up and flew past when we got too close. The sparse houses and barns along the floor of the valley leaned away from the wind, stoic against the passage of time, yet resigned to slowly bowing to the will of nature. Distant groups of cars coming from the north flashed their lights, and the ominous drops of rain on their glossy paint reflected in the dull, daytime sky.

8

Several miles outside of Cody fat drops of water began to slap onto the hard pavement then fell faster and faster until we were in a full downpour. Each time a drop of rain hit my face it slapped my wet skin with a sting and reverberated through my tense body.

We slowed and then stopped at a dirt turnout on the side of the highway. Bryan pointed across the road. About 20 yards away from us, near a fence and a line of scrubby trees, was an old, white-frame church and we parked the bikes and ran for it.

It was short and square, mystical in its utilitarian appearance. Angled boards covered the tall windows, and the rusty metal nail bled red streaks onto the wood. The paint on the outside was chipped and peeled, revealing long lines of gray wood underneath, running the length of the building from the roof to the stone foundation. Bryan pushed onto one of the wooden doors, and it opened with slight resistance.

We took shelter in the empty room. A fine, light dust covered the floor and floated through the dark, musty air. Vagrant drops of rain snaked through the cracks in the ceiling, dripping onto the wood floor.

At the far end of the room, I hung my wet leather jacket on a nail by the altar, then sat on the floor with my back against the wall. Bryan folded his jacket, dry side out, into a pillow and lay on the floor. He stared up at the rafters, tapped his folded fingers to the beat of the rain, eyes closed.

"This is a strange stretch of road, my friend," he said, "and I don't know if we're heading in the right direction."

"Let's get to Cody and find a hotel tonight, and find your cousin tomorrow. We'll both feel fine once we have a real roof over our heads and a decent drink."

"Sounds good," he replied.

With the beer still coursing through his blood, he dozed off and quickly fell into a light sleep. I pulled my copy of Whitman from the pocket of my coat and opened it, and read quietly to myself.

As I ponder'd in silence,
Returning upon my poems, considering, lingering long,
A phantom arose before me with distrustful aspect,
Terrible in beauty, age, and power,
The genius of poets of old lands,
As to me directing like flame its eyes,
With finger pointing to many immortal songs,
And menacing voice,

I stopped, and Bryan stirred slightly in his shallow sleep. I put the book down and closed my eyes, losing Walt to the troubles in my own mind. I revisited my old worries: the job, the house and the girl. Now, though, there was this sense of supernatural deterrence that I picked up at that gas station. I worried that the shadow, which I had only assumed was the past trying to catch up, might be something else entirely. Soon the patter on the roof began to slow, then stopped. Bryan sat up, roused by the peaceless silence, and soon we were back on the road, to make the last few miles to Cody.

The Irma Hotel in downtown Cody was a tragically-arranged tourist trap. It dripped with the history of the old West, but the reckless attempts to preserve its frontier spirit had corrupted it. However, it was the only hotel in the city that still had a vacancy; there was some early summer festival going on that week. Our options were to either stay at the Irma or sleep outside, so we decided not to quibble.

We checked in and settled into the rooms, then found a table in the corner of the hotel bar to relax and hide from the wearing of the day. Outside we heard the tap of rain and the loud claps of thunder. Everything in the hotel felt cold and dark, and it left me with the odd feeling of some place from another world.

In the hardwood shades of the old bar, we met two brothers, Austin and Shaun Parker, who were in the transport business and on their way to Canada. They were twins from Sonoita, Arizona, a tiny collection of buildings just a few miles north of the Mexican border. They didn't elaborate much on their employment, but I assumed that they were drug runners, making their way from Mexico. They had a certain reserve about them, and the unwitting fearlessness of two boys in their youth, with nothing to lose. I suspected that we should approach these two with caution, as there was something in their edgy manner that felt troublesome. We all sat and laughed at old stories as the rain fell outside.

This was when things began to get strange. We left the bar, and went to shower and dress for dinner. As I stepped out of the bathroom the phone rang and I answered. It was Bryan.

"Hey, man," he said, "when you finish getting ready, come over to my room. The twins are over here and they have a little something for us that might make the night more interesting."

"Done," I said.

I was up for anything. There was something vaguely strange about the pair we had met, but in the end I forgot about the feeling and went to Bryan's room with a kind of interested expectation. The door was propped open a couple of inches by the exposed deadbolt, and

I went into the room. The three of them were standing in a circle around the desk.

"There he is," said Shaun.

"Gentlemen," I said, "tell me, what craziness have you brought to us?"

Austin motioned me to come over. I approached them and saw four small brown pieces of chocolate sitting on a wrinkled bed of tin foil on the top of the desk.

"What do we have here?" I asked.

"Well," said Bryan, "these are chocolates with a little of the old fungi mixed in."

"Mushrooms?" I asked.

"I told you things were going to get interesting," he said with a smile.

They each picked up a square, and Bryan handed me one. I hesitated as they all swallowed theirs, then I tilted my head back and dropped the chocolate into my mouth chewed and swallowed. It was too late to go back and I was fully committed to whatever was going to happen next.

"Okay," said Austin, "we have about 30 minutes before the demons take us. We must venture out into the world for supplies, and meet back in our room. You two will find a store and get water and lots of cigarettes, and we will find beer and ice. Ready, break!"

Bryan and I left the hotel together. The rain had stopped, and the air was cool and smelled of musty, wet pavement. A large group of people stood on the long covered porch at the front of the building watching a reenactment of an old West gunfight in the street. We walked past the crowd and onto the sidewalk, toward the distant lights of a small market. Bryan motioned toward the spectacle of several men shooting each other.

"I hope that doesn't happen to us tonight."

We went into the store with a sense of urgency, knowing that very soon, we would be feeling the effects of the mysterious potions. Bryan picked up a few gallon jugs of spring water and I bought a carton of cigarettes and a box of matches.

"You don't want to get those," said Bryan, looking at the matches.

"Why not?" I asked.

In the back of my head and throat I began to feel a slight lifting sensation, and the hinges of my jaw tickled as I spoke.

"Have you ever done 'shrooms before?" Asked Bryan.

"No," I said, "I can't say that I have."

"Well then trust me, you don't want anything that requires any kind of dexterity."

I went back into the rows of aisles and found a pack of six lighters, and we left the store and returned to the hotel. Time was quickly running out. The town around me and the mountains beyond started to change, as I fixated on the steeple of a church at the end of the street; not a spinning exactly, more of a swirling. The sensation was something like the curious notion that the back of my brain was trying to roll over the top of the front, and my heart was beginning to beat loudly. I asked Bryan about it.

"We'd better get you back to the room before you start to freak out," he said.

By the time we got back, the fear had begun to set in, at first gradually and then faster and faster. Without even a pause to admire the feeling I slid past the point where the drug felt pleasant and into the great gulf, the black hole where all things felt scary and foreign. Instead of being a transcendent experience full of insight, it was a horrifying relapse into nearly every bad memory I had. My body felt as if it were spinning, and I couldn't look at one particular object for too long before it began to bend and swirl, so I looked at several objects per second, casting my eyes in broad circles about the room.

The other three sat in a circle and began a ranting tirade of everything that was going through their minds. All I could do was stand in the corner with my back to the wall and listen to them. They sounded like madmen and I was cowering, not afraid of them, but of what they were saying. Amplified, as it had always been present, was my fear of truth.

"All right," said Bryan, "I've got it. We will sit here and I will say anything that comes into my mind and we will respond to it, yes, we will go with it as the soul moves us, it will be the mushroom revival, and you all will be my congregation."

"Why do you get to be the guy?" said Shaun. "You know, the man? Why do you get to be the man? We are not the purpose of your wandering exaltations, man."

All things were sinking further into the abyss. What had I done? Why was I with these crazy people? My heart began to pound, and then I wondered if it was even my heart. What if I were hearing someone else's heart and it was the broken heart of someone I had hurt in the past? What if it was someone lost, what if it was some-one dead and their dead heart was beating in my head? I shuddered at the thought.

"This is true," said Bryan, "and I see your point, but you two seem vaguely singular in purpose and I am a wanderer you see, and an explorer, and as such my enterprises being more noble in their pur-suits, I have an obligation to take my role as religious arbitrator in this activity, this exercise, and guide us all in comfort of the process until we drift back unto the world. Do you understand?"

I closed my eyes and saw a string of faces, all from my old life, and they were laughing, and I could not stop them, and all the while, remained that damned beating heart and its terrifying echo. The spirit of the road, the great man, the purveyors of the journey in dark reds and greens walking across the dotted lines of some dark highway in an ancient, concrete forest. The voices of the others became low waves, and I could see their inflections on the backs of my eyelids, and beyond that was the memory of myself from birth to that not-so-dis-tant death.

It came to me in fearful waves that I was as close to the end of my life as I ever had been, and there was nothing for me to report, there was nothing redeeming about it. I felt as though there were an expectant judge in the deep recesses of my head, demanding answers, and there was nothing to give except the fact that I had abandoned my family and those I loved. I beat my fist against the floor.

Across the room, their voices came back into focus, then stopped as the three of them sat in a circle and laughed. I stood up, and felt the overwhelming desire to leave the room as quickly as I could, to get away from my horrible past, to close the door behind me. Through the veil of hypnotic flashes and colors, I knew that I had to leave the past, get ahead of the shadow and stay ahead of it. The shadow was the past, everything bad in my life, and now that I was out on the road, I had the opportunity to finally get ahead of it.

If I stayed ahead of it, then running from it would be my motivation to keep going deeper into the journey and deeper into life. I wouldn't need Bryan anymore; I could strike out on my own, see all, remember, live, love, die and be reborn far away from this hell. The heart stopped, the faces were gone and there was a low rumbling, and a scream building, rising in volume.

"Do you guys hear that?" I asked.

I stood up, and the rush came. I steadied myself and jumped over the corner of the bed to the nearest door, but it was locked and I couldn't open it. At once, there was a sinking feeling, all things growing dark. My head felt detached and it drifted through the impenetrable air to the soft bed below. It was over, it was done and it had been a terrible idea. I lay on the bed feeling time tick away as minutes became uncountable hours. The loud discussions and laughter from the other side of the room faded and disappeared, and a kind of peace settled over the hotel.

When the morning sky began to brighten the room under the veil of the clouds, I sat up and looked around. The twins had left late in the night for some unknown reason. They left behind all of their luggage, with the exception of one large duffel, and disappeared. We would never see them again in person, but catch them on the news not long after they left us. They were arrested trying to smuggle marijuana into Canada.

I went back to my own room to try to sleep. Bryan knocked on the door shortly before noon, and when I opened it, he could only laugh. The strange night had passed, and we had survived. He came into the room and I lay back on the bed. There was a long silence before either of us spoke.

"I'm never doing that again," I said.

"Why, what happened?" asked Bryan.

"I don't know how to describe it. It was like everything I have ever been afraid of came to me at once. I was scared shitless the entire time."

"That, my friend," said Bryan, "is what we call a bad trip!"

There was a quiet pause.

"Well, I guess we're not going to Yellowstone now," he said.

"Why not?" I asked.

"I called the restaurant my cousin works at, and they said that he hadn't been to work in over a week. I guess he just didn't show up one day."

"Jesus," I said. "What is it with your family? Do you just have a genealogical history of disappearing for no apparent reason?"

"I guess," he said, shaking his head.

"So do you have any idea where he went?"

"The guy I talked to said that just before he took off, he met a girl from Denver. She was staying at the hotel with her family, and they hooked up. I could see him following her—that's totally something he would do."

"Well," I said, "I guess we're going to Denver?"

"Sure," he said. "That's a damn good town. Besides, we need to get out of Wyoming. There's just too much weirdness going on here."

"Yeah," I said, "but I think weirdness is going to follow you no matter what state you're in!"

With the madness seemingly behind us, we headed southeast toward Denver, riding in the pleasant day with the sun high overhead. Toward the end of the afternoon, we reached the outskirts of Laramie, Wyoming.

9
===

Laramie was, to be kind, not what I expected. A ring of hills surrounded a large, beautiful valley, but the town itself was dirty and rustic, like a ghost town that refused to submit to its inevitable fate. The buildings themselves looked old and worn, but there was still a sense of adventure in the people who walked its streets.

There was a rodeo going on in town and the festival atmosphere provided an innocent, comical relief to us after our experiences in Cody. We checked into the Travelodge Motel on 3rd Street in the downtown district, once again the only place with a vacancy. After seeing the lobby and the general shape of the hotel, I understood why.

I felt an odd attraction to the festive spirit of the people in Laramie and a desire to explore the town. I convinced Bryan that it was a good idea, and we began our revelry at the bar next to the hotel. We had parked our bikes in front of the bar anyway, so it seemed like a good idea to relax there with a few beers before setting out to experience the town.

About 12 beers apiece and four bars later, we had made a short circle and ended up at the same place in which we had started. It was early in the evening still, but already getting dark. The grand spirit of the citizens had not diminished, but we had gone as far as our own spirits had allowed.

We sat at a tall table nursing a pair of drinks and I announced my concern with finishing the night in a bar that we had already been to. Bryan suggested that, given the lack of suitable female companionship thus far, we might as well finish as much of the night as possible at a bar close to the hotel.

"That way," he said, "it will be an easy stumble to sleepy time!"

Bryan went to the washroom and I sat at the table thinking about what was going on at home. Inevitably everyone I associated with knew about what I had done, and I was trying to guess what their reactions had been. My thoughts were interrupted when, wading through the tables and the crowd on his way back to the table, Bryan stopped, rushed over to me, grabbed my arm and pulled me toward the front window.

"That cop from asshole Nebraska is outside!" he said over the crowd.

"That's ridiculous," I said, pulling him to a stop. "You're paranoid. Besides, even if he was here you were so hammered that night how could you know what he looked like?"

"I'll remember that fat bastard's face for the rest of my life. Now come here and look at this."

We walked to the window and looked out onto the sidewalk. Bryan was right, the fat sergeant and Deputy Buchanan were standing in the street looking at our bikes and scanning the crowds. It was impossible to think that we could cross vast stretches of the West only to randomly stumble on these two cops, but there they were, both dressed in bright cowboy clothes-obviously in town for the rodeo.

"No shit!" I said. "What fucking luck!"

"Yeah, man, I don't think I need to tell you this, but we have no business letting those two assholes find us."

"Look," I said, "maybe they're just admiring the bikes. Besides, they're from Nebraska and we're in Wyoming. It's not like they can arrest us for anything!"

"Yeah, but they could kick the shit out of us. Then the local cops would come, then I would get arrested and shipped back to New York in fuckin' shackles."

"They found us in that chicks Jeep," I said. "They never saw us on the bikes."

"I'm sure they saw the bikes at some point. Besides, I don't want to chance it!"

I knew that what Bryan was saying made sense. How many bikes like ours came through McCook, Nebraska? It was true that they might not recognize them, but given Bryan's situation it wasn't worth the risk to stick around.

Outside the window Deputy Buchanan disappeared into the street and the fat sergeant walked toward the door of the bar.

"Well, let's get the hell out of here, then," I said.

"Fine by me!" said Bryan, who was already five steps toward the back door. "Feel like sleeping outside again tonight?"

"I don't give a damn, as long as we can get out of here!" I replied.

We watched from the back hallway, to make sure the sergeant actually came into the bar before we tried to make our escape. When he did, we ran like hell out the back door and around the building, through the alley between it and the hotel. Bryan stopped near the entrance of the alley and pulled my arm.

"Slap me in the face," he said.

"What?" I asked, surprised.

"Slap me in the face! We're going to have to ride fast and I need to sober up."

Not wanting to waste any time arguing about it, I pulled my arm back and flung it forward, connecting hard with his left cheek. He winced, then returned the favor with a hard slap to my cheek.

"Damn," I said, holding my jaw. "That was a good idea!"

We got on the bikes, which we had neglected to unpack in our drunken stupor, and started them. Bryan shot out onto the pavement and down the busy street. Out of the corner of my eye, I saw the unmistakable shape of a fat man in starched jeans elbowing through a group of people in the doorway of the bar and running toward me. I gave

him a quick wave and a smile and disappeared down the street, following the distant glow of Bryan's taillight.

Without stopping or even pausing to look at the map we put
Laramie, Wyoming behind us, disappearing on a two-lane road toward
the mountains southwest of town. As we rode through the darkness,
I let the cold air crest over my uncovered head, embracing its ener-
gizing and sobering effect. The night was clear, and the sky was full
of fat stars. The city lights quickly faded and Bryan's posture changed
from stiff determination to relaxed triumph. He looked back at me
and we started to laugh. We had gotten away, at least for now.

Once Laramie was mostly out of sight, we slowed down to a man-
ageable speed and began to look for a remote spot to spend the night.
After a half hour, we came to a bridge spanning a small river. Just on
the other side of the river a dirt road lead off the highway and under
the bridge to a little beach. We slowed and turned off the highway,
stopping under the bridge. We shut off our engines and sat still, listening to the cold echo of the river against the concrete pillars.

Soon my eyes began to adjust to the darkness. I began to hear
and feel the presence of other people and noticed a small group sitting around a fire on the beach, about thirty yards away from us. A
truck was parked near the fire and the radio was playing an old Willie
Nelson song. The figures around the fire appeared to be young people
and they were drinking beer and talking, sometimes in shouts and
whoops. We stood motionless for a minute and watched them.

Periodically, one of them would turn around and look in our
direction, but they generally gave our arrival very little attention.

"Why don't ya'll come down here?" one of them eventually yelled
in our direction.

Bryan and I looked at each other. He shrugged his shoulders, and
we both started down the road to the beach.

We made our introductions to the group and sat down on a large
rock near the fire. They were all in their late teens or early 20s, and
were very excited to hear the stories of the two strange bikers who
had shown up in the middle of the night. We were honest in our
storytelling and elaborated as little as possible.

They were very intrigued and listened to us attentively. They accepted us into their group and offered us beers from their coolers. Bryan went to his bike and pulled a bottle of Crown Royal whiskey from his saddlebag, and we all began to pass it around the fire.

A used-up but roughly beautiful blonde girl sat to my right. She looked older than the other kids sitting around the fire, and I began talking to her. She told me about how she had left Laramie for Las Vegas with dreams of being a dancer, but had only managed to land a cocktailing gig in an off-strip casino. By the look of her, she had evidently fallen into the hard-living Vegas lifestyle.

She had shadows under her eyes, and her stringy, blonde hair was dry and distressed. She wore a pair of light-colored jeans, frayed at the cuffs, with holes in the knees, and a faded purple tank top. On her exposed left arm was a dark bruise, and from her ears hung long, glass earrings, cut to look like diamonds.

Soon the subject turned to which one of us could drink more. We both stood our ground on the issue, adamantly defending that we could out-drink the other.

"I am a survivor of a college fraternity, a Catholic high school and an Irish family," I said. "I was bred for drinking, and I don't think it's a good idea for you to challenge that."

"Well I," she said stoically, "have lived in Las Vegas for almost three years and have probably done more partying in that time than you ever have. Also, I grew up in Laramie and there really isn't much to do here when you're a teenager, other than get fucked-up every weekend."

We both had compelling arguments, and in the end agreed that there was only one way to settle the issue. We hijacked the bottle of whiskey from the rest of the group and began to match each other shot for shot, in an attempt to prove the other wrong. I would take a shot and hand the bottle to her, then she would take a shot and then hand it back. We passed the bottle back and forth for a while and the faces of the young people around the fire grew long as they watched the game. I never took my eyes off her, but from behind me, I could feel Bryan's smile.

"Yes, yes, yes," he said, "you show her what you're made of, my friend."

We sat close to each other, and as she tipped the bottle back, I caught the look and shape of a small woman who had been through a lot in her life. She was a few years younger than I was and small, with tiny legs and narrow hips. Like the barmaid in McCook, she looked as though she had once been beautiful but the passage of time had not been kind. The exotic life she had left to find never discovered her, and the difficulties of chasing an impossible dream showed on her scarred body. In the end, she won the game and I was left to finish the evening as best I could. My memory faded and my night ended.

———

When I woke in the morning, I was safe in my bedroll near the smoldering remains of the fire. It was light, probably mid-morning, and Bryan slept soundly on the side of the fire ring opposite me. A slight wind kicked up a small cloud of dust, which I felt in my eyes and on the tip of my dry tongue. The kids were gone, and only the scattered remains of the dying fire and their empty beer cans remained to tell their story.

I walked down to the river and tried to wash my headache away in the cold water, but the pain was fierce. I was due for a shower, and I took off my shirt and began to wash my neck and underarms in the clear, cold water. When Bryan finally woke up, we broke camp and looked at his map of the central and western United States. Together, we marked the route to Denver. We had to guess where we were, but by the map, there looked to be a town along the river very near to us, and the promise of a meal prompted us to seek it out.

By noon, we reached the foothills of the Snowy Range and rode into Centennial, Wyoming. The town wasn't much more than a small, rustic collection of dilapidated buildings, a few houses and several mobile homes.

We stopped for breakfast at a touristy restaurant in the center of town, a large, red structure built to look like a barn. It had life-sized wooden carvings of horses in the front yard and a multi-colored picket fence. On the inside, pieces of antique farm equipment and repro-ductions of road signs covered the walls, attempting to create the long-forgotten mystery of the West.

I didn't like the falseness of the atmosphere, or the restaurant's ridiculous attempt at nostalgic décor, but it was really the only decently clean place in Centennial to eat. It had been quite a while since our last good meal and I began to feel a want for those orgiastic portions that only American diner food could offer.

There were a few people scattered around the restaurant, and Bryan and I ordered quickly without saying anything to each other. We each quietly poked at our breakfasts for a little while without speaking, and generally avoided eye contact. I was still feeling the sour sting of a hangover from the night before and Bryan was lost in thought about something far off in the distance.

I had a realization in Cody that eventually I needed to experi-ence the adventure alone for a while. It felt as though I had reached that point, the time when Bryan and I would part ways. Though I didn't know it, he was of the same mind. It wasn't as if there was any kind of negativity behind our mutual feelings, it's just that there are times when the journey must be made as a solo affair.

After we finished, Bryan looked at me and smiled. We didn't say it, but we both knew what was going to happen. I didn't want to slow him down, and I think he felt concern about putting me in close trou-ble with the law.

"Hell of an adventure in a short time, huh?" he said.

"Yeah," I said. "It kind of sucks because I don't know if I'll ever see you again."

"Oh, I think we'll run into each other again," He said.

"Maybe," I said, "but for now, I don't think this will be an easy friendship to forget."

Bryan reached into his pocket, pulled out a pen, and began to write on a napkin.

"Here," he said sliding the napkin over to my side of the table. "This is the number to an answering service in New York. I check it periodically—if you ever need to get in touch with me this is where to call. There's also a physical address and an email address, so if you send me anything, it should find me eventually."

"Thanks," I said sadly, folding the napkin and sticking it in my shirt pocket.

"By the way," he said. "My family also owns one of the largest shipping companies in the country, and I would love for you to come to New York with me when this is all over. Maybe we can hop a slow boat and wander our way across Europe or something like that."

"That would be great," I said. "We definitely need to do that."

There wasn't much to say that we hadn't already implied in action. My experiences with Bryan Hillary had come to an end for a time, and I was curious where the road would take me next. He stood up and laid a $20 bill on the table.

"I'm going to the restroom. You pay the waitress and I will meet you outside," he said, looking around the room and out the window.

"All right," I answered, and he disappeared around the corner toward the washrooms.

A few minutes later, as the waitress was digging in her apron for change, I heard the sound of a bike engine starting, and then the long, popping sound of it accelerating down the road, growing softer as it sped away. I stood up and ran outside, with the waitress calling out behind me.

"Hey, what about your change?"

I spun around as I ran.

"Keep it," I yelled.

Outside the front door of the restaurant, I caught the glare of chrome and Bryan's unmistakable dark figure on the road, heading east toward Laramie. He was on his way to Denver, I imagined, to find his cousin, then to whatever destiny awaited him.

"He doesn't do goodbyes," I said aloud, remembering the conversation from when we'd first met. He topped a small rise in the distance and then dropped out of sight into the shadow of the hills. I kicked a small rock across the gravel parking lot in the same direction.

10

Bryan Hillary disappeared over the rolling hills to the east, and I mounted my bike and started up into the mountains, and the Snowy Range pass, to the west, toward the tiny town of River Park. I felt sad at the loss of my friend. He possessed the simple wisdom and strong character of a man at the end of a journey. He gave me a sense of stability at a time when I was most fragile, and gave me the strength to continue long after I would have normally turned around. We had made promises, but the reality was that I would probably never see him again. That's the way it goes: we make extravagant promises to take the pain away from the parting.

I wound my way up the two-lane mountain road until it began to level, and stopped in a parking lot near the sign marking the top of the pass. At the edge of the lot, a small dirt path led downward to a stone observation platform. Along the path fat boulders sat amongst patches of coarse alpine grass, and the wind blew stiffly over the treeless ridge behind. I walked up the steps to the top of the deck, stopping to catch my breath in the thin mountain air. The stone platform was perched on the edge of a sloping valley, and over the lip of the railing, it disappeared into a narrow gorge below.

In the quiet air, I stood staring out at the jagged peaks of the Rocky Mountains and the wild frontier of my imagination. The laminated maps bolted to the stone rail of the platform told me that I was looking at the Routt National Forest in northern Colorado, and the westernmost peaks before the Continental Divide where the waters flow west to the Pacific.

"Incredible," was all I could say to myself.

I stood in the cradle of the platform and contemplated all. As the wind echoed through the expanse, I tried to imagine that I was the first person to stand here and see this rugged beauty. Behind me was a long ridge that swept down in the shape of a bowl and held the observation deck in its fingertips.

It was an amphitheater built by the gods, to show the glory of the sweeping chasm. It was the grey stone monument to the power of our being. It was a steadfast reminder that all things of man are temporary when compared to the limitless convictions of the earth. To stand in that place was to put into perspective those boundless ideas that I had long forgotten. One only has to look as far as the ground below to remember the divine responsibility of life.

In the secretive world of our human endeavors, it is easy to forget everything that was on this planet before us and will continue to be here long after we are gone. The United States claims these mountains, these trees and these rocks as our own, but the reality is that they belong to no one. We have no more of a claim on these mountains than we have on the air, or the stars. The limitless mixture of earth and snow and sky is as free as anything in this world will ever be.

These mountains, unlike the roads and buildings constructed on their backs, will remain, as intended by the bending and flexing of the earth, forever. Everything else is only temporary, like all humanity.

I breathed deeply, bending my thoughts toward the sloping grandeur and romantic seclusion I had finally found within this incredible desolation. I hadn't been on the platform more than a few minutes when a crowd appeared on the trail from the parking lot. It was a group of excited children, bouncing about and screaming into the void, followed by two parents who held the look of a thousand years of child bearing in their eyes.

My moment was gone and I returned to the road and the bike that had carried me there. I sat on the seat for a moment, watched the family at a distance, and sardonically admired their white and gold mini-van parked a few spaces away from my motorcycle.

The observation deck appeared to have changed into a flea-circus-looking thing in the distance. The children, distant specks from where I sat, were bouncing around the two larger specks with the ferocity of electrons in random orbit. I thought about the fact that, not too far in the future, this could have been my mini-van, and those could have been my children, and that could have been my wife standing there, and me with no notion of her infidelity.

After a moment of reflection on this prospect I left the scene on the pass and started again toward the west, into the valley below, to the tiny town of Ryan Park, where I stopped for gas and a map of Colorado. Before I left, I called my friend Lance in Buena Vista, Colorado, and let him know that I would be in town in a few days.

When I reached the bottom of the valley, I came to a four-way intersection and was about to make the turn south when I saw a young girl standing at the corner. She had a small canvas bag crossed over her chest, with a faded nylon jacket folded over it.

She stood with one hip cocked and her thumb in the air, looking straight at me. Her tight, faded jeans spilled their torn cuffs over the sides of her brown leather shoes. She wore a small, white t-shirt and her curly blonde hair had been tied into a bun on the back of her head. Her sunglasses left the complete contour of her face shaded in mystery, but she was clearly a very beautiful and rugged girl.

"Want a ride?" I asked. "I'm going south but I don't know for how far."

"Perfect," she said as she hopped onto the bike. "You can take me all the way if you want."

━━━━━━

On the south side of Riverside, a small town close to the Colorado border, my newest passenger and I pulled into the Buck Snort Tavern. It was a small, wooden structure just off the highway, on the southwest bank of the Platte River.

That same river had crossed my path before, in Nebraska when I was with Bryan, just after we had met in McCook. Its waters were much clearer here, and the river ran faster and narrower. The map showed that we were not far from its ultimate source. The water rippled along the rocky shore and I tried to imagine all of the places it would go before finally dropping into the sea. Life is comprised of rivers that run the course of the continent to the ocean only to someday return to the mountains and streams from whence they came. Those waters would have been forever altered by the distance and experience of their journey, in the same way that humanity is forever altered by its journey.

From the gravel parking lot, I looked through the open door and into the bar. It looked as if a strong breeze would send the place flying along the valley floor. From inside, the smell of stale cigarettes and beer drifted out beckoning us to come in and rest.

"I find that stopping for a few beers once in a while helps numb a person's ass to the vibration of the road," I said, remembering Bryan's justification for drinking on the road.

"I've never been one to dislike a little vibration on my ass," she said suggestively, "but I will have a beer with you, cowboy."

We stepped out of the bright day and into the dark tavern. The bartender was an older man with a thick handlebar mustache. He wore a faded flannel shirt with the sleeves rolled up above his elbows, and dark blue jeans.

At the far end of the bar a solid column of dusty light illuminated the back of the room from an open door at the end of a hallway.

A small, dirt path led out the back door and disappeared around the corner of the building. Beyond it stood a grove of aspen trees and the rippling river.

The bartender approached us.

"Bud Light," said the girl, smiling with her chin resting on the palm of her hand.

"The same," I said.

The man turned around and filled two mason jars from the tap near the middle of the bar.

"Where are you going?" I asked my mysterious new companion.

"With you," she said, smiling.

Through the window to my left, I could see the dusty street. Across from the bar was a post office, an old frame building with wood siding and a bright new American flag hanging limply from an old metal pole that was stuck in the ground near the front door. A child came out of the building with a small box in his hand and ran diagonally down the street, then disappeared between two houses. Beyond the buildings was a slow rise, with golden grasses and shrubs clinging to the steep bank.

"Well," I said, "I'm running away from a whole long list of things."

"You're not running from *me*, though," she said, pulling her sunglasses off and sticking the end of one of the arms in her mouth. "I'm too cute for that."

She was right about both assertions. I was running from something completely different and it had nothing to do with her. Nothing at all.

With her sunglasses off I noticed, for the first time, her brilliant blue eyes sparkling in the dim bar light. Her thin eyebrows led into a gently sloping forehead, and her hair was unkempt and dirty in a very sexy way. She sat on the old stool, her feet propped on the brass rail at the foot of the bar, her body turned slightly toward me. Our knees were touching.

The day was warm, a perfect temperature, and lust drifted in the air. The breeze outside exhaled the heaving spirit of early summer, and the faint smell of distantly blooming flowers floated in and around us. My eyes met hers and she looked back at me with desire. This girl and I had found each other randomly in the prodigious reaches of the road, and we had a single-minded purpose in the meeting.

"I'm going south," I said, "to look up an old friend in Colorado. I can't really say where I'll go after that."

"I'm going to New Mexico. I left a guy up in Cheyenne and now I'm on my way back home."

"I left home, too," I said. "I had this thing going on there and… you know, I don't even really know why I left. It just felt like it was time to go."

"Sometimes," she said, "it's just that simple."

There are many reasons people leave who and what they love. Sometimes, it really is just as simple as the need to go forth and explore, and yet we invent all of these complicated reasons for wanting to do it. I began to realize, after meeting Bryan Hillary, and now this young woman, that I had been far from alone out there.

At any one time, there are thousands of people on the back roads and interstates of America, and they are all leaving one thing and arriving at something else. Coming and going, often in groups, but for their own reasons and with their own expectations. We constantly writhe in the complexities of the modern world and it is only when we have stepped out of our own front doors that the sacred spirit of life presents itself.

I was looking for something that I couldn't describe and though the young woman I picked up didn't say it, I knew she was, too. If that was all we had in common, it was enough to hold us together for that short time.

From the moment I picked her up, through the long conversation in the bar, and as we headed south along the highway toward Colorado, we never thought to exchange names. In the end, there is no relief in those subtle nuances of identity. Ours were two lives that were in the same place and, by chance, intersected on the side of a lonely mountain highway in southern Wyoming.

As is the case whenever two things intersect, they meet briefly, then return to their own paths. The meeting of two people on their own respective journey was often a temporary thing, but would always leave resounding memories. I knew that was to be true for me and this young woman, but I also felt that our time together ultimately always belonged to us.

On the road again, we watched as the foothills dissolved into the plains, and I pushed my old bike hard and fast. We rode through the curved and wide-open valleys between the mountains of Wyoming and northern Colorado. She held her hands tightly around my waist and rested her chin on my shoulder. Loose wisps of her hair flicked and tickled the back of my neck.

11

To the southwest, dark clouds touched the tops of the distant mountains, forcing us to stick to the roads leading to the south and east, avoiding the flashes that lit up the distant sky. North of Steamboat Springs, Colorado, the storms caught us and light rain began to fall as the wind brought a chill from the mountains. The rain came harder and harder, and when we finally arrived in downtown Steamboat it was time to stop for the day. I parked in front of the Portsmouth Hotel and we dismounted and stepped under the awning by the front door to escape the rain.

"I'm going inside to see about getting a room, so I can dry off," I told her, "and I would be delighted if you would join me in waiting out the storm."

"Hmm," she said in an exaggerated Southern accent, "a strange man inviting me into his hotel room right here in the middle of main street in front of everybody. A lady would take offense, sir."

"Now ma'am," I said, playing along, and delicately lifting her hand, "I assure you that my intentions are only for the sake of your health and safety. Now I must insist that you join me in this comfortable establishment so that I can assist you in being as pampered as you most rightfully deserve."

"Well, my darling," she replied with a curtsy, "your argument has won me over. I shall wait out here and look after your steed until you have secured us suitable accommodations."

I kissed her hand and left her under the awning, then disappeared up the stairs into the hotel. The building was old and narrow, four windows high but only two across. The lobby had been recently renovated, and smelled of plaster and wood stain. The clerk behind the desk watched me carefully as I approached.

After a week and a half in the saddle I had developed a stiffness in my legs, which produced less of a walk and more of a swagger. The rain had forced me back into my leather chaps and jacket, and I wore one bandana on my head and one around my neck, which I had used to cover my face during the rain. I was also extremely dirty and soaking wet.

The expression on the clerk's face as I approached reflected my appearance, and my impression was that she thought she was looking at a heathen. That *was* the look I had been going for, but I knew it would only hamper my attempts at getting a decent hotel room.

"Can I help you?" she asked in a superior tone.

"Yeah, do you have any rooms available?"

"Um, all we have is a suite, but it's $200 per night."

I produced my wallet full of credit cards, and her tone changed from smugness to one of perfectly trained, and perfectly fake, customer service.

"Do you take Discover?"

"Of course, sir," she said as she began working on her little computer.

Her sudden change in attitude struck me. This little woman in her trendy, themed, v-neck sweater and scarf, treated me with complete disdain until I pulled out my credit card to prove to her that I was "in the club." That, I decided, was completely wrong; that her attitude toward me changed so dramatically not because of our conversation or an exchanged pleasantry, but by the contents of my wallet.

I had been in this situation several times before. Through most of my early life, my appearance had never really matched my tax bracket, but this time, it really bothered me and I felt myself growing angry. Yet, the notion of the rebellion that I would enjoy tempered my emotion.

It gave me a sense of satisfaction that while this woman was sleeping soundly in her pretentious, comatose existence I would be upstairs in her tidy little mountain retreat, in a suite, participating in deviant behavior with a bottle of whiskey, which I intended to purchase, and the free-spirited woman I had ridden into town with. Rebellion, even in its simplest and least intrusive form, can be so very sweet and so very satisfying.

The whole transaction felt wrong, like it was against everything I had been trying to prove to myself. But the desire to stay in a comfortable room quickly overcame my disgust. I swept the keys from the desk, gave the woman a searing look for having corrupted my sensibilities, and went outside.

The girl was leaning against my bike, enjoying a break in the rain, and a cigarette, while she watched the traffic move through downtown Steamboat. The whooshing sound of tires on wet concrete rose and fell with each passing car. Scattered groups of people were starting to emerge from the stores and restaurants.

I folded the receipt that the woman had given me and stuck it in my pocket.

"Are we in?" she asked.

"Yeah," I said, in an aggravated tone. "That little tramp working the desk looked at me like a complete vagrant until I produced a wallet full of credit cards."

"Sweetie, you *do* look like a vagrant, and that's what I love about you."

She grabbed my arm, stood on her tiptoes and kissed me. We walked down the street together, admiring the quaint atmosphere of the town, until we found a small liquor store tucked between a t-shirt shop and an art gallery. I bought a bottle of whiskey, some champagne and a pack of clove cigarettes. As we walked back to the hotel, the rain began to fall again with renewed intensity, and I felt it soak through my leather and deep into my tired body.

I left my bike in front of the hotel and grabbed my saddlebags, tossing them over my shoulder as we walked into the lobby. The woman behind the desk looked at the girl and then at me, as if I had just left the hotel and picked her up off the street. We stopped, and the girl turned toward me and grabbed the collar of my jacket.

"You're right," she said, loud enough for anyone in the lobby to hear, "that woman is *terrible*. But when we get upstairs I'll make you forget *all* about her."

There was something strange about this girl, but I didn't care to know what it was. We were both in the same place right then, and our mutually troubled pasts didn't matter at all. All that mattered was that we needed each other, if only for a short time and in a primal way, but it was just as real as anything else. It was the kind of relationship and understanding that felt plainly comfortable and innocent—the physical explorations of two young creatures that had found each other in a dark and lonely world.

It is impossible for mankind to define love, because love is only one word used to describe an infinite set of mental, emotional and spiritual connections that people can have for each other. During the time I was with this girl I was in love with her, and she loved me, and it was for a fleeting, completely unstable and semi-permanent reason.

We went upstairs to the room, and she disappeared into the bathroom, glancing back over her shoulder with a smile and a flirtatious wink. The fatigue of too many miles washed over me as I sat on the edge of the bed and pulled off my wet boots and socks. I looked back on the events of the day, thinking about how I had exchanged one kind of companion for another and wondering whether it was a good decision. In the end, though, I felt safe knowing that these were all marks of fate, and that none of it was really my decision at all.

Through the partially open bathroom door came the loud blast of water hitting porcelain. Through the narrow opening I saw her standing near the claw-foot bathtub, holding her small, dark hand under the steaming stream of water, and then she disappeared behind the door. I leaned back contentedly against a mountain of soft pillows and listened to the rain tap against the windows and the roof above. The scuffing sounds of clothing came through the open door and I sat up to look at her. The room grew quiet, but I couldn't see her. I leaned far over and caught a glimpse of her standing, looking out the open window, lost in thought, with her back toward me. There appeared to be something on the distant horizon that occupied her mind completely.

She wore nothing but a towel tied loosely around her waist, revealing her perfect, young hips and her smooth, tan skin. Two small dimples on the small of her back pointed gracefully toward her neck and her smooth, soft shoulder blades flexed as she untied the ribbon around her hair, letting the long, blonde curls fall between her outstretched arms. The gray light from the window cast a dim line around the shape of her breast and the outline of her delicate face.

The white walls around her glowed with the flash and color of the passing storm and the dull shadow of her beautiful body fell across the black and white tiled floor. Fat drops of rain drifted slowly down the window glass, or clung to it with hesitation, as if they too admired her mysterious beauty. Steam from the bathtub faucet billowed around her back, and her big blue eyes radiated with light as she turned and looked at me.

Sometimes in life, there are moments that freeze still like images in the picture book of your mind that you will remember forever as clear, simple and perfect snapshots of what makes our world beautiful. This, for me, was one of those moments.

She elegantly dipped a hand into the half-full tub, lightly splashing the water, then turned off the faucet and disappeared behind the door again. I lay back and rolled the vision of her around in my head.

"Get undressed and come in here," she said, "and bring those cigarettes with you."

A faint splashing echoed from the room as she sank into the bathtub. I took off my damp clothes and looked into a long mirror on the back of the door. My hands and face were much darker and dirtier than the rest of my body and I felt shy about my worn appearance.

I filled two glasses with the whiskey, grabbed the cigarettes, and went into the bathroom. She motioned to me, and I went to her, standing over the tub. She looked up at me with clear eyes and our naked bodies seemed to feel each other before they ever touched.

She reached for one of the glasses, I gave it to her, and she took a long drink. I felt calm and unafraid. I didn't notice the absence of anxiety that usually comes when you allow someone to see you in your naked form for the first time.

"Now get in here with me," she said with desire in her voice.

I stood over her, facing her, and slowly lowered myself into the hot water. It seared my damp skin, then covered me like a soothing blanket.

Her knees rested against the sides of the tub, sticking out of the bubbles that hovered on top of the water. I sat down and turned to lay back between her legs, resting my head against her right shoulder as she stroked my hair with one hand and reached over to the table with the other. She put a cigarette between my lips and lit it. I took a long drag and let the smoke sit deep in my lungs, then blew it out in a cloud across the dark room.

I held the cigarette between my index finger and my middle finger, resting my elbow on the side of the tub. She moved her hand on top of mine and delicately pulled the cigarette away and took a drag. I picked up one of the glasses and took a small drink, letting the warm sting of the liquor roll slowly down my throat.

Outside, the storm grew more intense. The lightning threw sheets of color on the wall in the growing twilight, like a flashbulb going off in an erratic sequence. A few seconds later came the thunder, booming low and dull in the distance. There was a quiet calm in the room, the kind of peace that I had been looking for since leaving home. It was a peaceful, beautiful calm, and the distant notion of its temporary nature was my only resistance to its intoxicating effect.

═══════

The rain lasted for almost two days. Our only contact with the outside world was the occasional visit from a small dark-skinned man who brought us the room service that we ordered in indulgent quantities. Each time he came in, he smirked at the sight of us: I wore a towel around my waist and met him at the door, while she sat on the edge of the bed with a sheet wrapped around her, smoking a cigarette and looking far away outside the window. It must have been an unusual scene for him, but to us, it was the picture of perfection.

During those two days, we made love and talked about our hopes and dreams. We talked about our never-ending search for the right thing, whatever that may be, and the right person, whomever that may be. We knew our time together was not meant to last, but we never talked about what would happen at the end. We never tried to make plans or promises.

The beauty and mystery of a new lover is never spoiled by an awareness of the short time that you have together. In the acceptance of that frailty, you make the absolute most of the time that you are given, and resist the temptation of trying to drag it out long after it has expired. Its innocence and excitement never dimming, not for a second, and leaving you changed forever when it's over. It's not the kind of love that lasts for years, but it is the kind of passionate companionship that you remember. On the morning of the last day, I woke up and she was gone.

She had left, and we hadn't allowed ourselves to become close enough to be vulnerable. I simultaneously missed her and didn't miss her. She was gone, and so was everything that we had shared physically and emotionally. All that remained in my mind was the memory of a girl shrouded in mystery and all the wonderful things that we had experienced together, along with the exhilaration that it gave to the both of us. A feeling of sadness came over me, not because of the end of this brief relationship, but from the passing of the moment.

12

The fantasy was over and the time had come to move down the road, into the sable hands of fate. I ordered a light breakfast and when the attendant arrived, he looked around the room, as if he were waiting for my companion to appear, and seemed saddened when she did not.

I ate as I packed, keeping one eye on the Weather Channel. The forecast predicted the next few days to be clear and warm from Wyoming all the way to Mexico, and I stuffed my leathers and gloves deep into my bags, knowing I would not need them. The rich promise of the day drifted through the open window as I went about my routine, and soon I left the room for the first and last time.

As I walked through the lobby of the hotel I exchanged sarcastic goodbye looks with the woman behind the desk. There was no pull for me to go through the formality of checking out. If the charge on my card was correct, it was correct; if not, then to hell with it. I didn't want to deal with that horrible woman again.

The sun was high over the eastern mountains when I walked out of the hotel, and it bathed the tops of the emerald-green ski slopes in a mixture of shadows and golden light. There wasn't a single cloud in the sky, nor was there any trace of the storms that had passed through.

The bike was exactly where I had left it, and I hung my bags over the rear seat and tied their leather straps to the metal hardware on the back fender. The main street through downtown was, according to the map, the quickest way out of town, and I followed it as it curved to the south, and the buildings began to disappear.

One last twinge of sadness crept across the front of my mind as I left Steamboat Springs. I thought about the end of my time with the mysterious girl. It was temporary, and I had known that all along. Still, a part of me held on to the notion that maybe our love could have become permanent. Why would we not have just as good a chance at love as any other couple? What if I had been completely wrong in thinking that we were only destined to be together for a short time. I had been wrong before, about many things.

In the end, though, I decided it was only regret tugging at me. The reality was that while we had made it as brief lovers, we would have never made it as friends. As I left town, I smiled at her memory, and left my regret on the road.

━━━━━

I followed the main street out of town, into the wide valley slung between the two lines of tall mountains running from the north to the south. I turned onto a two-lane road that veered to the right and, according to the sign on the roadside, led south toward the town of Wolcott, which was a familiar name from teenage hunting adventures.

I knew that Wolcott was close to Highway 6, another two-lane road that snaked along the Eagle River, parallel to Interstate 70. From there, I could ride south to Buena Vista, and find my old college friend Lance Hamilton, and spend a week or two relaxing in the quiet comfort of a shady river town. It would do me good after so long on the road, I thought, to see a familiar face.

Yampa, Colorado, quickly came into view over the rolling valley floor. The business district of Yampa was a real Old West main street, with a sloping arch in the middle, separating two opposing lines of storefronts. The buildings on each side of the road were connected, and their porches formed a continuous wooden sidewalk which disappeared over the low rise ahead. I rode to the highest point of the street and surveyed the untouched ruggedness of the town. At the end of the street, where a busy-looking general store stood, the road turned sharply to the right and faded to the north and out of town. I stopped in front of the store, stood up, swung my long leg over the bike and stretched.

The few people on the street turned to look in my direction with cautious curiosity. They saw a shaggy, sunburned man in a white t-shirt and a faded, fringed, button-down Oxford, tucked in to keep the wind out, a new pair of jeans, faded chaps and dirty boots. I looked at my watch. It was high noon.

This town was a remnant of old Colorado, untouched by the slow passage of time, with no aspirations to adapt to the strange civilization that now surrounded it. I stood in the street, casting my short shadow onto the dark dirt in front of me. It seemed to me that I had wandered off the main road into a parallel world of ghost towns, dirt streets and outlaws. It was the old West of my dreams, and the idyllic image I had been looking for.

Inside the old store the floor slanted down and away from a long row of support posts running through its center. The wood shelves were filled with fresh produce and dusty dry goods. On the far wall an old map hung above a small pot of brewing coffee. Yellow pushpins, tacked to all four corners, held it to the wall. The paper was old, and depicted the town of Yampa, as well as the rivers and hills that surrounded it to the west.

There were three roads leading up the mountains, west of town, following the channels cut by snow-fed streams. There were small pieces of paper tacked to the faded map in various places along the rivers, and in the hills surrounding the town. One marked the spot where a 10-pound trout was caught, several others showed the locations of old mines and where relics and important sites were and one marked where a brown bear had been shot. Each piece of paper had its own name and date, the oldest being from 1962.

I bought a warm six-pack of beer, a small, collapsible, nylon cooler, a cup full of ice and a bungee cord. I put the items on the counter next to the register and asked the clerk, a young girl with sparkling eyes, to make me two ham and cheese sandwiches.

"I put extra cheese on there for you, but don't you go telling anyone," she said when she was finished.

"I won't," I replied, smiling at this amusing display of maternal affection.

I put the beer in the cooler and dumped the ice on top of it, grabbed the bag with the sandwiches and the bungee cord, and walked outside. I stuck the little sack into the leather saddlebags and secured the cooler to the backseat with the bungee cord. Before leaving town, I took a walk around the nearly deserted business district.

In this motley collection of cars and buildings there were no references to the current terror alert and only one politically motivated sticker, on the window of the hardware store, commenting on September 11th. There were no cell phone towers, no newspaper machines and no traces of corporate incursion. It was as if the outside world only slightly touched this place, and isolated local events and the passing of one generation to another were the only events to mark the slow progression of time.

These seemed to be people who spent their time the way their parents and grandparents had: living for the sake of taking care of their own, trying to create something out of nothing, and finding stability through simplicity.

For the sake of maintaining my perceived innocence of this little corner of the world, I left town by way of a dirt road, along a valley and into the mountains. Just after one, I stopped near the bank of a small, fast-moving river. I was completely alone except for the birds, and I spread my bedroll on the ground under an aspen tree.

I drank two beers and unfolded the wax paper that held my sandwiches. I ate them slowly, listening to the water bubble through the rocks and the wind push through the aspen trees behind me. I sat there for a couple of hours, not thinking about anything in particular, but meditating and feeling at ease with my surroundings. There was nothing complicated or deep about what I was doing, but it was very spiritual. I felt like I achieved a sense of solace and simplicity that the people in the town below seemed to exude.

After resting, I continued up the road, following it as it looped around two small peaks, then finally turned onto a small road leading down the mountain and back to the highway, south of Yampa. Again, I followed the pavement south and as afternoon turned to evening, I came to the small hamlet of State Bridge, Colorado.

The town was only a glancing intersection between Yampa, Kremmling and Wolcott. It was a key entry point for the whitewater rafting business on the upper Colorado River, and a mere two miles away from the Arapahoe National Forest.

State Bridge wasn't really a town at all, but merely a small store, a bar/restaurant and collection of small cabins, tepees and yurts. In front of the store, tacked to a post and stuck into a dusty flowerbed, was a small sign "For Sale—By Owner."

I walked into the bar, which was composed of three or four different styles of building that appeared to have been added together over the years; the different sections of the lodge reflecting the most efficient style at the time of construction. I sat at a table and an extremely attractive and slender girl, who introduced herself as Naomi, handed me a menu and took my drink order.

She spoke with an English accent, and her voice was soft and soothing. Her hair was long, brown and wavy. She wore a white tank top and a long, blue, cotton skirt. Around her neck was a string of beads that hung low to her flat, exposed belly, and she wore no shoes.

"What is this place?" I asked.

"It's a lodge now, but it used to be an old railroad and mail stop from the 1880s," she said, smiling and looking around the room as if to reexamine its place in history. "It's been added onto over the years and now it is a rest stop for wayward souls like yourself."

My mouth was dry and dusty. I ordered a glass of water. She disappeared and I sat back in the chair and looked around at the dark pine walls, and immediately felt relaxed and at ease.

Two men sat at the bar eating sandwiches and drinking Fat Tire beer. At their feet sat two large, dusty backpacks and they spoke to each other in low tones between bites. In the background was the calm, dull sound of an old jukebox, which sat in the corner spinning scratchy 45s. The song playing was of an early bluegrass variety, but I couldn't place it.

Naomi returned with my water and I ordered dinner and a bottle of the house red wine. As I waited I relaxed and took in the serenity of the place. As I looked around the room the idea of staying at the lodge for a little while flashed through my mind. When she returned, I asked if there were any cabins available.

"How long do you want to stay?" she asked.

"Oh," I replied, "I don't know. This place feels good to me. I think I'd like to stay a couple of nights."

"Well," she said, "I know that there are a lot of open spots right now, but there is a music festival here this weekend. I'll ask Debra, the owner, if there is anything available through the weekend."

"Thanks," I said.

When she returned a few minutes later, she brought the wine, already opened, and a small glass. She told me that she had talked to Debra and there wasn't anything open through the weekend, but that I could stay and see if anything opened up.

"That sounds good," I said. "I know I just got here, but I feel really relaxed and I think I need to stay here for a while."

"I know what you mean. I came here three years ago and I never left. I bought a little place between here and Wolcott, and I work here on the weekends and some evenings during the week."

"What do you do during the week?"

"Actually, I sell houses," she replied.

"You're a real estate agent?" I asked.

"Kind of," she answered, squinting her eyes. "I get people houses based on their spiritual connections with the places. I ask them what kind of house they can see and feel themselves living in, and I find it for them. I sell them a home more than a house."

"That is an interesting way of looking at it," I said.

"You look tired," she said. "There's a lot of strong light around you, but it seems dimmer than it should be."

"I've come a long way," I said. I felt a flash of energy exchange between us.

As I spoke, a group of four raft guides came in and sat down at a table near the door. They had noticeable tan lines around their upper bodies, in exactly the shapes of life jackets. They were talking loudly about the day's river conditions and the clients that they had taken on.

"Excuse me," Naomi said. "I have to go take care of these ruffians."

She walked away and as she began to take orders from the unruly group, she looked at me and our eyes met. She smiled. I felt a shock, one of those feelings that makes a person's heart warm and feel like it skips a beat.

"Wow," I said aloud to myself.

Immediately my fatigue and exhaustion were gone. I looked at her again and she was talking to the men at the table in a familiar way. I got the impression that they were regulars, which they probably were. All at once, I felt like an outsider, which surprised me even though I obviously was, and I began to lose the excited feeling. I looked in her direction again and saw that she was still looking at me, and the feeling instantly returned. It was coming from her, not from the place or the situation.

There was something about the woman that was completely and purely fascinating to me. I drank almost an entire glass of wine in nearly one gulp, feeling like I needed something to calm me down.

"Debra put you in cabin eight," Naomi said when she returned with my plate of ham and grilled vegetables, "and she said that you can come and fill out our little reservation form tomorrow. I'll get you the keys. The bathrooms and showers are between cabins six and seven."

"Thank you," I said without even looking at my food.

"What's your name?" she asked.

I told her and she looked up and over my head.

"Hmm," she said. "Well, I will let you enjoy your dinner. Don't worry about paying for it right now. I'll just put it on your bill."

"Thank you."

She began to walk away, then stopped suddenly and turned back.

"I'll be done here in a couple of hours. Do you want to go rest for a while and then meet me back here for a drink or two later?"

"I would love to," I said, trying to figure out what it was that was tying us together.

"Great," she said. "I would love to talk to you more."

I finished my dinner slowly and then the rest of the wine. The cabernet was dry, but it tasted good after my long weeks on the road. There was relaxation in its deep resonance, and my constant speculation of the eventual result of this adventure began to melt away. Of course, a whole bottle of anything was bound to help me feel better about my situation.

13

I walked out of the bar to a cloudless, star-filled sky, and a chill coming out of the valley up the long slope from the river, eroding the last of the daytime heat. The sound of the bubbling water drifted across the road toward the lodge, and the night smelled of pine trees and deep, dark earth. The hills and the tall rock faces above the bends of the river glowed in the last remaining light, then began to dim and hide themselves in the moonless night.

A thin layer of condensation covered the bike, along with my saddlebags and bedroll. I took my few possessions to the cabin, a small, wood-planked building with a modest, covered porch spanning the width of the front. Two large trees stuck out high in the air on either side, and dropped their heavy leaves downward, so that they swept back and forth against the shingles in the gentle evening breeze.

The cabin had two rooms: a sitting room that contained a small couch, a desk, and a fireplace, and a small bedroom in the back with a king-sized bed and a wide window. A sign on the wall in the front room reminded patrons to close their windows at night, so that no unwelcome guests came in. I assumed that they were talking about bears and raccoons, but then I considered that maybe there were strange people who would roam around at night looking for open windows so they could pay a visit. The wine was making me consider less logical possibilities.

With a stomach full of food and wine, I lay down on the bed and fell into a light sleep. I woke up a couple of hours later and walked out onto the porch. The night was quiet, and the sounds of the river in the distance mixed with faint conversation drifting out of the bar. The voices and the rippling swirls of the invisible water were almost indistinguishable from one another, creating a harmonic sense that the night was a living, breathing thing.

The cleanest pair of jeans I could find smelled damp and dirty, so I put them back and grabbed a t-shirt and my favorite Oxford button-down shirt, which by then had faded in the sun and developed a noticeably frayed collar and cuffs. I grabbed my semi-clean clothes and my shaving kit, and walked down the boardwalk to the bathhouse.

I took a long, semi-private shower and then dried off, dressed and walked back to the cabin, stopping briefly to once again admire the crisp, blue evening and listen to the sounds of guitar music added to the night's symphony.

Back in the cabin, I laid my shaving kit on a table near the door and put my dirty clothes back in my saddlebags. I pulled the rest of my wet clothes out of the bags to let them air out, and as I did I noticed a brown paper bag that I hadn't seen before in the bottom of one of them. I pulled it out, unrolled the top and looked inside. There was a piece of paper on top and I pulled it out to read it. It was from Bryan Hillary.

Brother,

I'm writing this by firelight, and I'm pretty drunk so don't give me any shit if you can't read it. You passed out not so long ago, and I can't believe you let that girl outdrink you! You are some piece of work, my friend.

If you're reading this, then we have parted ways and you are probably asking yourself some questions. I know we had to leave each other, but believe me, it was only because of my own past. I didn't want anything I did to cause you any problems.

I have enjoyed our time together. It was an unexpected friendship and I had no idea that I would meet anyone like you out here. I have never really been close to anyone and it seems to me that we've shared a good bond in the short time we've been together. I think we are two old souls traveling around, lost in this world. The fact that I was able to say the things to you that I did tells me that there is a strength between us that can never be duplicated, and I want to thank you for the opportunity.

Here are a couple of things that I want you to have. There is a bottle of whiskey in there that the girl, who kicked your worthless ass at drinking, gave me to give to you. Remember when you drink it that life is for celebrating. The second item is something that has always been with me in my travels. I have never been religious but I believe in the power of luck, and this medal has always served me well. It is a St. Christopher medal and it guides travelers through unfamiliar waters. I believe you need this more than I do and I know it will carry you far.

Farewell, my friend, and I know that we will see each other again. I have a feeling that we could go for years without seeing each other, but when we finally meet, it will be the same as if I saw you yesterday. You know how to find me, and please call to let me know where you are periodically. Leave me an address and I will stay in touch. Peace and love, my friend,

Bryan Hillary

I reached in the bag and pulled out the medal. It sparkled in the dim light of the cabin and I stuck it in my pocket, where it would stay.

The whiskey was a Basil Hayden's, an expensive brand. Through the glass bottle the hue of the liquor hinted of the Kentucky oak bar-

rels in which it had been stored. I put the bottle on the table, on top
of Bryan's letter, grabbed the keys to my room, and disappeared in
the cool night, down the boardwalk to the bar.

===============

The quiet restaurant had transformed itself, in my absence, to a bar
full of tanned faces and loud volleys of talk. A bright atmosphere radiated around the crowd, giving it a festive air that I noticed immediately.
There was a man on a small stage at one end, perched atop a tall stool,
playing the guitar. Stuck in the strings of his instrument, between two
of the tuning pegs, was a cigarette, and its smoke drifted through the
light and around his face, casting shadows on his shirt.

The bar light was dim, and I stopped in the doorway to look for
Naomi. A few of the patrons glanced in my direction, but the room
in general gave no notice of my arrival. I didn't see her, so I sat between
three empty stools at the counter and ordered a double Jameson on
the rocks.

I sat facing the mirror behind the bar. By then I had a thin, blonde
beard and I thumbed its bristles while considering the events of the previous days. I thought about Bryan, wondering whether he had made
it to Denver or not, and considered that perhaps he would want to meet
me in State Bridge for the festival. This didn't seem to be a place that
would be running loose with law enforcement, and he might enjoy the
kind of soothing experience we'd hoped to have in Yellowstone. As I
thought about this, a soft, English voice spoke from behind me.

"May I sit with you?" Naomi asked.

"Of course," I replied as I snapped out of my thoughts. I stood
up and pulled out the barstool to my right. "I was saving this for you."

"Thank you, dear," she said.

She sat down and put her purse on the bar. She wore a white shirt,
jeans and brown leather hiking boots. She turned and nodded at the
bartender, and he started to make a drink. She turned back to me,
put her elbow on the bar, and rested her chin on her hand.

"Oh, I am so glad that's over," she said. "So, how *are* you?"

"I'm very good," I answered. "I took a little nap and a shower, and I feel like a new man."

"Wonderful," she said in her beautiful accent. "You look a little more alive than when I saw you last."

"When did you finish up here?"

"Ugh," she said, "just now. I only had time to change, but I wanted to meet you as quickly as I could. I thought I'd better catch you before you decided to take off again."

"No," I answered, "I wanted to see you again."

She smiled. "Is that your motorcycle outside?"

"Of course," I said. "Don't I look like a biker?"

"You look too young to be a biker," she said with a quiet laugh.

"Damn it," I said. "That was the look I was going for."

"No," she said, "I didn't mean it that way. It's just that we get a lot of older guys on bikes in here, with beards and lots of leather and all of that. You look younger and more distinguished than they do. Anyway, you're the first biker who's ordered wine since I've worked here, that's for sure."

"Ok," I said, "I'll admit that I still have a long way to go before I'm a real biker, but I'm cute, though, right?"

"Oh, definitely," she answered. "Just not like a biker."

We both laughed at the exchange, and then paused. It felt like our words fed each other, and though we had just met there was the feeling that I had known her before. Our talk was easy and light-hearted. We both gave and took in turn. The words and stories flowed between us smoothly and comfortably.

"Where did you come from?" she asked.

"Do you want the short version or the long version?"

"I want it all."

"All right," I said, and began to tell her the whole story from the beginning.

I told her why I had left home, particularly what Beth had done, and my dissatisfaction with corporate America. As I spoke I began to feel like the story began much father back. Beyond the specific list of reasons that led me to travel west there was a long string of broken allegiances to my own heart that I hadn't yet considered. I told her about the wedding and the trip west and meeting Bryan, but there was much more to the story and she gave me the opportunity to let it go. There was a calm look in her eye, and as she listened to me, the true story flowed with poetic explosion.

"When I was a kid I had all of these things that I wanted to do, and I knew that I had a whole life to do them. I wanted to travel and see the world, be a pilot, a fireman, play music and be a writer. But I started to grow up, and as each year went by I traded in dream after dream until finally they were all gone."

"I think that happens to all of us," she said. "We all have these powerful things that we want to accomplish, but as we get older we realize that we can't do all that. Real life isn't about doing what you want to do, it's about doing what you have to. I don't like it, and I don't agree with it-but that's the way it is."

"But why?" I asked. "It doesn't make any sense! We spend the first years of life dreaming about what we'll do when we're adults, but when we finally grow up we have to spend the rest of our lives thinking about all the things we couldn't do. People constantly live day to day, with one eye on the present and constantly thinking about unrealized dreams. The only thought we give to the future is always just planning out subsequent years so they are as comfortable as possible. Then one day we realize that decades have passed and eventually we are too old for futile dreams."

"We can't all go off and be pilots and doctors and firemen though," she said. "I'm not saying I disagree with you, but I'm playing devil's advocate here. The world has to function, and that means that we all have to sacrifice dreams."

"I know," I said, "but we don't have to be robots! No matter what profession people choose they can't use it as an excuse to stop being human. People can live in both worlds I think-the world of dreams *and* the world of reality. It can't all be about populating the next generation and making money to spend while we're not at work. We have to make more of the experience."

"That makes sense," she said, "but how does that happen? How do you differentiate between the two?"

"I don't know," I said, and considered the question. "That's going to be different for everyone," I continued. "It's all about finding happiness and adventure within the confines of a normal life. It's about finding the things you can truly enjoy."

"So what do you enjoy?" She asked.

"Well," I said, with a pause. "I enjoy this. I enjoy talking to you. There's something about you…I've never talked this openly to *anyone.*"

Naomi smiled and looked at me. The depth of our conversation had silenced the activity in the bar, and for a second we were the only two people in the world. There was a long pause in which I felt like I was experiencing something that I had never felt for another human.

"You know," I said, "when I was a teenager I kept praying for the day when everything would become clear. I mean, when you're at that age you see adults as these powerful people and they seem so stable. Meanwhile I just felt so goddamn confused about *everything.*"

"Yes, but adults aren't like that, though," she said. "They're just as clueless, but they've been around long enough to know how to manage it, I think."

"Well," I replied, "either that, or they just give up and ignore the bigger stuff in favor of managing their own lives. When I was eighteen, I *really* thought that as I got out of college and into the real world, I would get to a certain age and everything would just…start to make sense, I guess. I just thought I would hit 30 or so and all the uncertainty would be overshadowed by all the answers I had accumulated."

"Yeah," she said, with a laugh. "That doesn't happen, though."

"Well… I know that *now!*"

As I spoke, she looked at me with interest, seemed pained when I spoke of bad things and smiled when the story had its comical moments. Suddenly, everything that had happened began to feel real, rather than just a series of fly-by events. It was as if all these events were distantly connected and at some point and I would find the thing that would tie them all together. There was a sense of impending reality setting in about the whole odyssey, and it felt like that shadow I had been running from was beginning to catch up.

Naomi listened to me with the attention that I felt my story deserved. In turn, I listened to her. She had little to say about herself, but she had a great deal to say about others, and what she said had a profound effect on my state of mind. What really drew me to her was the way she spoke of the energy that readily flowed between humans, which was a precept that I hadn't thought about in a long time. Her idea was that there was a subtle connection between all of us, and it was rooted in the basic sense of our humanity.

"Interactions between people," she said, "are what create all that energy we feel. When you meet someone you connect with, you can feel it deep inside, and that's when you know you've experienced something profound, and that is a feeling that you can never let go of. You just have to hold it. Your life is only just a series of moments, and they are what connect the past and the future. If you miss out on that, then you miss out on life."

What she was telling me was right, and it felt right. I gladly sat back and drank it in. We smiled and laughed for the rest of the evening, drinking wine and absorbing the energy that zigzagged between us, as we fell deeper and deeper into each other. The guitarist began to play an old, sad song and our eyes met over the light of the candle that sat between us on the bar.

"I would really like to dance with you right now," she said, smiling.

I had never been very good at dancing. It was a custom that I wasn't comfortable with, but I knew that missing this dance would be missing something important. There are few things better in life than a first dance, or a first kiss, or the first time that you hold someone you never want to let go of. I held my hand out to her and she took it, and we danced.

I took her left hand softly and put my right hand on the small of her back. When we came together, it was as if our bodies fit in a way I had never experienced with anyone else. She looked into my eyes, and we both smiled. We pulled each other close, swaying in the soft light of the bar. I could feel the warmth of her body against me, and closed my eyes as all anxiety quietly vanished.

Already, I knew that she was an amazing woman; her spirit was kind, carefree, magnetic and soothing. She had told me in the course of our conversation that she could see a great power in me, but that I had not found it yet. She was right; I had felt empty for so long in my old life.

Yet, something different was happening now. In talking to her, I stumbled on hidden feelings. There was something else in the world to look forward to now, and I blindly tried to search for where that thought was going to take me. I finally felt fate's hand again, and hoped I still had a bigger part to play in life.

During college, I had always looked at the possibilities of the future, as if there weren't any dream that I couldn't realize. Afterward, I'd strain to come up with anything I could do that would really make a difference in the world. Naomi's passion inspired me to believe in possibility again, and deep down, I hoped I would find it, and that she would be there when I did. She had reached out to me, grabbed on to that hidden corner of my soul, and dangled it in front of me. What I liked about her was the fact that her comforting words held a challenge in them.

The bar closed and we disappeared together into the night, down the long boardwalk toward my cabin. I had bought a bottle of wine back at the bar, and I carried it in one arm while she held on to the other. All around were the sounds of people leaving, the slamming of car doors and the starting of engines. As we walked, the sounds died down, and soon, only the quiet of the mountain night surrounded us.

She stopped just outside my front door and pulled on my arm. We stood facing each other, and she leaned toward me with her face lifted to meet mine. Our foreheads touched and I didn't know whether I should kiss her or not. I set the bottle on the railing and put my hands around the small of her back.

"Would you like to come in for a drink?" I asked.

"No, my dear," she said, as she backed away, shaking her head. "I don't think that would be a good idea."

"What do you mean?" I asked.

"We have a good thing going here, and I don't want to ruin it."

"Oh, great," I replied with a laugh. "Don't tell me that I've turned into *the friend* guy."

"No," she said, shaking her head. "It's just that…" She paused, and loosened her grip on my waist.

"What is it?" I asked.

"It's late and I have to work in Edwards tomorrow," she said, with a hint of despair. "I have to get home and get some sleep."

"All right," I said. "Well, at least we made some memories tonight."

I took her hands.

"Yeah," she mumbled, and looked up and away from me. "God, I don't want this night to end like this."

"I know," I replied, "but there is always tomorrow to face, no matter how long we would like the night to last."

"I want to see you again," she said, looking down at the ground, as if she were ashamed.

"You know where I'll be," I replied, strengthening my hold on her cold, delicate hands.

"I should be around here tomorrow night."

"Well, I hope I'll see you then. I would like to stay through the weekend, at least."

"I'm sure Debra will let you stay if I asked her. She always leaves at least one cabin open for friends."

"Good, because I want to see you again, too," I said.

"Yeah, I have some things to tell you before you leave," she said.

She looked at me worriedly, like a person who was about to tell you the worst news possible, but was searching blindly for a civil way to do it.

"Yeah," I said, "me too."

We leaned toward each other. She looked up at me with her deep, brown eyes and I bent down to kiss her. Before our lips touched, she turned, and we stumbled into an awkward embrace. It was an embrace that felt distant, as if the expectation of the moment had not been met and what had actually happened was only a weak alternative.

She shifted, moved in close and put her head on my shoulder, returning to the exact fit that we had found as we'd danced. She held onto me tightly, as if we were never going to see each other again. We held each other in the last minutes of the night, as the river gurgled behind us. There was an uncomfortable pause as I tried to disengage, an awkward moment when I tried to let go but she still held on. We pulled each other close again and then she let go, looked at me and smiled.

"Good night," she said in her beautiful accent. "I hope I'll see you tomorrow. You need to rest, and then we can see each other again."

"I will look forward to it," I said.

"Yeah," she said, putting one hand gently on my cheek.

She turned and walked away. My eyes followed her until she disappeared into the darkness, then I sat down in one of the chairs on the porch. The only thing I knew for sure was that I was going to finish the bottle of wine, and then maybe drink the whiskey that Bryan had left me. I knew that I had a lot to think about, but I also knew that the time to think was tomorrow, and the time to drink was now. So it goes: alone with my thoughts in the most beautiful place I could imagine, thinking about the most beautiful person I had ever met.

The night was cold, and I sat alone in the stillness of the valley. I lit a cigarette, and exhaled the smoke with deep resonance. The end of the evening had left me drunk and, against my intentions, I was thinking in profound leaps, but there were flashes of intuition within my confusion.

Outside of everything Naomi and I had shared over the course of the night, I could sense an almost deliberate distance in her. I could only speculate, but I understood that there was something more to this woman than what I knew. Without a doubt there was a strange and unexpected chemistry between us, but she seemed ill-at-ease with our connection. Something in her mind or in her life was preventing our natural behavior toward each other from running its course.

During our conversation, she had talked a lot about her spiritual views, but never divulged any personal information about her life or background. Perhaps, I considered, there was something that I should know about her before being that attracted to her.

In the flexing emotions of the night, I felt an overwhelming sense of repetition. This confusion was something I had already experienced. What was happening to me then had happened sometime before, sometime long ago.

14

I slept until mid-morning of the next day. All the time that I had spent on the road over the previous weeks had finally begun to catch up to me, and I slept long and deep.

The afternoon found the sun shining brightly through the thin, linen curtains separating the inside of my cabin from the outside world. I was alone, and the quiet of the room was sweet and pleasant against the backdrop of the road, which had provided me with little time to myself since leaving Kansas City.

Sitting on the edge of the bed, I stretched and looked out the window between the breaks in the curtain, over the porch railing to the river. Groups of people wearing life jackets hovered around several large, rubber boats on the opposite side of the river, at the boat ramp. They were receiving instructions from a very loud man who stood on a tree stump holding a paddle.

I dressed and walked down the boardwalk to the restaurant for breakfast. Behind the bar, which doubled as the breakfast counter, was a woman in her late 50s, writing in a ledger. I sat down at the bar and picked up a menu. The woman turned to look at me.

"Are you Debra?" I asked.

"Yes I am, honey," she replied as she continued writing. "Are you the guy in cabin eight?"

"Yes, ma'am, I am. Thank you for letting me stay the night."

"Yeah, well, don't mention it. Naomi told me about you. She said we were supposed to take good care of you."

"I would appreciate that. What do you recommend for breakfast?"

"Well," she replied, "for the hungover raft guide, I generally serve the whitewater special."

I gratefully accepted the suggestion and ordered the special, which was two fried eggs, cheese, bacon and sausage served on a toasted bagel, along with the strongest drink, she said, served in the Rocky Mountains. The concoction, she told me, was special and made using fresh coffee, grounds from the day before, plus a raw egg and a generous dose of Tabasco.

"It's guaranteed to make a dead man weep," she said.

"I'm not scared," I replied.

She smiled as she jotted my order down on a worn pad of paper that she had pulled from her back pocket. She clicked her pen and disappeared into the kitchen.

"By the way, honey," she said, sticking her head out of the swinging door. "You feel free to stay in that cabin as long as you want. We ended up with a cancellation for the festival this weekend, so if you want it, it's yours."

"Cool," I said. "I will take you up on that."

"Good," she said.

She disappeared through the door to get my order to the cook. When she returned, she had a clipboard and began to inventory the level of the liquor bottles, which sat in rows on the back bar.

"Is Naomi working tonight?" I asked. I tried to sound casual, as if I had only a moderate desire to see her again.

"Yes, she is," Debra answered. "She's taking the 7:00 to close shift." She turned and tilted her head down, resting her hand on the bar. "What's going on between you two, anyway?"

"Nothing," I replied weakly. "Why?"

"I just wanted to ask. Look, if you don't want to talk about it, that's fine, but I'm no fool. There's something going on between you two. I could see it in her face, and I see that same look in your eyes right now. I'm old enough to be able to see when two people are starting to fall in love."

"Was it that obvious?" I asked.

"Sweetie, you two might as well have posted flyers."

I put my hand on my thigh and turned slightly to look at the nearly empty bar. An elderly couple sat in one of the booths, poring over maps and brochures amidst half-empty lunch plates. The jukebox sat silently against the wall, and the room still smelled of stale beer and cigarette smoke. It was a sweet sight to see two people, in the winter of life, exploring remote parts of the west. They were seeing the earth before they once again became a part of it.

"I really don't know what it is about her Debra," I admitted, "but it has me scared shitless."

"Call me D," she said. "All my friends call me that, whether I want them to or not. Anyway, I asked Naomi about you last night and she started to act just as nervous as you are right now."

She paused.

"There are some things that you don't know about her, though," she said sternly, "and I hope that she tells you what you need to know before something bad happens."

"What does that mean?"

"Look, it's not *my* place to tell you. She'll have that conversation with you when she's ready, I guess. In the greater scheme of things, what she will tell you isn't 'bad,' but it will put a damper on this giddy little schoolboy notion of romance you've got right now."

She fixed her gaze on me, like a teacher looking on an insolent child, and then turned away for a moment and went back to her work.

D was quite a bit older than everyone else who worked at the lodge. She was probably in her late 40s or early 50s, and had the ruggedly beautiful look of someone who had lived in the mountains her whole life. Her black and grey hair was pulled back in a tight ponytail. She was full figured, with dark eyes, and her hands were rough. She told me that she had spent several years working as a guide on the Colorado River before buying the lodge.

There was a gentle nature in her eyes which made her very easy to talk to. Yet there was something about her look that told you not to mess with her. Her advice was profound in a purely simple way, complemented by an eerie ability to correctly identify people based on facial expressions and body postures.

"Humans are animals just like any other animal on the planet," she would say, "We have all that fancy psychological mumbo jumbo, but at the end of the day we are still just animals. You can count on it."

Her philosophy was that most people were easy to read if you just took time to study their body language, and what better place to see that in its purest form than in a bar?

"Alcohol takes away some of the inhibition that sets us apart from animals," she said to me. "It allows our predatory instincts to shine. The true nature of our animal heritage is only evident when we've had a few."

Though her speech and manner felt like they came straight out of the backwoods, there was no getting around her intelligence. During our conversation I had learned that she held a PhD in biology from Tulane, and had actually come to the Colorado River in the early '80s, to study migratory bacteria in the alpine ecosystem, and had never bothered to leave. The strange mix of intelligence and back-road philosophies had created one of those one-of-a-kind women who a person of any age readily listened to.

"Well, I guess she'll tell me in her own time," I said. "Say, I meant to ask you—what's with the 'for sale' sign out front? Is that for real?"

"Yeah," she said, "in case you hadn't noticed, I'm not getting any younger and there's still quite a lot I want to do out there. I'm hoping I can get some traveling money by selling the place, and maybe the new owners would let me work here in the summers or something like that."

"Anyone knockin' at your door?"

"Not really, just these corporate fuckers wanting to turn the place into some trendy backwoods resort, but they can go to hell. I don't give a damn how much they want to offer for it; I want to wait until the right person comes around. I always fancied a young couple taking it over and making it their home, or something like that."

She walked around the bar and approached a pair of travelers who had sat down at a table near the front door. I reached into my pocket, pulled out the St. Christopher medal, and rubbed it with my thumb and forefinger. I wondered what Bryan's advice would be in this situation.

I stood up and walked toward the back of the bar, to a short hallway that led to the restrooms. On the wall opposite the doors hung an old pay phone, which was covered with a residue of sticky drinks and had old numbers scratched in the wall around it. I opened my wallet and took out the phone number that Mr. Hillary had given me as well as my room key, which had the address of the lodge stamped on the key chain.

I made the call using my credit card, and I leaned against the wall by the phone, waiting for it to connect. When his voicemail answered, I smiled. Hearing my friend's voice again was comforting, and I immediately began to miss his sardonic opinion of humanity and his independent but troubled spirit.

"Hey, Bryan," I said, "it's me. I'm in this small town in central Colorado. I haven't made it very far since I saw you last, but I've seen some great country and met some interesting people."

I went on to tell him about the girl in Steamboat, the trip south and my blissful experiences with Naomi. At the end of the message, I gave him the address and number of the lodge, and asked that he get in touch with me when he got the chance. I also thanked him for the letter, the medal and the bottle.

I hung up the phone and stood still for a while, looking at my distorted reflection in its chrome faceplate. The napkin with Bryan's number and address sat in my hand, and I felt a sudden stab of loneliness. I missed him, and this uncertainty about Naomi was making me feel unsure about the source of my feelings for her.

Was it loneliness that was letting me feel so deeply for her this early on? Perhaps my strong attraction to her was the result of some intense hatred of being alone. I began to think that all those long days on the road, combined with everything that had happened with Beth in Kansas City, were beginning to cloud my judgment.

I could really be falling for Naomi—or, perhaps, my recent experiences with loss and pain forced me to become attracted to the idea of her, or to the idea of falling in love. I was confused, but was determined not to let Naomi know about it. I hoped that I could spend the rest of my time there getting to know her and enjoying her company.

I felt no rush for anything physical to happen between us. I was content with seeing her and learning more about her beautiful outlook on the world. I decided that I would allow myself to relax, and ignore the possibility that something bad *could* eventually happen between us. For once, I decided to let events unfold in their natural order instead of forcing them to their uncertain end. The decision felt right, and my feelings of loneliness gave way to excitement.

I went back to the bar with a smile on my face. When I sat down again, breakfast was waiting for me. I ate quickly, and drank two large glasses of water and a cup of the thick, spicy coffee—which felt a lot like being hit in the face with a rolled up phone book. I fished a $5 bill out of my pocket and laid it on the table for a tip.

"Thanks, D!" I yelled. "I'm going into the mountains for a while."

"Okay," she said. "Keep your calendar clear tonight. We're having an after-bar party."

"Absolutely. I will be there."

I left quickly and went back to the cabin. I grabbed my copy of *Leaves of Grass*, hopped on my bike, and took off up the wide dirt road that led toward the mountains and away from the main highway.

The gravel surface of the road had been compacted so much with heavy logging traffic that it felt like riding on concrete. I was alone in the valley except for the occasional mountain biker and the steady stream of dories and rubber rafts on the river below.

The road ran parallel to the river, rising above and away from it occasionally when the water disappeared into some of the narrow canyons that dotted the valley. High, rugged mountaintops surrounded the low, grassy hills. Above the tree line, the last of the winter snow clung to the rocks in windblown patches.

At the top of a pass the road intersected with a smooth forest road. The crossing road led to the top of a narrow ridge, toward a snow-covered mountain. I turned and slowly traversed the backbone of the ridge, upward toward the jagged and rocky peak. Creeping slowly through the damp alpine dirt, I was careful to keep the bike steady on the uneven ground. As the road rose higher and strong gusts of cold, thin air swept down the ridge, and the strong rocky aroma of the mountain surrounded me.

I came to a small clearing and stopped on the side of the road. A narrow path disappeared through the line of tall pines and I walked into the veil of trees to follow it. The trail was short and led through the thick pines and to a large grove of aspen trees, beyond which lay an alpine meadow. I surveyed the long, sloping field.

The flat grasses sloped down toward the valley and in the distance, I could see the road and the river, running their parallel courses down the valley toward the lodge, which was just out of sight behind a fat shoulder of rock. I stood on the promontory of my kingdom and let the breeze fan across my face.

Everything around me had an air of brilliant newness, reflecting the beauty of the season. It had rained there recently, and the air was heavy with wet earth and old wood. The sun was low in the sky but its beam still covered my body, and bathed it in delicate warmth. The wind was at my back, rustling the trees and flying through the grasses to the valley floor.

An enormous expanse hung between the past and the present, and brilliant images of my life on the road filled the void between that old forgotten life and this sublimely uncertain new one. It all came back, every memory of the road, in one satisfying sigh.

There were the people: Bryan, the McCook girls, the cops, the devil in Wyoming, the twin drug runners in Cody, the girl in Steamboat, and, of course, Naomi. The road and the open sky, the smell of the rain, the expiration of the fading day and the memory of a long string of forgotten promises left in the place I had once thought of as home.

What had happened to me, and what was happening, were deliberately hiding my decision to leave without closing any doors. The farther I traveled into the surviving frontier, the more paradoxically I became aware of the freedoms I would never find, and the future that would inevitably come when the shadow finally found me.

I had hidden behind thousands of miles of dark nights, shady bars and strange people, and kept the real world at bay through a haze of drinking and casual affairs and friendships, which had done nothing but afford me a false sense of peace. All the while, life seemed to look back at me with the same cruel indifference. My particular corner of it appeared to be little more than an extravagant fabrication.

Eventually, darkness began to settle on the eastern sky. The earth cradled the sun on her rigid back, the high mountains to the west. In her arms were promises, and the late afternoon hour betrayed the uncertainty, which still weighed heavily on me. I turned away and walked back up the trail to the road, and coasted down the mountain to the lodge. I arrived shortly before dark, and went to the crowded main building to use the phone.

15

I had called my old friend Lance Hamilton a few days before I arrived at State Bridge to tell him that I would be coming to see him. After I called him, I intended to ride straight though to Buena Vista and spend some time off the road. The situation had since changed, and I had a feeling that I would be staying longer than I had intended.

Lance Hamilton was one of my oldest friends; we had met during the beginning of our freshman year in college. We lived across the hall from each other, and the first time I saw him I knew I wouldn't like him. As fate would have it, though, we eventually became the best of friends.

He was an unpredictable, smooth-talking guy who, despite being seven years out of school, continued to exude the type of adolescent indifference that he had carried with him since he was 18. Lance had left college halfway through his last semester and never looked back. He'd broken up with his girlfriend, quit his job, dropped out of school, sold his house and moved to Colorado to be a raft guide for a summer, with the intention of eventually returning to school afterwards.

That was seven years ago. Now he was still working as a guide during the warmer months and a dishwasher/ski bum in the lofty resort town of Vail during the winter. Before he'd taken off for the Rockies, he'd asked me to go with him.

"Come on, man," he said, "I'm only going out there for a summer!"

"No way, bro," I replied. "I have to graduate, and I have this real life starting right afterward. I can't run off to the mountains, as much as I'd like to. Besides, something tells me that you won't be back at the end of the summer."

Perhaps if I had gone with him, things would have been different for me. But that wasn't how life had worked out, so it didn't make sense for me to sit around and cry about what could have been. In the end, what *could* have happened, or what *should* have happened, were just a small part of everything that didn't happen, and nothing more.

I gave him a call to update him on my plans.

"What are you up to?" I asked.

"Aw, you know," he replied, "nothing good." His voice was rough, like a saw on wet wood.

I told him about the supernatural side trip in Wyoming and the road to Steamboat. I didn't tell him about Naomi, other than a passing mention. Lance wouldn't have been interested in passion or love. The only thing that would have concerned him was the size of her breasts and whether or not she looked good naked.

"I blew into this little place called State Bridge," I said, "and I'm going to stay for a few days."

I started to tell him more about it, but he quickly and excitedly interrupted me.

"Hell yeah, man," he said. "I love that place! We take clients up there to float the Colorado River sometimes. That place is the shit! I hang out there all the time! Are you staying up there this weekend for the festival?"

"I think so," I replied.

"Excellent! I'm coming up there too. There's also a buddy of mine from Austin coming up. He's a musician, and he's playing in the festival. You'll dig him, man, he's a smooth guy to party with."

"That's badass, man—what a small world! I'll look forward to it. Say, your voice doesn't sound too good, man, you feel all right?" I asked.

He laughed. "Let me tell you," he began, "what happened to me last night."

═══════

After talking to Lance I went back to the cabin. In the valley surrounding the lodge, the air had taken on a different tone than the one I had left it with.

People were beginning to arrive for the weekend, and the noise of the gathering festival had disrupted the seclusion of State Bridge. It was pleasant for me to remember the former serenity of the place, but I was looking forward to the distraction that the festival would offer.

Perhaps I was missing the atmosphere of a city, with its large groups of neatly attended people and the lively air that circulated the streets in the late hours of the weekend nights. The part of the country that I was in did not offer the grand spectacle of a large city, but the lodge held the promised coming of lively nights, and the opportunity for slightly erratic behavior.

When I returned to the cabin, I closed the door, leaving the lights off, and laid down on the short couch in front of the fireplace. I thought—I tried to think—profoundly, but my mind was wrecked, and soon I was asleep. I did not dream; I only felt the light touch of the dream world in the darkness. Some distant glimpse of the alternate world that comes at night brushed against me like a feather, but gave me nothing more than a subtle hint of pleasant escape.

By the time I woke up it was well after midnight, and the new moon cast a long shadow across the wood floor of the cabin. I could hear the sounds of revelry coming from the bar, and I sat up on the edge of the couch and rubbed my face. There was uncertainty in my head as I sat still, soaking in the sweet delirium and hovering somewhere between being awake and asleep. Should I stay in the cabin, or venture out into the world of the bar?

It was late, and I would be far more sober and serious than any-one in the lodge, and it was inconceivable that I would be able to lose my sensibilities fast enough to catch up with the other patrons. Naomi would be there, and the promise by D of an after party, both of which were pulling me in the direction I knew I didn't want to go. It was better for me to stay away from the bar, and so I did.

I picked up the empty ice bucket from the dresser and walked down the boardwalk, and around the back of the bar. The door near the big dumpster was unlocked and I stuck my head inside. There wasn't anyone in the kitchen, so I tiptoed to the ice machine quietly, so as not to be heard over the scratchy noise of the crowded room. Through the swinging door, I caught sight of Naomi. She was not working, but was sitting at the bar, smiling and talking to Sarah, one of the other bartenders.

She looked exactly as I remembered her. She was soft and deli-cate, with that bright fire in her eyes. The other faces in the room melted away and I saw only her. I wanted to be with her, talking to her, enclosed in the private embrace of our minds.

Once I had the ice, which was my primary objective, I retreated out the door and back to the cabin. The bottle of whiskey that Brian had left me was already out, and I poured some ice and a generous portion of it into a paper cup, and took Whitman and the drink to the couch to read by the light of a dim bulb dangling from the water-stained, plaster ceiling. Around the glowing globe of orange light danced the shadows of two moths, locked in a clumsy, circular dance around the top of the room.

As I ponder'd in silence,
Returning upon my poems, considering, lingering long,
A phantom arose before me with distrustful aspect,
Terrible in beauty, age, and power,
The genius of poets of old lands,
As to me directing like flame its eyes,

With finger pointing to many immortal songs

I was periodically distracted as I read by the story that Lance had told me earlier in the night.

Apparently, though he never said specifically why, he and his coworkers had found reason to celebrate, which they did with stunning efficiency. He and two South African raft guides had gone up a mountain four-wheeling trail late in the evening, and drunkenly wedged his car between a tree and a rock. They'd walked back to the bar and Lance had used the experience, and the fact that he no longer had a ride home, to convince one of his friends to let him shack up with her.

They had a fun night together, according to Lance, but in the morning she left early to go to work, and Lance was stuck without a car. She lived ten miles from the highway and had no phone, so Lance had to walk back to town. The only article of his clothing he could find were his pants, and so he headed off down the road with no shoes, and a shirt that read, "Well behaved women rarely make history." Eventually, he was able to thumb a ride with one of the other raft companies, and by evening, everyone in town had heard the story.

This was a situation that only Lance could get into and out of gracefully. As the night air began to cool, I withdrew to the interior of the cabin with my book, thoughts of Lance's story and the vague recollection that he had reserved a room at State Bridge for the weekend under the name Ken I. Doer.

There was a still and pleasant quiet in my little room for a long time, then staggered steps on the boardwalk, and a fast and firm knock on my door. The clock on the wall read 2:30 a.m. I opened the door, and on the other side stood Naomi and Sarah, and a young man whom I did not know.

"Hi," I said, surprised to see the strange and motley group on my porch.

"Darling," said Naomi, gripping the doorpost and leaning into the room, "you must let us in, we brought wine!"

I stepped back and the group trotted in with mixed laughter and the ends of stories they had brought from the bar. The three strangers came into the cabin, and I went about picking up piles of clothes and straightening the room. Naomi introduced me to Sarah, and to the young man they had brought with them. He was tall and slender, and didn't look anything like the usual guides and backpackers who frequented the lodge.

"This is my new friend Steven," said Naomi, as she approached me with her arm around him.

He had an innocent countenance, tall and tan with a good build and a sweet face. I introduced myself and he shook my hand with nervous intensity. He was dressed like the corporate offspring of America, well-appointed and carrying himself with brash dignity.

"You didn't come to the bar, darling," Naomi continued. "I wanted to see you, but I met this guy instead. He's from Vail, here for the festival."

"Let's drink," said Sarah, as she pulled the cork out of one of the already opened bottles.

I brought four porcelain coffee cups and she filled them all, emptying the bottle. We all went out onto the porch. Naomi sat next to me on the railing, with the young man standing expectantly on her other side.

"Baby," she said, with the hint of a strong kind of liquor on her breath, "you must call me Baroness Cobian from now on. It suits me to have a title. Steven says that I must have some kind of title to be unique."

I looked at the young man, and he smiled, staring only at her.

"You're drunk," I said to Naomi.

"Don't be like that," she whispered. "We have friends here."

I stepped back, feeling strange and uncomfortable. Steven leaned over and whispered something into Naomi's ear, and she laughed loudly and fingered the hem of his collar. Sarah stood on the other side of the porch, leaning against the railing. I walked over to her and sat down.

"She doesn't mean anything by it," Sarah said. "She's drunk and pissed that you didn't come to see her tonight, that's all."

"That's ridiculous," I said. "I didn't know she knew me well enough to get pissed at me."

Naomi broke away from her conversation with Steven and leaned into the circle. "Sarah, what the hell are you doing? You have to come drink with me."

Sarah went to Naomi, and Steven came over to my side of the porch. He leaned against the railing toward me.

Naomi was behaving badly, as if she were trying to prove a point. She had brought Sarah, and a guy who obviously had some sort of expectation about her. She was trying to prove a point and I didn't like it.

"These girls are fuckin' crazy," he said, leaning in close. "How do you know them?"

"I don't," I said as I stood up and put my hand on his shoulder. "They're all yours, friend."

I stepped out onto the boardwalk and leaned against the railing, away from the loud giggles of the two girls and the territorial countenance of the guy from Vail. There was a sweet silence on the other side of the railing, of which I drank slowly, and then I heard footsteps on the boardwalk behind me. Naomi put her arms around my shoulders and pressed her cheek against mine.

"Let's send them away," she said. "I want to be with you."

I turned and put a hand on her hip. I was confused about the situation and I couldn't quite figure out what was going on.

"Who is he?" I asked.

"He's nobody," she said as she ran her fingers through my hair and held the small of my back tightly. "We met him at the bar and he wanted to hang out with us. He's young but he has a great heart. He's not you, though."

I was immediately jealous, knowing that she was sharing the best of her heart, the same she had shared with me, with him, a strange man from obvious affluent backgrounds. I didn't know how to feel.

"Am I falling in love with you?" I asked.

"I don't know," she said with her head bowed.

She paused, and the distance in her voice was gone.

"I think I love you," she said, but her voice slurred, and it was hard to take her seriously.

She turned away when she saw the look in my eyes, and walked out onto the porch. She whispered something to Sarah and the young man, and they finished their drinks. Sarah and Steven stepped onto the boardwalk, and he shook my hand. He turned toward Naomi expectantly, but she just looked at him, then buried her head in my arm, saying nothing. They disappeared into the darkness and a moment later a car started in the muffled background of the night. Naomi walked to me, slowly and seductively.

"We're going to take off," she said, with a slight stumble. "I wish you would have come to the bar tonight."

"I just fell asleep, that's all," I said, pulling her tight against me. "I've been on the road for a while and I'm catching up on my sleep. I thought you wanted to send them away."

"I have to go," she said, "but I want to see you tomorrow. I'm sorry about tonight."

She stood on the tips of her toes and leaned forward. Her lips touched mine and they were soft and dry. Then she hesitated and turned away, holding my hand as she bent toward the boardwalk. I let go, and our hands slid apart. She turned, smiled, and disappeared in the direction of her waiting friends.

I stood listening in the darkness until I heard the car leaving, wondering if she had a late night future with the young man, and then I went back into the cabin. I lay on the bed, fully clothed, and fell asleep.

16

Saturday was the official start to the festival, but most of the guests at the lodge were scheduled to arrive the night before. During the day on Friday, the lodge was alive with preparation for the coming crowds, the comings and goings of rafts on the river, and the in and out of the summer tourist lunch crowd.

The whole valley transformed into a living, breathing monster drawing its last breath before the coming of the festival. New faces in black shirts buzzed around every corner, carrying large stacks of cases and cables to set up for the concerts. The stage sat just behind the main building, where the gentle slope of the foothill made a natural amphitheater. All things in the lodge were moving in preparation for the festival, slithering along the boardwalks and corridors with unabashed purpose.

The staff was on the move as well, winding around the twists and turns of every corner of the lodge-preparing the bathhouses, cleaning cabins, and all other manner of menial, festival related tasks.

Naomi wasn't working—she was in Edwards, at her day job—and the whole place felt strange and foreign without her there.

I woke up early, and floated into and out of the vast array of activity circulating through the coarse veins of the valley. I watched distantly, trying not to interrupt the machine. It was powerful, and difficult to avoid. I began to wish I were somewhere else, and decided to take off on a ride over the foothills to the south.

I went into the restaurant for breakfast. There were no menus, only a small buffet arranged with eggs, bagels, cheese and various breakfast meats: the ingredients for D's bagel sandwiches, a quick solution she'd designed for the raft guide on the go.

After breakfast, I asked D if I could use her laundry facilities, and she easily agreed. She led me up a narrow path to her house, and I stuffed my small pile of clothes, smelling of dampness and the road, into the mouth of a bright yellow washing machine. Satisfied that all was well with my clothing, I left the confusion of the lodge and took off on my bike, following the two-lane blacktop highway that meandered toward the Eagle River and Interstate 70.

There were only about 18 miles from State Bridge to Wolcott and the bottom of Vail Valley. The road was narrow and curvy, and I took my time so I could see as much of the landscape as possible. Far above the road, in the mountains surrounding the valley, were the unmistakable rings of aspen and pine trees, but along the road, the land resembled more of a desert country. Short scrub bushes dotted the ground and contrasted dramatically with the exposed, red sandstone rock faces that disappeared up the low slopes on both sides of the road. The air was dry, and the warm temperature and still air made it the perfect day to ride. A phrase from Whitman floated back and forth in my head as I rode away from the lodge.

Yet now of all that city I remember only a woman I
casually met there who detain'd me for love of me.

What did Naomi want from me? Where did I fit into the context of her life and situation? It was very possible that I loved her, but was it because I allowed myself to see perfection where I had never experienced it before? Was I projecting all the bad blood that had gone on between me and Beth into everything that was right with Naomi? Was she doing the same thing to me?

Then again, maybe I had been wrong about all of it. Maybe we were in love, really in love. However, since I had never been in love, I couldn't possibly know what it felt like. I couldn't know if I had the ability to separate love and lust.

There were two routes to take to the east, toward Edwards and Vail. There was Route 6, a two-lane road that snaked through the valley with the river. Then there was Interstate 70, which ran nearly straight, cutting the corners of the winding valley and beating the wild sanctity of the valley into submission. I was still interested in avoiding the interstates, so I went west on the two-lane, which had, until recently, been the only road to traverse the passes and canyons of Vail Valley. However, thanks to President Eisenhower and the German-inspired interstate system, the pollution-belching monster that was Interstate 70 had long since supplanted it in the name of economic and military efficiency.

Route 6 took me into Edwards, Colorado, and I stopped to look at a curious collection of trendy stores and restaurants known as the Edwards Riverwalk. It was essentially a strip mall that had been dressed to fit the upscale, affluent architecture of the Vail Valley.

The buildings sat with their backs to the Eagle River. The term "Riverwalk" was a misnomer because there was a good twenty-five yards worth of flashy, showy building between the walker and the river. In order to get to the water's edge a person would have to find one of two unmarked staircases that would lead him to a nearly unused park next to the river.

If capitalism and economy were kings of the country, then Vail Valley was a jewel in their crowns; a bright, glowing showpiece whose only function was to attract attention. Dotted along the once wild and mysterious valley were mountain vacation homes, grand hotels, boutique shopping centers, art galleries, ski slopes, gourmet restaurants and all other necessary facets of the upscale ski industry.

As I rode away from the heightening confusion and tenacity of Vail, I turned south into the quiet serenity of the Fryingpan Wilderness. Up and over the two-lane switchbacks south of Minturn and past the abandoned mining town of Gilman, with its long rows of decaying houses and stores perched precariously on the side of the mountain. All the buildings had been left as they were when the mine closed, giving passersby the feeling of transcendence into some future, post-apocalyptic world.

I kept riding fast, over the heaving roads, through Leadville and up Independence Pass, still covered with snow except for the road, which was clear and dry. Aspen passed by in the dry, warm afternoon, then Basalt and Glenwood Springs, where I stopped at the grave of Doc Holliday to pay my respects to an old boyhood hero. Then, finally, I turned and made my way back to State Bridge.

By the time the road brought me back to the maternal protection of the lodge, the last strands of sunlight were trickling over the rim of the valley. The boisterous commotion from earlier in the day had begun to slow. As the noise and movement around the lodge faded, the smell of food and the sound of soft music and talk began to rise, carried by the light breeze from the bar along the row of cabins.

There was nobody at D's cabin when I knocked, so I went inside cautiously and picked up my clothes, which she had put in the dryer sometime during the day. They were still warm, and the smell reminded me of my long ago and far away home, which left me with a hollow sadness as I folded underwear and mated socks.

When I got back to the cabin I stacked my clothes on the edge of the bed, and retired for a few minutes of peace on the front porch. I sat in one of the metal chairs with my book, and watched groups of people walking along the boardwalk to the restaurant. That loop through the wilderness had taken me nearly six hours and over 200 miles, but its effect felt far greater. The air had been cool and dry, and the sun shone over a cloudless sky. I had returned to the lodge with a sense of solace and unspeakable admiration for the beauty of the desolation-the kind of feeling that only a trip though mountains in summer could give.

As I sat alone, thinking about the day, the sound of quick footsteps coming toward me brought Naomi into view in the corner of my eye. I continued to stare blankly at the pages of my book, playing childish games with the situation.

"Hello, stranger," she said, leaning against the porch railing and resting her chin on her folded hands.

"Hey there," I said. "What are you doing?"

"I have to work," she said. "Did you have a good day? I missed you."

"Well, I did some laundry and took a long ride through the mountains. I just got back a few minutes ago."

"Yeah, I just wanted to come by and apologize for last night," she said quietly. "That was...um..."

"Forget about it," I said, interrupting her hesitant explanation. "We all act drunk and foolish every once in a while. I'm sure I'll pull the same thing with you at some point."

"I knew you would be cool about it," she said. "I was kind of trying to make you jealous, I guess. That was so childish of me!"

"Really, don't mention it," I said. "Besides, if you were trying to make me jealous, that must mean that you're into me."

"I did miss you," she said again, "and I wanted to talk to you last night, but I got scared. That's why I left like I did."

"What do you want to talk to me about?" I asked.

"Look, there's something you need to know about me," she said. She turned away, looking out over the river.

"You can tell me, Naomi," I said, holding her hand. "You can tell me anything."

"It's about my husband."

There was a long pause, and I searched for the right words. I was expecting the worst, but even in all my speculations, I never considered that she might be married. I never even thought of it as a possibility, and I felt myself growing cold. How could she do this?

"I'm sorry," I said. "Your husband?"

"Look," she said, pulling away and rubbing her hands together nervously. She stared at the ground in a kind of trance. "I should have told you before, but it's not really a simple matter. I think you're an amazing person. I don't know how *you* feel, but what happened the other night was completely unexpected."

"I had a feeling there was something you weren't telling me," I said. "Why the hell didn't you mention this before?"

"I haven't been able to stop thinking about you," she said, her eyes welling, "but you have to believe me that this isn't a simple thing at all."

"It never is," I said, "but you have to level with me. I mean, I have to know where you're at if I'm going to feel anything for you. We had this great night when I got here, and then all that weird shit last night happened. I mean, I can't stand this back and forth bullshit."

"Don't be like that," she said. "This isn't easy for me, you know."

She paused and took a long breath, looking over my shoulder, Then she stepped closer and reached for my hand. I felt my heart grow light, and fluttery-almost the sensation of nervousness. It had been a mistake for me to assume that the world would always take good care of us.

"I came to this country to go to school," she said slowly. "I loved America, and I met so many wonderful people but my visa expired, and I was about to have to go back to England. I had this guy in my life, he had always been a close friend to me, and he offered to marry me so that I could get my citizenship. We'd already had a daughter together, so getting married seemed like the next logical step. We went to Vegas one weekend and we were married."

"Sounds romantic," I said.

"Oh, shut up!" She paused "So that was three years ago. Last year he took a job in Denver. He moved there, and I stayed here. He takes the baby most weekends, and other than that we don't see each other. We didn't really split up, we just went our separate ways."

"Why?"

"Well, I loved him, but I wasn't in love with him. He's a great person, but I always thought there might be someone else out there. I think maybe I was waiting for you."

I let go of her hand and stepped back.

"I need some time with this," I said, turning away from her. "Just let me think about it for a little while."

"Sure," she replied. "I'll give you all the time you need."

I turned away from her and stepped off the porch, and down the boardwalk toward the lodge. Over my shoulder I saw her leave the porch behind me and disappear down a small trail between the bathhouses.

17

As I walked, thinking about Naomi, the sound of a motorcycle zipping through the valley filled the air, growing louder as it approached. It was vaguely familiar, and I leaned far out over the porch railing to see down the road.

Coming around a hill was a dirty road bike with a bedroll strapped to the handlebars and a tall, dust-covered figure sitting low in the seat. The bike was brown with dirt and mud, streaks of orange paint showing through in spots. The rider turned onto the dirt road in front of the lodge and into the parking area. He stopped, dropped his kickstand, stood up, and removed his sunglasses. It was my old friend from the road, Mr. Bryan Hillary.

"Bryan!" I yelled from the railing.

We moved toward each other, faster as we got closer, and I hopped the railing to the dirt parking area below. I held out my hand and he grabbed it and threw his other arm around my shoulder. We embraced, and then he pushed against me, holding me at arm's length.

"What are you doing here, man?" he said.

"Nothing," I said. "Trying to find the answer to life. What the hell are *you* doing here?"

"Well," he said, "I happened to be in the neighborhood. By the way, it took me a bloody hour to find this place. I think I passed it twice!"

"Man, it's damn good to see you, but I had no *idea* you were coming."

"Yeah, like I said, I was in the neighborhood. I was in Moab, Utah, and I stopped at this little shit-hole diner and called my answering service. When I got your message, I pulled out my maps and figured I could probably make it here before you moved on. Sounds like you have a pretty good reason to stay, though."

"She's married," I said bitterly. "It's a long story, better told over dinner."

"Can you offer a man a shower first?"

"I don't usually offer men showers," I said with a smile, "but you look like you could use one."

I grabbed his bag and bedroll and we turned toward the cabin.

"How long are you going to stay?" I asked.

"Tonight for sure, maybe a couple of days. I'm on my way back to New York."

"Really? That's good to hear, man!"

"Yeah, I think it's time to go home and face the music. I'm going to take my time getting back, though, and I thought I'd stop in and say hello."

"Well, I'm glad you did."

I showed Bryan the showers and then took him to the cabin. We talked for a while, then I gave him some clean towels and told him to take his time; I would meet him in the bar for dinner.

═══════

The restaurant was crowded, and I found a table in the corner. Naomi looked at me from across the room and approached with an air of caution: as if she were trying to size up my reaction to her.

"What can I get for you, sweetie?" she asked nervously.

"Just a beer right now," I said. "Do you remember that guy I told you about who I met on the road?"

She nodded.

"He showed up here right after you and I finished talking. He's going to stay here for a couple of days."

"That's so awesome," she said. "I'm so happy you guys get to hang out. I can't wait to meet him."

"He'll be here in a little bit."

She disappeared around the bar. While she was gone I thought about the whole situation: her husband, my journey and the possible temporary nature of our association. I decided to let it go, and she and I would be friends. It would be good, and anything that happened in the future would unfold as fate allowed. A few minutes later she returned with my beer.

"Hey, I've been thinking about our conversation earlier," I said. "Let's just be friendly, and enjoy the rest of our time together. We obviously get along well, and I want to experience this weekend with you. We can just keep it simple and forget about everything else."

She tilted her head and smiled, putting her hand on my cheek.

"I'm so happy to hear you say that," she said. "It's been tearing me up all day."

"Does that sound like a good way to go on?"

"Yes," she said, "That sounds perfect."

She turned away and melted into the crowd of strangers. As I thought about the previous night, and the strange alteration of Naomi's feelings, and the evolution of my own, a heavy hand descended on my shoulder.

"Ken I. Doer checking in. Why don't you grab my bags for me, son?"

I turned around in my seat and looked up to see the smiling face of Lance Hamilton hovering over me. He was taller than I remembered him, with frayed, baggy clothes and a thick patch of long, curly blonde hair. His smile was confident and comical, and he blended perfectly with the crowd.

I stood up and shook his hand. He spoke fast as though he were constantly on the move. His speech was deliberate and direct, but fast enough so that he came across as eternally aloof and distracted.

"All right, don't let me interrupt your dinner party," he said. "I'm going to check in and clean up and all of that bullshit. It is essential that I come back down here as soon as I can make myself presentable, and we will commence with whatever this evening has to offer. I'll meet you back here in two hours for cocktails. Cool?"

"Yeah, man," I said. "I'm going to have dinner with a friend who just showed up out of the blue. Hurry your ass up, because I want you to meet this guy."

Lance snapped his fingers, gave me a thumbs-up and disappeared into the small lobby adjacent to the bar. There was the sound of brief commotion, like the fox had just walked into the henhouse, followed by the shrill voice of a girl who was evidently waiting to see Lance, then the sharp slam of a screen door.

Bryan came into the bar a few minutes later and sat down at the table. We ordered dinner and a bottle of wine, and got to the business of catching up. It had been over a week since we had parted ways and I desperately wanted to know what he had been up to, and why he had suddenly changed his mind and decided to return home. I had considered, as I'd watched him disappear over that low rise in Wyoming, that it could have been years before we connected again, if ever.

It was fascinating to be sitting across the table from him, sharing wine and our own versions of true stories. I was eager to tell him everything that had occupied my mind in the last week.

Bryan, like Lance, was a wandering spirit, and though it would have been painful, I wouldn't have been surprised if I never saw him again. We had both gone great distances mentally and physically, and now there we were, having dinner. Strange things happen on the road. Chance encounters, random meetings and odd discoveries are, to me, an essential part of the adventure.

After dinner, we walked out into the courtyard where the main stage was, and finished our second bottle of wine and a cigarette. There was a sparse crowd outside, and a man sat on the stage with a guitar, and a strange spotted dog that would sing along with him. The music was bad, but the night and the air were beautiful.

The stars were bright in the sky, and the moon hung low over the mountains, showing their contours as shadows against the deep, distant blue. The fat band of the Milky Way stretched from one side of the valley to the other. I tasted the wine, and it mixed well with the subtle smells of the night—pine trees, and the pinching sensation of the coming cold. In the distance, below the sound of music and laughter, came the slow roar of the world, the deep intonations of life.

"What are you going to do when you get home?" I asked.

"I don't know," Bryan said dejectedly. "I guess I'll go to work for my old man. I don't know if I'm ready to go back, but I have a lot of ground to cover before then, so hopefully I'll be ready to be home when I get there."

He paused. "Why don't you come back east with me?" he asked.

"I don't know, man," I said. "Let me think about it. In the meantime, though, it's damn good to see you again."

"You too, buddy."

We talked through the rest of the bottle of Woodbridge and part of another, until Lance descended upon us. He walked out into the courtyard with a confidant strut. His arrival always seemed to be invasive, yet energetically uplifting. I didn't ask, but he had the look of a person who had just gotten laid.

"Whose ass do you have to kiss to get a drink around here?" he yelled as he walked, his heavy footsteps echoing against the wooden walls of the courtyard. When he got to where we stood he stopped and gave me brief, psychotic smile, then began to size up my companion.

"Bryan," I said, "this is Lance. Lance, Bryan."

"Hey, man," Lance said, shaking Bryan's hand. "Damn good to meet you."

"Yeah, you too," said Bryan.

Neither Lance nor Bryan enjoyed making small talk with members of the same sex. There was something territorial in their approach to meeting new people, as if they were attempting to establish dominance. However, I knew that their similar personalities would soon allow them to dispense with this formality and engage each other as likeable equals.

"All right, lads," said Lance. "There are some hot-ass chicks in that bar and I heard there was going to be a party tonight. I say we quit screwing around and have some fuckin' fun."

"Yeah, man," said Bryan, smiling. "Let's do it."

Lance grabbed the wine bottle off the railing and took a long drink, then pulled it out of his mouth and spit a sizeable quantity on the ground.

"First things first," he declared, looking at the bottle. "We need to get some real drinks."

Bryan turned to walk into the bar, and Lance and I followed.

"Do you know that girl Sarah?" Lance asked. "That little blonde girl?"

"Yeah, she works the desk. Big boobs, not too bright?"

"She totally raped me when I got here," he said.

"I'm very happy for you, Lance," I replied, shaking my head.

"You should be-I hear you're having some trouble closing the deal!"

I should have punched him for saying that, but at the time I could only laugh.

"You're a prick," I said, "and you always have been."

"Takes one to know one!" he said, and trotted to catch up to Bryan.

"We need to get this guy a shot or something," Lance said, looking back at me with his arm around Bryan's shoulder. "He's so uptight, I think you could pull diamonds out of his ass."

The two of them laughed. I smiled, glad that Lance and Bryan were beginning to feel comfortable with each other, and winked at Naomi from across the bar. Soon all I would have to do was sit back and watch the show.

The three of us lined up on stools at the counter, like old barflies. We told stories from the working world, stories from the road, and stories from the river. The most interesting tales had to do with drinking and poor decision-making. Amidst the lies and jokes were casual flir-tations with other patrons, and playing grab-ass with the waitresses. Most everyone in the bar either knew Lance or knew his reputation, and everyone else got a good idea about him by the end of the night.

Sarah came behind the bar to swipe a credit card, and Lance howled at her. She turned around and gave him a high-five.

"Nice work earlier, tiger," she said.

"Anytime, baby," he replied with a sly smile.

Bryan looked at me and I shook my head as if in disbelief.

Naomi finished waiting tables at about eight, and began to work behind the bar. She served us double drinks and took shots with us periodically, never once telling us to slow down or shut up. To her, we were the only people in the bar.

"How do you know this loser?" Lance asked her, pointing in my direction.

"Didn't he tell you?" she asked, grabbing my hand. "We're in love."

Lance laughed and made a comment about my inability to fall in love. Naomi winked at me and our eyes met, and we held that gaze for a moment before I turned away. Staying only friends with her was going to be more difficult that I had envisioned. Lance leaned back in the stool and laughed again.

"Holy shit," Lance said. "She wasn't kidding, was she?"

"Yes, she was," I said, and then I took sip of my drink and looked away.

Naomi put her head down and stuck out her lower lip, making the cutest pouting face I had ever seen. Then she smiled and turned away to help another customer.

"You dog!" Lance whispered.

"Whatever," I said.

"Tell him about the other thing," said Bryan, referring to her husband.

"Shut the hell up," I said, "both of you. You guys mind your business!"

They both laughed and I left to use the restroom. When I returned, I caught the tail end of Bryan's story that Lance and Naomi were laughing at.

"So this chick starts talking shit," he was saying, "and she's like, 'Hey, I'm from Vegas and I can outdrink anyone,' and our boy here starts getting a little pissed about it so they start drinking."

"Oh, man," I said, "don't tell this story."

Bryan ignored me and continued telling Lance how the girl had continued drinking while I gave up and passed out. The two of them enjoyed the laugh and I pretended not to pay attention. For the rest of the night, when it came time to order shots, Naomi would bring me pink ones with little umbrellas because, as she would remind me, I drank like a girl.

The night went on, and the bar filled with people. Naomi and I forgot our earlier conversation for most of the night, and we talked and flirted as if it had never happened. She kept serving my drinks topped with little sculptures made of limes and bar napkins, straws and toothpicks. We played games with each other, mixed with smiles and expectations.

Lance and Bryan were talking loudly and I listened to their conversation with interest. They were getting drunk, and their subject matter rapidly became too strange to understand.

"No, no, no, my friend," said Lance. "You can't relax in a place like this. It's too much work between watching the mountains, finding suitable women and running around the bars that are so spread out that you can only enjoy them one at a time. It's better in the city, and it's easier. The girls there know what the expectations are, and you can visit dozens of bars and meet hundreds of women. You actually have to work at it here."

"You obviously haven't been to New York City," answered Bryan. "People there expect you to act like you know what you're doing. It's all competition so see who's more worthwhile to go home with. If you don't have a nice car or a penthouse on Park Avenue, then you better have a magic penis or something to make up for it."

"Well, well, I guess I would do *all right* in New York then," said Lance. "But, I can see that you're getting to a point here, and I'm trying to see what it is, but you don't know me and I don't know you and the truth is that we both have the same plan, but we're going about it in different ways."

"I'm sorry," said Bryan. "What the hell are you talking about?"

"I'm talking about getting laid, man!" Lance answered with a frustrated tone, as if he were trying to rationalize with a child.

Getting laid was Lance's sole and permanent goal in life; all roads led to that objective. He made no apologies for it, and in his mind, he saw that it was good.

"Ah yes," said Bryan, "of course. You know, there is nothing better than finding yourself in the hands of a good-looking woman who knows what she's doing. You don't want to take her home to mom, and you feel kind of bad for taking advantage, but, well, usually a woman like that knows what she's good for and probably made the decision to be the way she is knowing that people will use her for it. It's a win-win situation for you."

"That's right, that's right," said Lance. "Now you're speaking my language."

Bryan's talent was that he could talk to anyone about anything. He had an introspective nature, but he could carry on endless, two-dimensional conversations as well, as he had with the girls in McCook when I'd first met him. His natural beliefs and complexities ran much deeper than that, and I knew that he didn't share Lance's often shallow opinions, but Lance didn't know that. It was on this common ground that the two formed an understanding, and in the end, a friendship of sorts.

Toward the end of their conversation, a short, well-built man with dark hair, hipster clothes and cowboy boots came into the bar. He carried a guitar in one hand and a backpack slung around his shoulder. He leaned against the counter, setting his guitar on the ground, and made eyes at Naomi. She walked over to him.

"I'll have a whiskey," he said, "and you better get that funny-looking fucker down there a glass of milk before he gets drunk and destroys your bar."

Lance spun around and stood up quickly, knocking his stool over. Everyone within hearing distance turned toward them, and Bryan looked at me expecting trouble.

"What the fuck do you know, cowboy?" demanded Lance. "Why don't you get back on your horse and go back to your boyfriend!"

The two men looked at each other until neither one of them could hold their laughter in. They hugged and then they both turned toward Bryan and me.

"Gentlemen, this is my friend Mark McDaniel."

According to Lance, Mark was a musician from Texas. The two of them had grown up near each other in Dallas and were decently close friends. Mark had left school to be a musician and had spent some time in Nashville, but now lived in Austin. He was doing well for himself.

The two of them looked over at me and Mark and I shook hands.

"I went to college with this guy and apparently he can't hold his liquor for shit. This is Bryan, he's some kind of road warrior guy."

"Damn good to meet you guys. I'm going to check in and drop this stuff off in my room, and then let's get some drinkin' done."

"Amen," said Lance.

We went back to our seats and took care in ordering strong drinks, which would give us the optimum state of mind to revel in the atmosphere of the growing crowd. Mark returned a while later and we carried on, even as the apex of the bar crowd began to recede and the people slowly began to trickle out into the darkness.

When the bar closed, we went to D's house for the after-party, along with Sarah, Naomi and a few other employees. Mark got his guitar and we gathered around a steel fire pit behind D's house. The party was loud, and soon attracted the attention of some of the other guests who were still awake.

We were joined by a couple from Texas, Dave and Katie, who made a yearly trek to the mountains for the festival. A little while later four fishermen from Denver, who introduced themselves as JD, Scott, Chris and Ben, emerged from the thick brush behind the lodge. Mark picked at his guitar quietly, and we stood in a broken circle around the fire, playing off the mood of the night.

The four fishermen had brought a large bottle of Jim Beam whiskey, which we passed around, and D brought some beer from the bar. Dave and Katie were fans of Mark and his band back in Texas, and sat around him listening and quietly admiring the energy of the group. I stood with Naomi, holding her hand, and talking about the beauty of the night. Lance, Bryan and Sarah were in a small circle on the other side of the fire. They were planning something, but I couldn't tell what it was. D was stoking the fire and a few of the other bartenders hovered in a group, smoking out of a long, brightly painted glass pipe.

The night drew on, and the crowd around the fire dwindled. Naomi and I talked for a while about nothing in particular, until she and D left to go to bed. Bryan and Sarah disappeared without telling anyone, and Lance gave me a wave and a wink, and then disappeared with a different waitress.

Mark and I remained at the fire with the strange collection of fishermen and their giant bottle of whiskey. The group had come from their camp not far up the river, having heard the commotion from the bar; they set out to find the party, had gotten lost, and stumbled out of the woods at the exact spot where the fire was. We sat around the circle and, amidst stories and obscene jokes, finished the bottle. When it was gone, our four new friends disappeared back into the brush.

18

At the absolute end of the night, Mark and I were the only ones around the fire. As the early sun rose and the night gave way to the morning, we sat near the dying flame and talked. We were both very drunk, and the conversation was muddled. Our philosophies were similar, and we both saw life as possibility. His own journey had started much the same way mine had, and we bonded in our shared experience of leaving corporate America for a foreign way of life.

His own departure had been a marked success. He had a blooming career and considerable renown as a musician. The fact that we had similar beginnings, and that he had found success within the pages of his own journey gave me hope. There was the possibility that this journey was serving some kind of purpose.

The sky turned bright, and we sat in the quiet. I felt calm and unencumbered. My mind didn't race, and we sat in peace as the cool air in the valley warmed in the first rays of light as the stars disappeared. No grand spectacle awaited us with the coming of the morning, no grand illusions about the mystery of life, only the notion of the birth of morning and the riffle of the water as backdrop against the fading night.

"When are you going back to Texas?" I asked.

"Monday," he replied. "I have to spend some time back in the studio, then I'm back on the road in three weeks. I'll be out for a month."

"I'm going to stay here for another day or so," I said, "then go down to Buena Vista to spend a few days with Lance. After that, I have no idea."

"Look," he said, "I really need some help with my business. Why don't you come to Austin? You could hang with me for a little while and make some money while you work everything else out."

"Really?" I replied. "But I just met you."

"Yeah," he said, "I know, but my tour manager quit recently and I need some good people. I think you and I see eye to eye on a lot of things-and besides, I think you'd dig it."

"I'll think about it," I said.

When the restaurant opened, we stumbled down the boardwalk and into the quiet building. The room was scattered with people, both the extremely sober and the extremely hung over. We were both still extremely drunk and didn't fit well into the dynamic, but we did our best to behave as soberly as possible. The restaurant was serving a continental buffet, and we got into line and served ourselves. The other patrons, mostly raft guides and older travelers, quickly figured out our state as we fumbled through the array of foods and juices. Those who didn't, quickly learned.

In the process of trying to make a waffle, Mark jolted the waffle maker and it fell off the table, onto the floor. The machine hit the ground with an ear-splitting crash, spilling batter and blueberries in a wide, cone-shaped arc across the smooth wood. Heather, one of the lodge staff, came rushing out of the kitchen. She looked at us, then at the mess, and shook her head. We stared at her dumbly. She packed us a couple of take-out boxes stuffed with muffins and cereal bars, and ushered us out the door.

"What about the coffee?" Mark asked over his shoulder.

She glared at him.

"OK," he said, and we turned away from her.

We parted ways on the boardwalk, and I went back to the cabin. I went inside and Bryan was asleep on the bed with Sarah. I threw the box of muffins on the table.

"Breakfast!" I yelled, trying to reclaim my bed.

They didn't wake up and I sank onto the couch. There was a brief stirring across the room, and then the darkness consumed me.

━━━━━

Aside from the distractions offered by the swarming, excited crowds, the constant succession of parties and my anticipatory romance with Naomi, the whole festival was nothing more than a staggered series of goodbyes. The music was good and the days were warm, but the experience was marked by my quiet resignation. I was acutely aware that my circle was quietly disbanding, and that reality made full enjoyment of the festival nearly impossible.

While I had welcomed my time in State Bridge, and the hope that something tangible would be produced from the twisting emotions that ran between me and my married friend, I held a strong, secret desire to return to the road, where time and distance would help to smooth the past.

I had been in the company of wonderful people, and though I knew I would miss them, the advantage of remaining at the lodge had passed. The good that had come to me during my time at the lodge was beginning to feel like preparation for something that had not yet occurred.

Bryan Hillary was the first of our party to go. On Sunday morning he woke up, packed, and together we ate a quick breakfast in the main dining room. It was mid-morning, and the inhabitants of the lodge were still moving either slowly or not at all.

The music wasn't scheduled to start until the afternoon, and the crowds and river patrons had not yet begun to arrive. The valley was quiet, and together we walked across the bridge to the large beach across the river. We sat together on a large log in the water. The air was dry and cool, and we sat in silent admiration of the beauty of the young day.

"What do you think you'll do when you get back home?" I asked.

"Well, like I told you," he said, "I'm going to straighten everything out and probably go back to work for my dad." He turned toward me. "Do you think there's something wrong with that?"

"Is that really going to work?" I replied. Bryan's face was sober and serious, and the ever-present power in his eye was gone. "I mean," I continued, "doesn't that make everything that's happened out here irrelevant?"

Bryan dug through the sand with a stick, and looked toward the lazy current of the river.

"No way!" he said. "You remember all of the crap that happened just before I left? Well, I was ready to spend time in jail, and it all seemed worth it because I had squared things away with my father. This feels the same. I could spend the rest of my life stuck in some office, but I will *always* have the memory of the road. I can always remember it, and it will all be worthwhile. Freedom isn't freedom until it's gone, you know?"

"I don't think I could do that," I said. "I couldn't just go back like that. I still hang on to the idea that there's something for me out there."

He stood up and walked to the water's edge, then turned to face me.

"Well," he said, "I don't know if it will work, but I owe it to my family to go back and try. Maybe everything I've been looking for is there, or maybe I'll find it on the way back. I just don't know."

I reached out my hand, and he grabbed it and pulled me to my feet.

"I hope you find it, man," I said.

"I will," he replied, "and you will, too. Shit, maybe you *have* found it," he said as he pointed his chin toward the lodge.

Naomi stood in the distance, leaning against the porch railing of D's house with a cup of coffee. The steam from the cup rose in delicate plumes around her face, and the sun over the notch in the mountains behind glowed around the outline of her body.

"Yeah," I said, looking back at Bryan. "I don't know what to do about her. I have this feeling about her that I can't get rid of, though, and it's making me crazy."

"Well," said Bryan, "you don't need me to blow sunshine up your ass about her, but you'll figure it out."

We started back to the lodge, where I noticed his bike parked in front of the steps, and it was already packed. When I'd woken up that morning, I'd half expected him to be gone already. He had distaste for goodbyes, and I was expecting his silent departure and another note stuck in my saddlebag.

"This is where I say goodbye, brother," he said, putting a hand firmly on my shoulder.

"I will see you down the road," I said.

"You bet your ass you will!"

He stepped a long leg over the seat, and I moved away from the bike.

"Wait," I said. "Where are you going after this?"

"I'm going to head down south, look up an old friend in Marfa, Texas, then head through the south and back up to New York. Why?"

"Well, I was talking to Mark about maybe going to Austin in a few days to hang out with him and possibly Lance. You think it over, but it'd be cool if you came there for a couple of days."

"Yeah, man," he said. "I'll think about it."

He started the engine, gave me a quick salute, and turned onto the main highway.

As he disappeared around the curve, I felt a burning in the center of my chest-pain at the passing of the blissful moments I had spent with Bryan and the rest of the strange collection of people I had met. It was the end of a moment, and for a second, I could feel that all was temporary.

I would miss his perspective and I knew that it would be a long time until I saw him again. Bryan Hillary was a man who never said goodbye, but on that day he did.

Mark was the next to leave. He, Lance, Naomi and I spent the rest of the weekend together, when Mark wasn't playing and Naomi wasn't working, and our friendship grew. Saturday night was Mark's last night at the lodge and we spent some time alone, after the bar closed, talking. The conversation turned to some of the more serious subjects we had talked about during the weekend; the summation of all that had occupied my mind for the last several years and had ultimately led me to walk away from my stable, secure life.

"You know," Mark said, "we're as young, right now, as we're ever going to be."

His assertion startled me and I sat back to think about it.

"Why don't people think about that kind of thing more?" he asked.

"I don't know," I replied. "I think that when people have time to think about it, they're still too young to care. I mean, when you're in your mid-20s, the end of your life seems so far away that it doesn't seem worth it to think about it. Then, somewhere, you get involved with the job and family and all that, and life just becomes a day-to-day kind of affair. You think about getting old every now and again, usually around a birthday or the death of a loved one or something like that. You think about it, then you get caught up in life again and you forget. Days become months, months become years. The next thing you know, you're almost through it all."

"Why is that?" asked Mark. "I mean, what's the point of even thinking about it when you're young?"

"It all makes evolutionary sense," I said. "When you're young you're developing into the *type* of person you're going to be when you're older, so it makes sense that you'll have a much broader scope. As you become more settled into your routine, your viewpoint begins to telescope in the direction you had planned for yourself, and you fixate on those few goals you started out with. Job, family—all those things map out your trajectory and you immerse yourself in them. You can no longer afford the distraction of contemplating the greater mysteries of life. I don't believe that this is the best way to do it, but it just seems to be what's happening."

"So if that's how we're supposed to be, then what's the point of trying to walk away from it at all? It sounds like that will be the inevitable end."

"Well," I replied, "We all need a sense of meaning and worth in life, so we turn to our accomplishments, religion, the families we create and so on. If we stumbled around through our entire lives only enjoying the geography in the world and searching for an overwhelming sense of meaning, then we would jeopardize our general progress as a species. That's why there are only a few who are philosophers, saints and intellectuals; their roles are to provide the rest of us with a greater sense of meaning. The population as a whole goes on its day-to-day pursuits with the idea that they perpetuate the world."

We went on in that fashion until after midnight, until there was a long quiet moment, and then Mark said good night. He was to leave on the express shuttle to Denver early in the morning. We shook hands and parted with the understanding that I would meet him in Austin sometime soon. He reminded me to think about the job, and disappeared into the night.

After he left I settled into the couch with a book. I put Whitman aside and thumbed through *The Kreutzer Sonata*, Tolstoy's scathing account of the absurdity of the interactions between men and women, and the pathetic nature of love, marriage and sex. The book engrossed me, and I barely heard the light tap on the door that came at two in the morning. When I opened it I saw Naomi standing under the porch light.

"What are you doing here?" I asked. "I thought you would be back home in Edwards."

"I want to stay with you tonight," she said. "I hope that's okay. May I come in?"

"Of course," I said as I stepped out of the doorway.

She walked to the middle of the room, then turned to face me. The light from the solitary bulb above cascaded over her delicate shoulders, and her long hair was pulled tight and hanging down her back. She was radiantly beautiful in the dim light, and she looked at me expectantly.

"I had to work tonight," she said, "and the only thing I could think about was seeing you."

We stepped toward each other and came together for the first time as lovers. There was nothing awkward about it, and our embrace lacked the hesitation that every embrace we'd experienced before had exuded. It never felt wrong. There was only the passion, the love and the harmony of two people meant to know each other in that way. There was magnificence about the whole affair, and all external restriction had gone.

For that short time, there was no one else in the world, only the communion of our two bodies, and the interlocking of souls in a confounded world. It was beautiful and it was permanent, and she was the first and last woman I would ever love. Afterward, we lay in bed, fearful to let each other go, and worried that if we did it would be for the last time.

"Can I come to Buena Vista with you tomorrow?" she asked.

"Of course," I said. "I would love to have you with me."

"I have some friends down there I want to see, and I couldn't bear the thought of you leaving just yet."

19

Naomi and I left the lodge late Tuesday afternoon, and just like that, I was back on the road. It felt strange to be putting miles behind me again. After spending any amount of time in one place with fascinating people, you feel a kind of pushing and pulling between the desire to stay and the need to leave. What I was experiencing could only be compared to homesickness. It was a disturbing feeling to leave a place like that, and I knew in my heart that my time there was over, possibly forever.

Lance had left earlier, and we were all set to meet in Buena Vista later that day, where we would spend some time in the quiet reclusion of the dry mountains. By afternoon, Naomi had secured enough time off to go with me to Buena Vista, and I had settled my bill with the lodge and said my goodbyes to the rest of my new friends who were staying behind.

The only thing left to do was leave. I loaded my saddlebags and Naomi's backpack onto the bike, and together we turned onto

Highway 131 heading south, once again toward the glittering expanse of the Vail Valley.

We followed the curve of the road and turned east onto a two-lane highway that paralleled the bustling monstrosity of Interstate 70. Edwards and Avon came and went in their long, blended lines of store-fronts, apartment buildings and restaurants. To my right, the long, upward drift of the green ski slopes brought back vivid images of Steamboat Springs and my sordid love affair with that mysterious girl. I rode on with a slight smile.

Before Vail appeared around the long scoop of a rocky canyon, we turned south again, through the once thriving community of Minturn. The town had been revitalized with the tourist boom, but we only stopped briefly for fuel, and to notice a dirty sport utility vehicle with California plates.

Outside and around the car a group of wild-eyed blond children ran in circles and screamed, and a tired-looking man tried to control them while pumping gas. I watched as Naomi went into the store, and a surgically handsome woman in her early 40s walked out with an air of smug superiority.

"Come on, guys," she said to the bubbling circus. "Leave your dad alone before he has another breakdown."

════════

Below the town of Minturn, the road dipped down and then rose in switchbacks above the floor of the valley, followed the curving draws, and descended past the town of Red Cliff, Colorado, where I had stopped a few days before.

"This is a ghost town!" said Naomi.

"Yeah," I said, "but it's a stubborn ghost town."

No sooner had we found Red Cliff than we lost it. The town faded behind us and I pulled the throttle. We traced the outside curves of the road, cutting into the left lane and breaking ninety miles per hour on the valley floor. Naomi laughed, and I felt the return of the road and its power-that end run from the ghosts of the past. It was the kind of freedom that had carried me in Kansas and Wyoming, a freedom only tempered by the memory of the lost life that followed shortly behind.

Across Tennessee Pass, the valley opened into a wide plain and we swept downhill, past a steady stream of traffic moving in the opposite direction. We passed through the quiet town of Leadville, which was surrounded by open fields that rolled gently toward the shining mountains to the west. Large bales and stock pens filled the open expanses around the borders of Leadville, and the smells of cattle and freshly cut grasses drifted across the road. The smells were a vivid reminder of the farmlands of Kansas. The turnoff to Independence Pass appeared and disappeared, and we were in undiscovered territory again.

The air was hot and dry, and the radiant sun filled the valley and brought its tastes, smells and magnetic brilliance all together into a vast sense of hope. Naomi tightened her grip around my waist and pressed her cheek into my shoulder. We were in love with the world that day, and the energy it gave coursed between us.

Past the reach of a small village, we caught the first glimpses of the Collegiate Range. The road meandered through a series of short canyons and small valleys, all the while paralleling the Arkansas River with its dotted population of rafters and fly fishermen. The valley was descending, ever so slightly, toward the high plains of southern Colorado. The drop was perceptible only in the foaming agitation of the river, which from the seat of the bike made no sound, a serene and beautiful spectacle. One of the canyons opened into a wide, v-shaped valley, and in the late afternoon we arrived in Buena Vista, having traveled just under 100 miles from the State Bridge Lodge.

We stopped, and I left Naomi at the River Runner Raft Company office to wait for her friends, who would be getting off work soon. Later we would all meet at Cyrano's for dinner. We both stood up, and she rubbed my cheek with her hand.

"I have a good feeling, my love," she said, "that we're going to have a great time together tonight."

She leaned up and kissed me, then held her soft, smoky brown eyes on me, and smiled. It was a smile of warmth and expectation.

It was an inspiring prediction, but it wasn't to be. She turned toward the door of the office, and I rode into town to find Lance.

At a gas station near a busy intersection downtown I stopped to search my pockets for the note Lance had left me. His writing wasn't completely legible, and the only verbal instructions he'd given me were sketchy at best. He had said that he would finish work at four, and then would probably be at a bar. Past these vague references, I was obviously on my own to find him. I guessed that he didn't have much faith that I would actually come to Buena Vista.

Before searching for him I checked into a small hotel near the highway. The room was a medium-sized hotel room with a large bed and indifferent furnishings, and as I unpacked thoughts of the day and of Naomi drifted in and out of my mind, like a carousel of post-cards in a roadside shop.

It had been a beautiful day, and she had seemed to smile at every turn. She'd held me close the entire way, and we'd exchanged quick looks in the reflection of the side mirror. She was even more alive and important to me than she had been at the lodge, and I decided that before I left Buena Vista, I would ask her to come with me to Austin, and further if she wanted. The idea of seeing the country with her brought more excitement than fear. It felt as if a new part of the picture had come into being, and I accepted it with all the feelings that new love could affect.

I left the bike, with my saddlebags still on the back, and went out to find Lance. I left the hotel on foot and wandered toward the small business district of the town.

An eager mix of the early evening tourist crowd and the young, rugged employees from the rafting companies filled the patios and porches of every bar and restaurant. I lazily searched the concentration of old brick buildings until I found Lance's damaged, yellow Land Rover in the parking lot of the Broken Paddle, a seedy dive bar. Once inside, I squinted to see in the brown light, scanning faces until I found him.

He was sitting at the bar with a young woman, who looked like a tourist who had wandered into the wrong bar. Lance was leaning into her, sizing up her features and telling a story. She winced each time he exhaled, and had a very bored look in her eye. Lance, who didn't notice her disinterest, continued to tell his story-probably of some recent adventure in which he'd behaved perfectly, while the forces of nature or man had acted solely against him.

He had a history of telling these self-fulfilling fantasies in the hopes of finding women impressed enough to go home with him. I approached him and his unwilling companion.

"Man," I said dryly in his direction, "they'll let anyone in here."

Lance turned around. "What's up, yo?" he said.

"Nada," I replied. "I just rolled into town."

"Well sit down and have a beer with me, you goddamn scholar!"

I sat down next to Lance, hoping that our conversation would offer his "friend" a chance to escape. Lance tried to divide the conversation between her and me, but was having little success, and within 10 minutes, she had found her window and left for the ladies room, never to return.

Lance was a strange sort of character and we were very different people, but complemented each other well. We were both aloof, but our strong points were polar opposites. While I thought about the more abstract nuances of life, he was more mechanically useful and practical. When he made a suggestion about how to fix something or a particular method of travel, I usually listened. As a result, I thought nothing of it when, just before we left to meet Naomi and her friends at the restaurant, he suggested that I leave my motorcycle with him and take his Land Rover to Texas instead.

"Look at it this way," he said. "You've been running that bike hard for over 2,000 miles and it's starting to sound like shit. You're never going to make it to the Texas border, much less Austin, without that thing breaking down. You should leave it here with me. I'll even get it fixed for you."

"No offense," I said, "but I know your tendency to drink and drive, and I would like to see my bike again in one piece. Not to mention that given your track record, I have no way of knowing if you'll even make it to Austin within the next year."

"No, listen—it's perfect," he said. "I've been looking for an excuse to get away from drinking and driving, and there's one thing I will never do: I will never ride a motorcycle drunk."

I cocked an eyebrow and looked at him.

"I will never ride a motorcycle drunk *again,* ok! Does that make you feel better?"

"Much," I said sarcastically. "Tell me this, then—when am I going to get my bike back?"

"I'm going back to Texas pretty soon, I think. Mark told me about the job he offered you, and I'd like to come down and try my hand at it. See where it takes me. We can trade back again in August. Besides, do you know how much trim I can score riding around here on a Harley?"

If there had been a possibility that Lance could get some action by pursuing a career in basket-weaving, he would probably have tried that too.

I told him I would think about it, and he left it at that. We settled our tabs and the two of us walked down a long side street to Cyrano's. As we walked, I told Lance about my feelings for Naomi, and that I intended to ask her to come to Texas with me. Lance isn't exactly a romantic, and he reacted predictably.

"Are you out of your fucking mind?" he asked, stopping and pulling my arm.

He had a smile on his face and I shoved him playfully.

"Look," I said, trying to bring the conversation back to his level, "some of us can like a girl for something more than a night wife!"

"Whatever," he said, walking away. "Just don't ruin my night with all that romantical bullshit."

We got to Cyrano's, and the place was full. It had a relaxed atmosphere with a large outdoor patio and several small interior rooms. One of the waiters, a friend of Lance's, approached us. They exchanged a handshake and the guy shifted excitedly in his sandals.

"Hey, Lance," he said. "How was the river?"

"Oh, you know," Lance replied. "Up and down, and pretty wet. We need a table for..." He paused and looked at me.

"Probably four, I guess," I said, "but we may need to add to it."

"Well, I have a six outside."

"That's fine, man," said Lance. "You guys look pretty swamped."

"No shit, Sherlock!" he replied.

The waiter took a stack of menus from the top of the host's podium and walked into the bustling dining room. We followed him, and he and Lance continued to talk, but I could no longer hear them over the loud voices and explosions of laughter around the restaurant. We sat at a long table near the edge of the patio, and Lance's friend disappeared into the room.

Lance ordered beer from our server, a girl in her early 20s. She was sweet to the eye, with a rugged innocence about her posture and dress. She brought the beer, and Lance and I waited for Naomi and her friends under the sagging branches of a pinion pine. The air was warm and still. The sound of the river in the distance was a pleasant backdrop against the deliberate calm of the patio, which hovered over the deck like a cloud.

We sat and talked casually and in a few minutes, Lance's friend returned to tell us that one of the girls from River Runner's called to say that they would be late, and not to wait for them. They would meet us at the Broken Paddle in a couple of hours. When our server returned, we ordered, and Lance tried to make meaningful eye contact with her. She pretended not to notice.

As we ate, Lance continued to drink faster than the server could bring him fresh ones, and the conversation turned to the same rudimentary subjects that Lance enjoyed. By the end, he was quite drunk.

On the way to the Broken Paddle, we stopped at the Green Parrot to have few more drinks, and so Lance could talk to a girl he'd had his eye on. She worked behind the counter, and as the two of them talked, I picked up my drink and walked around the empty bar. Old photographs of people and landscapes covered the walls. The black and white faces stared back through the glass frames, as if they were trying to tell a story—an old story of an old Colorado—but no one was listening.

I came to a picture, hanging on the wall near the back door, of a couple sitting at the corner of a bar. They were holding hands and looking at each other with broad smiles. They had an antique, forlorn mystique about them that all characters in old photographs had, but beyond that, there was something special in the way they looked at each other. It was different from any of the other photos. Their eyes exchanged a deeper meaning, something not normally captured on film.

After looking at the photo for a moment I realized that the couple had posed for the picture seated at the bar behind me. I went to their corner and sat down. I felt their ghosts, and longed to see Naomi. I wanted to tell her about my feelings for her. I wanted to ask her to come with me, and then we would take off on that long road into the setting sun, and we could be together. We could make it work; through all the complications, there was something worth holding on to.

I nudged Lance and we left the Green Parrot for the Broken Paddle. When we got there, he went to the restroom and I went to find Naomi. She was at a table at the far end of the room with three guys and two other girls. I approached and she looked at me strangely. The others stopped talking and turned in my direction.

"Hey," she said, hesitantly. "Where's Lance? Is he with you?"

"Yeah," I said. "He's in the bathroom. How are you guys doing?"

The man sitting next to Naomi looked at me. "Who's this guy?" he asked.

Naomi introduced me to the table. "This is John, Cory, Sunny and Ellen," she said, "and this is Dan, my husband."

Lance came bounding up behind me as I searched for words.

"Hey, guys," he said.

The girls knew him from work, and he introduced himself to the guys.

"I've been here for one minute," he said, "and I already got a phone number. How's that for a good sign?"

Naomi looked at me with a pained expression and mouthed, "I'm sorry." I ignored her and turned to the waitress.

"I'll have a double whiskey and soda," I said.

I was talking frantically, and I felt my sensibilities collapsing. "Lance what do you want?" I asked. "Tell you what, get him the same, and do you guys want anything? Bring us a round of shots. And, I tell you what, get Naomi an extra shot. Put it all on my tab."

"Hey," Lance said. "what's gotten into you?"

"Nothing," I said, looking at Naomi with piercing eyes. "All of a sudden, it feels like a good night to get drunk!"

20

Naomi's husband sat next to her, laughing loudly at something one of his friends had said and slapping the table with the palm of his hand. He was a meaty man, with no redeeming social qualities that I could see, and I tried to imagine the reasons why she would have ever been attracted to him in the first place. His friends weren't much better—they all had superior airs and were loud and obnoxious to each other, the wait staff and everyone in the bar. They weren't the kind of people I would usually want to be around, but I tried to behave amicably, given the circumstances. The whole night was crashing down around me, and I wished to be anywhere other than where I was. Naomi left to go to the washroom, and I followed a couple of minutes later to catch her on the way back.

When she walked out, I grabbed her and pulled her into an alcove near a payphone. Her eyes were red and puffy, and she grabbed my collar and kissed me. Her hot, wet cheek pressed against mine.

"I'm so sorry, my love," she whispered into my ear. Her breath was hot, and her tears smeared across my red cheek. I pushed her away.

"What the fuck is going on?" I asked. "What are you doing?"

"I didn't *know* he would be here," she said.

"Yeah, right," I said. "Do you really think I believe that?"

"It's true," she said frantically. "My friend Jeannie told me after you dropped me off. That's why we didn't meet you at the restaurant. I told you, we have the same friends. I had to see him—she told him I was coming down. It's just a crazy, messed-up coincidence. I swear, I had no idea."

Against my better judgment, I believed her. The fact did little to minimize the damage to me, but it was still pleasant to know.

"I thought you guys split up," I said. "I thought you 'loved him but weren't in love with him.'"

"I know," she said, "but he doesn't know what's happening with us. He knows it's over, but he also knows I'm still his wife."

"I could fight him," I said.

"But you won't," she replied, looking away.

"You don't think I will?"

"No," she said, "you're not like that. He is, but you're not. That's why I love you."

"This is ridiculous," I said, feeling my body grow warm, and my voice rising. "Just tell him. Why won't you tell him? If you don't love him, and you don't want to be married to him, then end it! It's not that difficult to sort out!"

"It's not the right time. I can't do it now. Why are you being like this?"

I grabbed her arms, and held her close. "Because you're making me crazy! *This* is making me crazy!"

"I can't," she said. "I just can't. Not yet."

She broke away and went back to the table. When she disappeared around the corner, I went into the bathroom. I ran cool water over my hands and wet my face. The night was collapsing and I could only think about how fast I could get out of there. The door opened slowly and Lance came in.

"Hey, man," he said softly, "you okay?"

"No," I replied. "That's her fucking husband!"

"Yeah," he said, "I know."

"Look," I said, "I have to get out of here. I have to get back to the hotel, or back on the road or something. I have to get out of this bar."

"Don't do that," he said. "Just stick around, man, and shrug it off. We'll have fun tonight anyway."

It was bad advice—Lance's attempt to preserve the stability of the night in his own mind. To him, all things would appear normal if the status quo were maintained; the appearance of normality, to him, was just as good as the real thing. We went to the bar to have a drink before going back to the table, just to lubricate the unpleasantness.

I did my best to ignore the situation and enjoy the night. Soon three groups had formed at the table. The three guys were engaged in a drinking game. Each time a girl would walk by the table, they would drink if they wanted to sleep with her. If only one person drank, then he would have to buy the next round. If one person didn't drink, or hesitated, then he would have to buy the next round. I watched them, thinking of all that was unholy about them.

The second group was Lance and the other two girls. He was doing what he did best, concerned only with feeling them out to see with whom he had the best chances. They were all laughing and flirting. It was very tiring.

The third group consisted of Naomi and me, hovering somewhere in the baffles of the night, exchanging nervous glances, and I kept trying to talk with Lance and the girls, but Naomi kept looking at me expectantly.

Our group passed the evening in that way until the bar finally closed. They all left to go to an after-party and I broke away to go back to the hotel. As we parted ways, Naomi looked back at me. I stood under the glow of the streetlight and watched them disappear around the corner. Her husband had no clue that she and I had been exchanging looks all night. It was as if we had been blatantly discussing our private life right in front of him, and he had no idea-then again he *was* thoroughly occupied with evaluating the other women in the bar.

I walked back to the hotel alone through the dark streets, with the smell of the river hanging and blowing through the scratching pine trees. There were recurrent thoughts in my mind about the women in my life. I seriously doubted that all of my troubles with love were someone else's fault, and I began to worry that there was some part of me that was unlovable.

━━━━━

Sleep didn't come easily that night. Early in the morning, I woke and drank coffee in the hotel dining room before heading out. I felt as bad as I'd ever felt, and couldn't eat breakfast.

After finishing the coffee, I left the hotel to find Lance and exchange the Harley for his car, which would carry me east alone. I took everything I owned in the world with me: a few clothes, some books and a nervous heart. It was as if I had borrowed someone else's life for a time, and the old pains had finally caught up and fell upon me all at once.

I found Lance and we said our goodbyes. He was feeling badly too, but only because of his hangover, and our conversation was short. I was soon on my way, and glad to put that terrible memory behind me.

There was an outfitter on the side of the road near the south end of town, and I stopped to buy some shorts, t-shirts and a hat for the trip through the desert. There was a long rack of fly-fishing rods, and I grabbed one to take with me. There was something relaxing about spending time in a river, and after what had happened, it seemed like the most productive way to feel sorry for myself. The clerk helped me find some suitable flies, and I paid him and continued down the road.

Several miles outside of town, I came to a place where the river curved away from the road at some rapids, and sank into a deep pool. It bowed out to another set of rapids and then turned back toward the highway. When I came to the top of a third set of rapids there was a turnout on the side of the road and I stopped.

The banks were overgrown and there were no trails, forcing me to walk in the shallows, somewhere between the shore and the rapids that bubbled and gurgled in the center of the channel. The water was cold—fresh spring snowmelt that ran down from the peaks of the Collegiate Range and into the Arkansas River. Long flat stones lined the bottom and I noticed, for the first time, how pure and clear the water was.

The further I walked upriver, the echo of the rapids became softer. My ears adjusted to the variations of sound and heard the next set of rapids upriver; they were louder and more troublesome. I stopped and found a small clearing on the side of a large pool. The dirt was soft, and I sat down between the branches of the shrubs to prepare my rod.

As I assembled the pole and threaded the delicate line through the eyelets, the sense of touch returned to my feet and the sun warmed my body. The soothing sounds of the river provided a peaceful music, and I immediately began to relax.

I pulled two mayflies out of the plastic cup, putting one in my shirt pocket and tying the other to the end of the line. I had forgotten my book of knots but made do with a good, tight square knot, which I doubled five or six times. It was heavy, but it would hold. I chewed the excess line from the end and stood up, being careful not to tangle the rod in the low-lying scrub brush that bordered the river.

I waded into the deep water until it was less than an inch from the bottom of my shorts, embracing the cold with a meditative cringe. I pulled the orange line from the reel with my left hand, and held the rod with my right.

After glancing over my shoulder to judge the distance to shore, I brought the rod tip up, letting some of the line out, and brought it forward. I repeated this motion, each time springing my leader farther out over the flat water as the line speed increased. When the line was three-quarters of the way across, I increased my range of motion, allowing the fly to lightly touch the water, simulating a mayfly landing on the surface. The line fanned three or four light touches and then landed, and the orange line followed, coiling in the water near the fly and making a small ripple.

The fly drifted slowly downstream, and I waved the end of the rod in a circular motion to straighten the line, waiting for a strike. Nothing. Fishing always had a calming effect on me, and bad memories began to drift away.

I pulled the fly closer to me by gliding the loose end through the eyelets with my left hand, and popped the end of the rod up. The fly was airborne again. I brought the rod tip up over my head, spinning the line behind me, and then heaved it forward, feeling the force of the bending rod in my hand. I twirled the fly in the air, above the spot where it had previously landed. Before I let it touch the water, there was a slight ripple as a trout broke the surface with its long body, dove under with a small splash and flipped its tail in the air.

The fly touched the surface once, then twice, and then landed. There was a sharp splash and the leader disappeared under the surface, pulling the orange line with it. I jerked the rod tip up, setting the hook, and began to feel the fish struggling and pulling the line toward the deep water. I adjusted the drag, held the tip high in the air, and waited for the fish to tire.

I laughed aloud and gave the trout a long line on which to wear himself down. As the pull began to decrease, I brought the tip down slightly and brought in a few inches of line, raising the tip of the rod as I reeled, then repeated the motion and pulled the fish in closer.

Each time he got close to me he would renew the fight, running repeatedly toward the deep water, forcing me to repeat the process. Every time he fought, though, he would stop shorter and shorter, until I brought him in close enough to grab. I locked the line between my forefinger and the pole and stood the end of the rod up, parallel with my body, bringing the fish to my knees. I reached down and pulled him out of the water.

The long trout struggled little as I rested the end of my rod on the river bottom, and used my elbow to keep the tip from falling into the water. I held the fish with one hand and backed the hook out of his mouth and dropped the fly into the water with the other. It was a rainbow trout about 15 inches long with a thick build. I lowered him back into the river and moved him back and forth against the slow current. His tail twitched and I loosened my grip until he hovered on his own. His tail began to move, slowly and uncoordinated at first, but in a few seconds he found his equilibrium and darted off to the deep water.

I stayed in the river for another hour and caught two brook trout and five more rainbows, and each fish was smaller than the last. When I felt sufficiently detached from the events of the previous night, I hooked the fly around one of the eyelets, tightened the line and waded through the shallows, back to the car. The sound of the small rapids ahead grew louder and I walked carefully over the rocks in the ankle-deep water until I came to the beach.

I dismantled the rod and put it back into the case. I put the case and the cup of flies on a rock near the trail, knowing that I wouldn't use them again, and returned to the road. The highway ran along the edge of the river, through a staggered series of wide valleys and narrow canyons.

There is a subtle difference between a highway and the road. The highway is the surface on which I traveled. The road is the experience of it.

As I drove lower, toward the high plains, the air became hotter, and the land transformed into something like a desert.

21

By the late afternoon, I was on the edge of the plains, descending into Pueblo, Colorado. To the southwest, above the distant mountains, a violent storm gathered and quickly moved to engulf the foothills with a terrifying swirl of dark clouds and rain. The bright flashes of blue lightning penetrated the earth and illuminated the purple sky. Claps of thunder echoed across the prairie and the storm gathered itself in a long reach toward town.

Pueblo had two distinct and very different parts. The first was the old side of town, the original city center that surrounded the small road that lead out of the mountains. A few miles away were the bright and shiny, plastic, collapsible corporate buildings of the new side of town that surrounded the bustling interstate. I drove through the old city and found a decent hotel somewhere between the two sides, near the highway.

The hotel was dirty, and a musty smell drifted around the property. I went into the lobby and leaned against the desk. It was a dark, despairing place and the odor of burned coffee and cigarettes hung in the air. A bored-looking clerk with gray eyes appeared from a room behind the desk, looked at me, and began to type on his computer.

"What, haven't had enough of this town yet?" he asked.

"Excuse me?" I said, taken aback.

"City boy, right? From Denver, come down here every now and again for some girl?"

"I'm just passing through, man."

"Uh-huh. Look, I just don't want any pissed-off husbands or boyfriends showing up tonight looking for you and whoever you're shacking up with here. What I'm trying to say is that I don't want no trouble. I run a quiet place here and I don't want any more of you philandering city boys up here causing problems."

"No way, man," I said with a crooked smile. "It's not like that. I'm just stopping in for a quiet night."

"Whatever, dude. Just remember what I said. The room's $25 a night. Sorry, but we don't rent by the hour."

"That's fine," I said.

I filled out the register and, after exchanging cold stares with the clerk, got the key to the room and went outside.

There were small tufts of grass growing from the cracks in the cement, and a stray dog meandered across the lot under the glowing arc of a large, fluorescent light, hanging from a pole. Thunder echoed from the distant foothills and he stopped, his ears perked slightly. Then he disappeared into some trees that bordered a small creek near the edge of the hotel.

The storm came and the wind began to howl around the corners of the building. Dust from the parking lot rose in small swirls. I found the room, threw my bags on the floor, and went across a side street behind the hotel to a small market.

I bought 12 bottles of beer, a pack of cigarettes, two ham sandwiches and a bottle of the most expensive red wine they had. The clerk scanned each item slowly, and my mind and body ached with anticipation. I was hoping to get back to the hotel before the rain, but the more excited I got, the slower his movements became.

"That's a pretty big storm comin', huh?" he said.

"Yeah, looks like it's going to be a bad one," I replied.

"Yup, worst one of the season so far, 'cordin to the radio," he answered in a slow drawl.

He scanned the last item and I handed him $40. He counted the change slowly and deliberately, and my patience began to disappear, as if the fast wind outside were carrying it. It was already beginning to spit fat drops of rain and I knew it would only be minutes before the storm engulfed the store and hotel.

He bagged everything except the beer, which he started to hand to me. He dropped his chin, and before he let go he spoke to me in a low tone.

"You don't want to get caught up in a mess like that," he said, motioning toward the rolling clouds. "If you don't get ready *before* the storm, you're never going to make it. You'll just end up blowing across the prairie like a tumbleweed. You have to take the weather, so it don't take you."

I stopped, and I was no longer in a hurry, no longer rushed. What he said made sense; if you don't prepare for the storm then you will be swept up by it. The same went for life I supposed. Perhaps the situation with Naomi would have been more tolerable if I hadn't been so blind-if I would have been prepared for all possibilities.

"Holy shit," I said. "You are absolutely right."

"I know," he replied. "You don't think I got this old by having my head up my ass, do you?"

I smiled and turned to walk out, then stopped before I got to the door. There was a direct and forceful simplicity to his logic.

"Where's a good place to get a drink around here?" I asked.

"I always drink at Phil's Radiator Service and Beer Garden, but that's just me."

"You going to be there tonight?"

"I reckon."

"Good," I said. "I need to buy you a beer."

"Can't say no to that, young fellar!"

I nodded and went out the door. Outside, the wind began to calm, but the storm was still moving fast. I walked quickly across the parking lot and into the hotel room. The slender trees bobbed and weaved, showing the light undersides of their leaves and straining under the force of the wind. The rain began to fall harder, and I watched through the window with excited curiosity.

When my attraction to the storm had gone, I sat on the bed near the nightstand and called Bryan on the hotel phone. I left a message with his answering service, telling him where I was, and to call me back when he could.

I hung up the phone and lay back on the bed, feeling small. Though I was tired, I did not sleep. A thousand miles away, in the buzz of Kansas City, my old life carried on without me. Life in State Bridge carried on as well, and Naomi with her husband. The whole machine carried on and gave my passage little notice. I felt sick that I had to live with myself for the rest of my life.

I closed my eyes under the force of the realization, and after a few minutes the phone rang. From the other end came the soothing voice of Bryan Hillary. He told me he was exploring Big Bend National Park, an enormous swath of land in southwest Texas along the Rio Grande. He was calling from the town of Lajitas, a small town on the border and almost a thousand miles directly south of Pueblo.

"Hey, man," I said. "I've been thinking about some things and I wanted your advice. I'm thinking about heading back home."

"What?" he replied. "Why? I thought you were going to stay out there. You know, discover what you're made of and all that."

"Yeah," I said, "I know, but something happened. Something happened and it made me think this whole thing is just a waste. I should just go back. I should be with Beth. I should get my old job back. At least that was all permanent."

"Did something happen with Naomi?" he asked.

"Yeah," I said, "something bad. How'd you guess?"

"Come on, man," he said. "You can sugarcoat all of it by talking about falling in love, and the fact that she and her husband were split up and all this nobility bullshit, but the fact of the matter is that you were involved with a married woman. That kind of shit never goes too far without a cave-in."

"I know," I replied, "but I thought this was different. It felt right. It just…I thought this was special."

"Yeah," he said, "I'm sure everyone thinks that. So what happened?"

I told him about the last night in State Bridge, the ride to Buena Vista and meeting her husband. He listened quietly until the end of the story.

"So, what'd you do?" he asked.

"What do you mean?" I replied. "I just told you."

"No," he said firmly. "How did you act? How did you act when you met her husband?"

"Oh," I said. "Badly. I was with Lance and he convinced me to stay around and try to have fun. You know Lance—he's always the diplomat. So I did the next best thing. I got drunk, and everything went on from there. No one knew what had happened except for Lance, and he didn't seem to care. It was awkward as hell, Bryan. I didn't know what to do."

"I like Lance," he said. "He's a fun guy and he has a great, liberated kind of personality, but let's be honest. He's not the guy to be alone with when something like that happens."

"I know. They all went to an after-party and I went back to the hotel. The next day, I left. I did a little fishing on the river to relax, and drove on to Pueblo. It's kind of a crossroads town, you know?"

"I don't think you should go home. I think that's the absolute last thing you should do."

"Really?" I replied. "Why?"

"Well," he said, "I know it's rough, but you can't just turn it into a reason to tuck your tail and run away. That's the kind of shit that got you into this in the first place."

"But what about you?" I asked. "You're going home."

"Yes," he said, "but we're not talking about me. Don't change the subject."

There was a long pause.

"Look," he went on, "if you want my advice, which you obviously do or you wouldn't have called, I would say that you should go to Austin. Take the trip to try to work it out. When you get there, call her. I'm sure you and she have some things to talk about."

"So what are you going to do?" I asked.

"I'll meet you in Austin in a few days. You don't need to be left alone with Mark and Lance if shit goes south."

"I like it," I said. "That sounds better than my plan. So what about you? You come to Austin, then what?"

"Then back to New York, I guess," he said.

"You're still set on that?"

"Yeah, I have some things to straighten out with Pop, but other than that, I don't know what the hell I'm going to do. Go back to work, but I hope I can last. I mean, it's the right thing to do, but I just don't want to feel caged-up again."

If anything, Bryan wasn't the kind of man who would put up with feeling stuck anywhere. He had a free spirit, more so than anyone else I've ever known, including me. I was afraid that he would stay in a place he did not love only out of obligation to the people whom he did love. I could see his situation turning sour quickly, and by the sound of his voice, it was apparent that it was already beginning to happen.

His voice was dry, and without the passion that had first drawn me to his commanding personality. He was cornered in his life by the pressures of the world, and I didn't know if there was anything I could do to help him. He had held my hand when I surely would have gone back, and helped me to understand the road. He had guided me along with the Naomi problem, and I hoped that if he ever needed me, I would be there in the same capacity; In fact I had the feeling that I might have to save my friend in much the same way he saved me.

We finished the conversation with warm assurances that we would see each other soon, and then the line went dead. I held the phone to my ear, half wishing the conversation weren't over.

Outside, the storm subsided and broke up over the plains to the west. The rain continued as a light mist, punctuated by a few fat drops, and then stopped. I opened the door to the room, walked outside and lit a cigarette. The smell of wet earth and pavement filled the air, bringing to mind the sad relief that came to me as a child at the end of a storm. There was an excitement that I was safe and alive, but sadness that the intense and passionate excitement was gone, fading in the distance as passions often do.

I went back into the room and washed my face and my hands, letting the water run over my sunburned arms under the scratchy glow of the old fixtures, in a cracked ceramic sink. I ran my wet hands through my hair, leaned forward on the counter and stared into the mirror.

The person in the reflection looked different now. Though my face retained its general shape, it seemed older and more distinguished. My skin was tan and weathered, and a line stood out around my eyes where sunglasses usually sat. On my forehead and cheeks small freckles had begun to pop up, the result of prolonged, unprotected exposure to the sun. The stubble on my face, my chin, and below my nose had grown longer and was bleached almost white by the sun. My eyes were bright and had a radiance deep within them that I had never seen before.

With the rain gone and the sky clearing I left the room and began to wander down the black street. I searched for Phil's Radiator Service and Beer Garden. I was hoping to run into the old man from the market and talk to him. The guy looked like he'd been around, and I had reason to think he might have some good advise for me- one wanderer to another.

The hotel sat on the edge of the old downtown business district. Since the construction of Interstate 25, which ran from north to south along the eastern edge of town, commerce had gradually drifted away from the city center in favor of the booming, high-volume industries that clung to the highway like clustering mold spots on a tile floor.

Like so many downtown areas across America, however, old downtown Pueblo was trying to breathe life back into itself—a kind of cross-country renaissance of old town America. The area was attempting to counteract the natural tendency of urban sprawl and interstate highway commerce in favor of the eclectic, small-town atmosphere that these old buildings provided. Storefronts that once held necessary venues of worldly commerce now contained theme restaurants and gift stores, art shops and flea markets—all businesses that fed the travelers' overly nostalgic curiosities, and their attractions to the quaint and long-gone spirit of the rural American city center.

As I left the hotel, stars began to pop out behind the clouds, against the arc of the city lights. The streets quietly came alive as the after-dinner crowd drifted out of the restaurants. I found Phil's at one end of a busy line of brilliantly lit buildings, and went inside. It was an old gas station and garage that had been converted into a bar, with an open patio flowing out of the wooden bay doors.

I went inside and sat at the long counter, ordered a beer and watched through the window the passing of the small crowds. Their sweet and satisfied dispositions brightened the evening, making me feel calm and collected. The old man never showed, and I was disappointed that I would never get the chance to find out more about him. I quietly retreated from the bar and returned to the hotel to sleep, and then to continue south the next day. I had an appointment to see Mark in Texas, and I was going keep it.

———

A taxi took me to the hotel and I lay down on my dingy bed, staring blankly at the off-white ceiling, letting my mind run away with everything that had happened. In the beginning, the alcohol was making it difficult to produce coherent and meaningful thought. But as I stared at the cracked plaster above, things slowly became clear.

I had been living as a fugitive did: day-to-day, finding short periods of comfort but always fearful that my past would someday catch up with me. It finally came to me that I would never have the possibility of success and happiness in love if I continued to carry around the same emotional baggage everywhere I went.

Somehow, the last of the whiskey that Bryan gave me had survived the recklessness in State Bridge. As I dug through the bag to find the bottle my hand brushed against an envelope that was folded and stuck in between two of the books on top of a stack of wrinkled clothes.

I sat on the corner of the bed and pulled a small stack of neatly folded pages out of the envelope. The letter was written in a delicate hand and the shapes of the letters made reading it seem as if she were talking to me; I could feel her soothing nature in the loops and wavy lines.

> My love,
>   I know how all of this must feel. Believe me, I didn't know that it was going to turn out like this. Ever since I met you, I just can't stand talking to him. There's no way I can continue this charade of a marriage. I will be back at the lodge in a day or so. Call me when you can. We must talk soon. I am so sorry again, my love,
>
>   Naomi

I folded the letter, stuck the envelope in my pocket next to Bryan's medal, and put my head in my hands.

Tears came, but there was relief in them. As crossroads come and go, it's difficult to know which is the right path, where it comes from, or where it will lead you. Often, the wrong path is the exact opposite direction from where you want to go, and that becomes clear when you are confronted by the decision of which way you *should* go.

The right path is somewhat less clear. While the beginning of it feels right, the resulting turn of events is completely unknown and may be either good or bad, and you cannot know until you have traversed its length and breadth. The wrong path, on the other hand, bears no false pretense.

22

The next morning was difficult, like so many mornings I experienced out there. I woke to the sound of an excited knock at the door. On the other side was the brightest of sunlight, and the tanned face of the housekeeping attendant.

"You staying longer, or you check out?" she asked in a thick accent.

"No," I said, my voice dry and scratchy, "I'm leaving in an hour or so."

"Oh, ok," she said dejectedly. "I come back."

I closed the door and paused, strangely worried that my life had suddenly become a series of strange hotels and painful hangovers. I showered, put on another set of dirty clothes, and sat on the corner of the bed. The phone rang and when I picked it up, a gruff voice called out my name in the form of a question.

"Yes," I said.

"Checkout was an hour ago. If you don't clear out, I'm going to charge you for another day."

"Look, man," I said, massaging my head, "you do whatever you have to do."

I hung up the phone, then quickly picked it up again. I called the offices of the Mark McDaniel Band in Austin, to tell him that I was on my way and would be there in a few days. Mark wasn't in the office, but his bookkeeper/receptionist was, and she had been expecting a call from me.

"Do you want to leave a message for Mark?"

"Yeah," I said. "Tell him I'm on my way, and to leave a time and place to meet him for drinks on Friday evening. That should give me enough time to find my way to Austin."

"Sure. You will be calling us when you get to town then?"

"Yeah," I said. "you can just leave me a message when you find out where I'm supposed to meet him."

She agreed and I gave her the number to my voicemail, which I would be able to check from the road. I thanked her and hung up the phone, then I stood up and looked around the little room.

I felt dirty, and the best option I could consider was to head south before I changed my mind. I packed my duffle bag, walked into the parking lot and loaded it into the backseat of the Land Rover.

Now I had some time. I was to turn once more to the road, but this time, I had a destination and a few distant prospects. Aside from wanting to talk to Naomi, I knew that things were slightly brighter. Now, I decided, it was time to pick up and start the next chapter. The best thing to do would be to get to Austin, and call Naomi then.

I navigated the yellow Land Rover through the streets of downtown Pueblo until I found the interstate. Once I found it, I turned south and wound my way into the southeast corner of Colorado.

Raton, New Mexico, appeared on the other side of a low mountain pass. It was little more than a crossroads that travelers used to access the tourist destinations in the Rocky Mountains. The town was a scattering of middle-income houses, truck stops, economy hotels and cheap restaurants; there was nothing of significance in this place that an outsider could see, with the exception of the surrounding foothills and distant peaks beyond the west end of town.

The buildings and streets seemed to follow the interstate as trees cling to the banks of rivers for their sustenance. A town settled in the hills, settled as a crossroads, with aspirations of nothing.

About 10 miles outside of Raton, I saw a young man standing on the side of the road. I didn't feel like making the long drive into Texas alone, so I stopped and asked him if he wanted a ride.

"Yeah," he said as he threw a faded, green duffle bag into the backseat through the open window. "Thanks man, I've been standing out here all day and you're the first person to stop!"

He was a young man, in his early 20s, and carried himself proudly. He was tan and muscular and wore a dirty pair of boots, a faded pair of ripped up jeans, a ribbed undershirt and a denim snap-shirt that hung over his long legs, unbuttoned and untucked. His sleeves were rolled up to just below his elbows. On one hand he wore a watch with a large brown leather band, and on the other was a faded blue bandana, wrapped around his wrist like a bracelet.

He climbed into the front seat and I pulled out onto the highway, to the sound of loose gravel spitting and clicking through the small dust cloud that rose into the air from the shoulder of the road. We were quiet for a short time, and then I turned toward him.

"Where are you coming from?" I asked.

"L.A.," he replied.

"You're a long way from home, friend. Why are you all the way out here in the ass of nowhere?"

"L.A.'s not home. I'm from Louisiana. I went to California to get a job as an actor, but that didn't really pan out. What about you?"

"Well," I said, "I'm just out here wandering around. I'm on a pilgrimage of sorts."

"I'm Randy," he said, and held out his right hand. I shook it and told him my name.

"So," he said, "we're both out here alone on the road, huh? Any particular reason you're here and not somewhere else?"

"Sometimes, you just have to get out and see the world," I said. "If you want to stay home all the time, then you're better off being asleep for the rest of your life."

I left it at that. I didn't want to go into the full story, as I had with so many other people I'd met along the way. I had been thinking about it with such intensity over the previous week that I no longer wanted to talk about it, especially to a stranger who probably wouldn't have any interest in my personal problems. What was the point of thinking about the past? It didn't seem right to sulk about it when life spread itself so sweetly before me.

For the first few hours, we talked sporadically about unimportant subjects, like the weather, and how long he had been waiting for a ride. We shared information like where we were from and what we had studied in college. As the road flew past and the late afternoon turned to evening, we sat in a long and comfortable silence, which was broken only by the periodic reference to sights or towns that we passed.

"Check that out," said Randy, pointing to the side of the road.

Off the highway, in a field, was a tall billboard, painted black with large, white letters. It read:

> *"DON'T MAKE ME*
> *COME DOWN THERE!"*
> *—GOD*

"I wonder," said Randy, "how much they charged God for that billboard."

———

We drove past the last group of fat, low mountains. Now, there were only a few rocky rises dotting the landscape on either side of the road, and flat, open plains in front of us. The air was dry and hot, and we kept the windows down. My new traveling companion held his face in the breeze, which swirled through the open cab. He rested his arm on the door, letting the passing wind lift his hand and drop it down as he looked away, over the landscape and into things that only he could see on the horizon of his mind.

I tuned the radio to an AM station that was playing old, scratchy bluegrass tunes, and the beat of the music matched the speed at which we traveled, slow and smooth across the border of New Mexico and into Texas, to the steady rhythm of the New Grass Revival singing "Sweet Release." The evening turned to night, and still we held the long pause that was only slightly more comfortable than the obligatory small talk.

We both seemed to project the same disinterest in the subjects of history and origins of the other. We had taken one another's cues to speak only when we had something important to say. It was quiet, and yet we were learning about each other. We seemed connected in the desire to think, and to discuss only what came from within. I had an important story, and I had the feeling that he did too, but we were waiting for the right time to let them out.

Late in the evening, the lights of Dumas, Texas, came into view in the distance, over the flat shadow of the open desert. I had come only 160 miles since leaving Raton, but the day was wearing on me and I felt an acute exhaustion. I leaned forward, holding my chin above the steering wheel, and looked at the stars above, perched atop the magnificent void. The dome of light above the town hid the tail of the Big Dipper, which pointed toward it like an arrow, leading me to a place where I could rest.

Randy had fallen asleep some time before, with the seat reclined and one foot propped on the dashboard. I felt a pleasant calm from having someone in the car with me, even though we hadn't spoken much. He was the first person I had traveled with since Buena Vista. That seemed like years ago now, and it was good to have someone along on the road again.

There was a cheap-looking hotel just off the highway, and I turned off into the driveway, over a high hump in the pavement, which startled Randy awake. He sat up and looked around, batting his eyes with the strange confusion of someone who had forgotten where he was. I stopped under the awning in front of the door leading to the lobby.

"What's going on?" he asked, his voice scratchy.

"It's time to call it a night," I said. "I've done all the driving I can do."

"Cool, are you getting a room?"

"Yeah. I'm going to clean up and get some food and maybe a drink. You interested, or are you moving on?"

"Well, it's probably too late to get a ride anywhere. You mind if I crash on the floor?"

"Hell, man, if you don't have anywhere to stay, then I'll get you a room. It looks like you've been living hard on the road, and a quiet night alone under a roof might be good for you."

He smiled and looked me in the eye. "Thanks, brother," he said. "That's mighty Christian of you."

I left Randy and went into the lobby, which reminded me of the hotel in Pueblo in its rustic charms. But it was cheap, and I was trying to budget my remaining cash to last me as long as possible. I paid for the two rooms and asked the clerk for directions to a place to get some food and a good drink. The man at the desk was helpful and courteous, and it was endearing to know that there were still people who valued the art of good service. Outside, Randy was standing by the car stretching and looking up at the sky. The fluorescent floodlights surrounding the parking lot obscured the stars.

"Are we in?" he asked.

"Yeah," I answered. "I got us two rooms on the ground floor and the name of a good bar that serves decent food."

"Excellent," he said. "but, you may have to go alone tonight. I'm flat broke."

The young man, over the course of our few hours together, had begun to seem to me like a younger and more introverted version of Bryan Hillary. I remembered how well Bryan had taken care of me on our first night together, and I felt pride in being able to do the same for Randy.

"Look, let's get to the rooms and clean up. We'll meet back up in about an hour and go out for some food and, more importantly, a couple of drinks. I'll take care of the tab."

"I've already mooched a ride and a room off you. I can't accept that."

"Hey," I said. "I know how it feels to be in your position, and it'll probably be good for us both to kick back for a little while. I'll get it. I insist."

"Okay," he replied. "I appreciate it."

I parked the car and we grabbed our respective bags and went to our rooms, which were next door to each other. Inside I had an overwhelming sense of *déjà vu* about the room and the town. It felt as though I had been in this same place before.

This was the same hotel in the same town that I had stopped at every night during my time on the road, with the exception of State Bridge. Every little town and dirty hotel along the way had been the same. Only the people had been different.

23

An hour later, after a comfortable doze and a long shower, I walked outside. Randy was leaning against the hood of the Land Rover and drinking a beer, watching the traffic pass by on the road. A six-pack sat on the roof of the car, having recently become a five-pack.

"I thought you were broke," I said.

"I am *now*," he replied. "I figured the least I could do would be to throw my last few bones into the drinking till and get us a couple of beers before we go to the bar."

"I can't argue with that," I said, and he threw one of the full cans at me.

We stood in the parking lot, drinking the rest of the beer and talking about the prospects of finding some girls in this town. We both agreed that, given the nature of the place, it probably wouldn't be worth our time.

After the last of the beer was gone, we got into the car, drove into the downtown area, and found the Tumbleweed Bar in an old brick building on 12th Street. We sat at the bar and ordered a couple of burgers and a couple of cold beers.

The bar looked older than the town itself and I appreciated its significance. The food was bad and the service was slow, but it didn't matter because it was still a meal, and the first hot one I'd had in a while. Besides, we were there for the drinks first and foremost.

After we finished the burgers, we ordered two more bottles of beer, and each smoked one of the last two cigarettes that I had left in a pack that I'd bought at Phil's in Pueblo. It was the satisfying kind of smoke that comes with a full stomach and the taste of cold beer, and we both sat back in the bar stools and relaxed in a collected silence. We finished the smokes and the beer and ordered two more and another pack of cigarettes.

The bartender, an older man in a faded, blue-and-white snap shirt and jeans, brought them to us. They were Pall Malls, the only kind they sold in the bar.

"Sir," I said to the gentleman, "can I have two shots of Crown Royal?"

"You don't have to call me sir, son, I ain't royalty. You can call me Vic, and yes, you can have all the whiskey you want as long as you don't burn down the place or start a fight."

"We'll try," I said.

Vic brought the whiskey. Randy and I touched glasses and I felt the warm sting of the liquor as it rolled down my throat and entered my fragile body. For a second, my stomach turned and my mouth began to water, then the liquor stayed and the sickness passed. I turned to my companion.

"So, what's the deal?" I asked Randy. "Where are you coming from?"

"It's kind of a long story," he replied, breaking eye contact and staring into his beer.

The young man seemed to get increasingly nervous and edgy as the night continued. He struck me as drastically different from the hitchhiker I had picked up earlier in the day. It was as if he were waiting for someone or something to catch up to him. I wondered whether

I had perhaps brought some kind of unneeded trouble into my life by picking him up. Still, he looked like he needed help, and I was hearing Bryan's voice telling me to be charitable. I looked around the bar, which was mostly deserted.

"Well, I would say we have some time tonight," I said. "Let me hear it."

"I guess it would be good to talk about it. I haven't really told anyone the whole story. Maybe it would be good to lay it all out."

"I've always thought that if you just get it out, you'll be better off in the end. Then you won't have a whole lot of loose bullshit rolling around in your head."

"All right," he said, still uneasy. "I went out to L.A. to get a job as an actor, but it didn't work out. Now I'm on my way back home to Louisiana."

He stopped, as if he were waiting to see if I would let him off the hook, and he could leave the story at that. I kept my gaze fixed on him expectantly.

"I drove out to California," he continued, "after I graduated from college. My parents told me to go out there and be wild for a little while. I was supposed to start law school a year after I graduated, so my parents gave me a bunch of money and a new car and sent me out to California to take some time off."

"That sounds pretty cool," I said. "Just to be able to get out and blow off some steam before grad school."

"There's a little more to it than that," he said cautiously. "You see, my dad is an attorney, and so are my older brother and uncle. I was under a lot of pressure to go to graduate school, but I just wasn't that into it. I've always thought of myself as an artist of some kind. I could just never think like an attorney, or a businessman, and I always thought that fate was pulling me in another direction. I figured that I could go to California, and I would have a year to prove to my folks that I wasn't just out here screwing around, that I was actually serious about working. I knew I wanted to try acting, and I didn't think it would be hard to get work. All I needed was one little break, and I would be set."

"There's a lot of risk in that kind of talk, my friend," I said.

"No shit!" he said. "I thought if I got a big enough break, my folks would see that I was serious and help me financially until I was able to support myself. I had a job as a waiter during the evenings and at the library during some days. I went to auditions and worked hard, but I also partied hard and missed a lot of chances as a result. Eventually, I fell in with a girl. She was one of those loud, obnoxious, materialistic, L.A. types."

"Letting a girl like that get into your head tends to throw a big wrench in things," I said.

"By the time all this was happening, my year was almost up and my parents were pressuring me to come home. I was supposed to go to law school at Mississippi State in the fall but in reality, I had no intention of going back. I ignored my parents and continued on. Eventually, they stopped calling."

During the last part of the story, Randy's eyes never left his beer bottle as it sat motionless on the old bar. As he fixated on his past his face grew increasingly bitter and pale. His feelings about his experience were evident in the intensity of his expression, and the story of his lust for life once again made me think of Bryan. It was as if the two of them could be brothers. I knew from his demeanor that the story had yet to find a happy conclusion.

He got the attention of the bartender and ordered another pair of shots, which Vic brought immediately. Randy and I toasted to the lost art of bar brawling and downed the shots, then slammed the glasses back down on the bar.

"So this girl I ended up with," he continued, "one day she walked into my apartment and started telling me that the reason I hadn't gotten my break was because I didn't act, dress or party like a celebrity, and that if I did all those things, I would have a much better chance at getting a job. So that's what I did. I took the money I had left, about fifty thousand, and sold my car for about thirty thousand. My parents are rich, so I was never really hurting. Then I just dove into the L.A. nightlife. We went to clubs and parties and I bought enough X and coke to get me high for a year. I met quite a few people, but

I never followed up on any connections. I just got too caught up in the lifestyle. Then, one night, at a place in Santa Monica, I laid down my last c-note on the bar top, and the party was over. My girl ended up leaving with some cheap, sweet-talking producer. I think he made porn movies. Anyway, I went into the bathroom, stared at my face in the mirror; I was pale and sweaty and I watched the blood drip out of my nose. That's when I decided to get the hell out of there. That was two weeks ago, and I've been on the road ever since."

"That sucks, man," I said, turning to look him in the eye. "I know what you mean, though, getting caught up in something that you don't really believe in. Then one day you get the wakeup call and you think to yourself, *What the hell happened to me?*"

Once he finished telling his story and we had talked about it for a while, I began to tell him mine. We talked until after midnight, and then we went back to the hotel. I was glad we had gone with that option instead of making finding women our absolute priority. After our talk in the bar, I began to lose my discomfort with Randy. He struck me now as more of a mix between Lance and Bryan, and I was glad to have his company. We parted ways and I went to my room to sleep, half drunk and half relaxed. I fell into the scratchy folds of the hotel comforter and its stiff mattress, and let the darkness cradle me until I sank into a deep sleep.

Though the night had been calm and relatively uneventful, we nevertheless slept in until well after three on Thursday afternoon. When we finally dragged ourselves out of bed we hit the road at a vibrant and excited pace, pausing briefly to eat in Amarillo, Texas. While we were stopped, I found a payphone and called Mark's office, to tell him that I'd definitely be in Austin the next day, probably late in the afternoon. I spoke with his receptionist who told me to meet Mark at Palo's Icehouse around dusk.

"Tell him I'll be there," I said, and hung up the phone.

On the south side of town, we joined Interstate 27 to Lubbock, squeezing in as many miles as we could, and stopping only for gas in Plainview. Plainview was a small highway town in the middle of the Texas Panhandle farm country, an oasis in a thick sea of scrubby cotton and skinny cattle.

After we got gas, Randy asked if he could drive, and I sat in the passenger seat for the first time during the whole trip. I leaned back and watched the flat Texas farmland roll by, with one arm hanging out the window and the other resting across my lap.

The land cruised by the window in the form of large cotton fields with handfuls of abandoned houses scattered among them— sad reminders of the incorporation of rural America-and large feedlots and pasturelands. The green smell of the lots hung in the air long before they were visible on the side of the road, and for miles after.

Wisps of loose, dry cotton buds from the previous year drifted across the highway like snow flurries during an indifferent winter. The entire time we drove steadily down the highway, low-lying clouds buzzed by in the air above, riding the wind like ghosts flying ever westward into the gathering orange hue of dusk.

We passed through Lubbock late that night without so much as a pause, despite the temptation of a nighttime adventure in downtown Lubbock with the early summer stragglers from the University. We continued on, hoping to reach Austin early the next morning.

Randy had a few friends in Austin, and promised me an adventurous evening if I was so inclined. I was. I was also filled with impatience to arrive in what was, by far, the biggest city I had encountered on the road. I yearned for the fabricated comfort that only a large city could provide. It felt as though I had been living in the Stone Age, and some time in a large city would do me good. Moreover, I was looking forward to talking to Mark, and starting on the next chapter of my little adventure.

Outside of the town of Sweetwater, we passed through a low line of hills that were topped by processions of giant wind generators, which stood close to two hundred feet above the ground. Their enormous blades cut long, slow circles in the dry air. A full moon shone down on them from an angle, and they cast mysterious shadows along the ground. They stood in rows across the open expanse, facing the wind like soldiers in formation, spinning to the rhythm of the wind.

We continued south, stopping again in the small town of Bronte. The land between Sweetwater and Bronte had been mostly arid farm country, but it began to change as we passed further southeast. The tops of the trees cast dark shadows along fields of green grasses. The deep blue glow of the moon made it feel like some kind of surreal, supernatural afternoon—a dark, twisted night out of a Dr. Seuss painting.

Low hills and rock outcroppings accentuated a landscape dotted with mesquite and other low shrubs. Above the ground, in clumps along fencerows and over the hills, were large, tangled, live oak trees. There was a rugged and wild beauty about the country, and I could see that the people who lived there took a great deal of pride in it: almost every home displayed large flags and signs touting the importance of Texas. The stars hung across the horizon and filled a sky that seemed more open, and bigger, than anything I had seen out west, or even back in Kansas. It was as if we were getting closer to heaven.

Between the towns of Brady and Llano, the landscape began to change again. Tall hills and thick groves of live oak trees reaching above the green grasses replaced the low fields and plains of west Texas. As night began its revolution into morning, and a glow tickled the eastern horizon, the trees grew taller and wider. We had arrived in the Texas Hill Country, and were getting close to Austin.

We began to count down the miles by the highway signs that charted the progress to our destination: 50 miles, 35 miles. We had been quiet for most of the night, but as we began to feel the city in the distance, there was an electric air in the car: 20 miles, 15 miles.

Just past the small town of Bee Caves, we turned onto Southwest Parkway, a broad highway that would take us into the heart of downtown. 10 miles. 5 miles. We drove through a series of curves and up a small rise. Ahead on the horizon, the glow was getting brighter as we climbed higher up the gentle slope. When we crested the hill we could see, in the distance, the tall buildings and bright lights of Austin.

Beyond the skyline of the city, the sun was approaching fast. Randy had been to Austin frequently when he was younger. He had family and a number of friends who had gone to school there, so he knew the streets and the highways well enough to navigate without the maps that we didn't have. He negotiated the nearly deserted streets of downtown until we found a suitable hotel on 5th Street. I booked us into a couple of rooms and we parted ways, with the promise that we would see each other the next day.

I went to my room, sat down on the bed and pulled the shoes off my tired feet. I began to think about State Bridge and everything that had happened since I'd first talked to Mark about coming to Austin. When I was still in Colorado, the idea of ending up in Austin seemed about as likely as ending up on the moon, but there I was. Before long, I was asleep, and a wave of mental and physical exhaustion swept over me like a shadow, and I drifted off, deeply and soundly.

24

When I woke up it was late afternoon, almost evening. I took a shower and dressed. There was no answer when I knocked on Randy's door, so I went to the elevator and rode down ten floors to the lobby. At the front desk, I asked directions to the bar, where I was supposed to meet Mark.

"What's your room number?" the clerk asked.

"Twenty-two fourteen," I replied.

"That's what I thought," he said. "I have a message for you."

He hunched over slightly, searching through the scattered papers around the computer until he found what he was looking for. He handed me an envelope. Inside was a hand-scribbled note from Randy, on hotel stationery.

Hey man,

I'm off into town. I'm going to hook up with my uncle to see about getting some money for the rest of my trip.

I promised a few friends I would party with them tonight, so if you want to meet up with us later, we'll be at Shakespeare's Pub on 6th Street. Try to make it if you can.

Later, Randy

I was glad to see that he hadn't left yet. I was also glad that he was going to find some money. If I kept trying to support us both for much longer, I would wind up broke a thousand miles from home. If I had to, I could call home and try to persuade my father to send me a wire, but I considered it a last resort. If necessary, I could take Mark's job offer, but I was still experiencing the pull to keep moving, and I wasn't ready to tie myself down with another job.

Palo's Icehouse, according to the man at the desk, was within walking distance from the hotel, and I began to head in the direction he pointed, trying to remember the names of the streets. Downtown Austin had a clean, cultured feel to it, and its tall, new skyscrapers contrasted with the short, stone buildings of the bar district. The opposing architectural dichotomy of the old and the new created a kind of intrinsic balance between the historic town center and the vibrancy of a new growth.

As I walked, I watched the buildings moving against the sky, and the rushing lines of thick traffic on the street. I didn't, unfortunately, watch the street signs, and soon I had no idea where I was. I stood on the corner of a large street, six lanes across. The two street signs said "Congress" and "6th Street," and I stepped out and looked up the street, to where it dead-ended at the tall dome of the state capitol, then down the street to a bridge and a long, upward-sloping hill.

The desk clerk *had* mentioned, "Congress Avenue" and "take a left" in roughly the same sentence, so I veered to the south, across the bridge and up the hill. It was hot, and I was still used to the dry air of Colorado. It was the kind of heat that makes your breath heavy, and makes your shoulders droop under the weight of it. When you walk your body swells and flexes over the reflective heat of the pavement. It was late afternoon, but still hot enough that the sidewalks were mostly deserted. The few people who were outside mostly clung to the shaded patios of the restaurants and coffee houses.

I maintained my laborious climb up the long hill, stopping for a moment in front of the Austin Motel to take a break and get my bearings. I turned and looked back the way I had come, and then up the hill. There was no sign for Palo's Icehouse, and I thought that I had gone the wrong way. Seconds from turning back to the hotel I looked across the street and between two short buildings was a red neon sign that read "Palo's Icehouse" in twinkling letters. The traffic stopped at a light and I crossed the wide street and entered Palo's. Inside, at the bar, sat my musician friend from the road.

═══════════

Mark McDaniel sat at one end of a long bar, twirling a small drink straw in one hand and skimming a newspaper, which he held in the other. His short glass held about three fingers of whiskey in it, resting smooth and undisturbed in the afternoon heat.

The world outside the musty building was bright and hot and the cars moved slowly on the street outside, as if they were carrying the heat like a burden that restricted their movement.

Inside, the air was dim, with a smell of beer-soaked wood and stale smoke. Only the hypnotic spinning of four ceiling fans, all moving at slightly different speeds, cooled the room.

Mark was the only person at the bar when I walked in, but he didn't notice my arrival. The bartender stood leaning against the dark counter with his back to the door, watching a baseball game on a TV that was perched high on the wall above the icemaker at the end of the bar. I walked the length of the counter and slid into a stool next to Mark as he continued to read.

"Did you know," he said, without even looking at me, "that the average adult man thinks about sex once every seven seconds?"

"No, I didn't," I replied, "but now I do and I have to say that I feel a little dirty about it."

"Oh, well," he said, raising his glass. "We all have our demons, but they are easily washed away, my friend."

"I guess so. Some leave more of a stain than others."

He turned and looked at me. "That could be a good start to a song, you know."

From what Lance had told me, Mark was a moderately success-ful musician, whose strange and curiously complex—though innately simple—mind had produced a couple of number one hits in the south and central United States. These records had won him minor celebrity and credit as one of the pioneering members of the Texas Americana movement that was only then beginning to gain national attention.

The baseball game cut to a commercial and suddenly, the bartender, a Latino man in his late 40s, was interested in conducting business. He turned quickly and with a great deal of implied impatience.

"What ken I geet you, sir?" he asked.

"I will have the coldest light beer you have," I replied.

"No light beer sir, just Lone Star and Shiner."

"I'll have a Shiner then, so long as it's cold, I guess."

"No problem sir, eets the coldest beer in thee bar."

I thanked him and asked to start a tab.

"Hey, Palo," Mark interrupted, looking up from his paper, "just put it on my tab."

"Okay, Mr. McDaniel, I geeve him discount, too."

"Thank ya, sir," I said.

Mark folded his paper and set it on the counter, then took a long drink of the whiskey that sat in front of him. It would have been a full drink for any normal person, but for Mark, it was a shot.

"Palo," he said, "can I get one of those cold beers, too?"

"Sure theeng, Mr. McDaniel," Palo said, keeping one eye on the game, "I geeve you the coldest one."

"Thanks, Palo. So," he said, turning to me, "how's the world look-ing to you today?"

Palo sat the beers down in front of us, and without even both-ering to record the transaction in his little notebook, he went back to watching the game, as if its outcome were more important than the financial success of his bar.

"It's hot, man. I'm just kind of here today," I said.

"Yeah, I know what you mean. I haven't had a worthwhile thought all day."

"It seems like a good day to relax in the comfort of a cool tavern," I said prophetically.

"So you made it into town ok?"

"Yeah, long drive," I said, "but then again, it's those long drives that do the most good."

"I hear you. I always write my best songs on the road. So, what's your story? You given any thought to the job?"

"Can you ask me tomorrow? I have quite a lot to think about and I just want to relax for a while."

I wasn't sure why I wanted to hold off on telling Mark the truth. I knew that taking the job would be a step in the wrong direction, and I had already decided in my mind that I wasn't going to stay in Austin very long. It felt like a better situation if I kept him in anticipation, though. That way the day would carry on without any negativity.

"Yeah, sure," he said. "What's the problem?"

"Nothing," I said, "nothing at all."

I didn't tell him about my Naomi troubles. There wasn't anything he could do to change it; besides, if he didn't know, it would be that much easier for me to forget. We sat and talked as the sun dipped low in the western sky and began to fade into twilight. Palo's game ended, and he sat on a stool behind the bar and the three of us talked about the life of a wanderer.

It was a subject that we all related to, and we talked for a long time about the uncertainty that rested in us. We were mostly strangers to each other, so we didn't speak too deeply from the heart. When you take to the road, you learn to protect your thoughts until there is a certain level of trust, so we did not discuss the personal reasons behind our wanderings. Rather, we distantly assured each other that between the two general ways of living, we had chosen the most fulfilling.

Mark was a wanderer by profession, Palo had wandered most of his life and I was in the midst of my own journey. We were spiritual vagrants, and as Mark and I drank several of Palo's coldest beers we spoke highly of the life. Yet, we never spoke of its two most important drawbacks: when you wander, you learn to deal with the absence of hope, and the difficulty in securing love.

The sun had mostly gone by the time our conversation began to slow, and the sluggish atmosphere of a city soaked in summer heat began to beat faster as day life turned to nightlife. The pulse of the traffic quickened and the number of people who passed by the open door began to grow. The bar, which had for so long held the silence of the afternoon, now began to reverberate with the sounds of talk and laughter as small groups of people trickled in. Back and forth across the sidewalk came the dinner crowd, the calm before the spiraling lewdness that was a Friday night in Austin.

"Palo, *deseo mi cuenta*," said Mark.

"No, Mr. Mark, you pay tomorrow," answered Palo, who walked by busily and retreated behind a curtain, into the back room.

"Fucking bartenders," Mark mumbled, shaking his head and fishing a wadded-up $20 bill out of his pocket. He laid it on the bar and we walked out into the street.

Mark stood on the edge of the curb, resting one hand on the roof of a parked car, and looked down the street into the oncoming traffic, which the green light of the intersection had just released.

"What's the plan, Mark?" I asked.

"Well, if what I think is going to happen tonight happens, then we need to eat. We'll take a cab to a little place I know. Serves a great mix of Italian and American food, and some spectacular wine. Good wine to start always makes a great Friday night."

He caught the attention of a cab, which did not pull over but put on its hazard lights and stopped in the middle of the right lane. The driver paid no attention to the line of cars forming behind him, and neither did Mark. We climbed slowly into the backseat, and the driver took a few seconds to finish writing something into a small notebook, then calmly, slowly asked where we wanted to go.

"La Mirabelle on Riverside."

"You got it," said the driver.

25

The taxi bumped down the rough cobblestone road, away from downtown and into the warehouse district. I pressed my forehead against the glass, watching the city and its people go by. Mark was talking to someone on his cell phone, but my attentions wandered away from the plans he was making. I snapped back when I heard the pop of his phone closing.

"Here's the deal," he said. "I invited a couple of girls to join us. I want to tell you, though, that these girls are hot, but not that smart. I just don't want you to have any surprises."

"So, what's the point of inviting them to dinner? I thought that weekend meals at good restaurants were all about good wine and good conversation."

"Oh, I completely agree with you," he said, "but it never hurts to bring a little eye-candy along. Look, it's good to have deep conversations over dinner, and these girls will let us do that, I'm sure. They'll be quiet because they won't understand what we're talking about, and they'll let us talk without interrupting. But it's good to have some loud, fun-loving girls to flirt with whenever there's a lull in the conversation."

"That's a good point," I replied.

"Trust me," Mark said, turning away. "These girls will be good for a laugh and a great evening. They're fun and *very* friendly when they drink."

The cab slowed and then stopped on the corner of a dim street, lit only by a short lamp that stood next to a small city bus stop. La Mirabelle sat on one corner of the intersection, and its quiet appearance was undisturbed by the absence of traffic. It was a one-story, white building with a small patio out front. A dark glow ballooned out of the tall windows, and a few small groups of people sat around the tables outside, drinking wine, smoking cigars and talking loudly.

The inside of the restaurant was small and casually lit. There were about 15 tables in the center, and a few booths along the far wall, near the kitchen door. A long row of wine racks covered one side of the room. Most of the bottles were grouped by vintage and covered in a fine, light dust. Two chandeliers hung from the ceiling and illuminated the tops of the white tablecloths. The host showed us to a booth in a secluded corner near the back wall.

A short, skinny waiter came to the table and we ordered two double whiskeys and a bottle of the Magnificat cabernet. The waiter brought the drinks and we relaxed in the comfort of our hidden table. The low waves of dinner conversation drifted over the high back of the booth, and the candlelight danced off the green leather of the seat and the rich, black wood of the paneled wall.

"So tell me, my friend," Mark said, glancing around at the sparse crowd, "how was your trip to Austin?"

"It was interesting," I replied. "After I left State Bridge, I stopped to visit Lance in Buena Vista. He says he's going to come back this way soon."

"He's been saying that for years. It's kind of an ongoing joke with everyone here who knows him. You can always tell when summer's almost over because Lance starts calling and telling everyone he's coming back to town. You can set your calendar by it. Then, something will always come up and he'll never make it."

"Well," I said nervously, "he better make it this time. He has my motorcycle."

"You gave him your motorcycle?" Mark asked, sounding incredulous.

"Well, actually we traded. He let me take his Land Rover and he promised me that he'd fix my bike up and bring it to Austin before the end of the summer."

"I'll let you figure out on your own," Mark said in a jokingly parental tone, "whether you think that was a good idea."

"He made a very compelling argument," I said, "plus he looked like he really wanted it. He was like a kid in a toy store trying to convince his dad to buy him something. I couldn't say no."

"Well," he said, "that will be your loss."

Mark and I continued to talk and drink. Soon we had finished the whiskey and a good portion of the wine, and then the girls descended upon us. They came to the edge of the table, and Mark and I stood up.

One of them was tall and blonde, and had a quiet, innocent look about her. She had a thin body and well-defined yet very proportional curves that showed through her long, white cotton skirt and tank top. The other was shorter, with dark, curly hair and dark skin. She had an expressive upper body and smooth, round shoulders. She was strong and athletic-looking, and exotic. Mark introduced them as Lacy and Nicki, and they politely but distantly acknowledged me.

To the girls I was an outsider, and had not yet earned the full compliment of their attentions. They slid into the booth opposite one another, and Mark and I on either side. I was next to Nicki, the darker one, and Lacy, the blonde, sat with Mark. She was leaning close into him and looking into his eyes. The waiter returned and looked at the girls, who were quite obviously under twenty-one.

"Some more wine!" Mark said loudly, turning in his seat. The waiter nodded and disappeared through a swinging door. He returned a couple of minutes later with a fresh bottle and two clean glasses.

After a few refills and some lively and lewdly entertaining conversation between Mark and the girls, the waiter returned and waited patiently for us to order our food. None of us had looked at the menus, and we were about to open them when Mark collected them and handed them to the waiter.

"I'll get this," he said, holding up his index finger.

"You're going to order for us? That's very sexist of you!" said Lacy.

Mark giggled, told her to shut up and turned to the waiter.

"What we need here" he said with ferocity, "is a dinner that we can pick at while we talk and drink wine. We need some cheeses. A couple of assorted cheese plates with some fruit should do it. Make it grapes, sliced apples, cherries and whatever else you can come up with. Get a bunch of different cheeses, but make sure Brie is one of them. We also need meats…yes…protein! We want some thinly shaved prosciutto, a big pile of it. Also, some sliced baguettes and balsamic vinegar. At the end, we want strawberries and cream with champagne."

The waiter scribbled furiously on his little pad, a confused look on his face, as if someone had just hit him on the head. The girls were giggling and Mark seemed immediately excited, as if his ego were feeding on the mere presence of the their bubbly laughter.

As much as he'd promised against it, the dynamic of the evening had changed dramatically. No longer did we engage in any kind of productive or enlightening conversation. The mood had evolved from one of calm, artistic consumption to one of carnal indulgence. It was difficult for me to relate, so I sat back and thoughtfully pretended to listen to the primal conversations that Mark was having with our two guests.

The food came and the four of us picked off the extensive plates as we drank. They sat on the tablecloth, spread out across the table amidst the wine bottles and glasses. We sampled the various dishes without silverware, and drank several bottles of wine. The three of them talked and laughed loudly, with complete disregard of the other patrons in the restaurant.

I was the outsider, though, and my companions were involved in discussing a lifestyle of decadence and debauchery, with which I was completely unfamiliar. I interjected into the conversation periodically, but I was never able to directly compete. Instead, I mostly listened, thinking of what a great story this sequence of events would one day be. This was a wild bunch, much more so than I had ever been. It was an odd group, different from the one in State Bridge, and its bonds had a fragility that the other did not.

Yet there was a feeling of obligation in their tone and subject matter, and it tempered the fervor of their behavior in my mind. It occurred to me that their spry spirit, while very compelling, was scripted, as if they were more in tune to how their lifestyle *should* appear than how it actually did. I wasn't yet sure if the way they really lived matched their colorful descriptions.

The four of us ate and drank to our content, and then flung ourselves onto the hot night with decadent revelry. We left La Mirabelle in a taxi and rumbled along the curved streets, toward the bright lights of downtown. Lacy sat on Mark's lap, and Nicki sat in the middle, turned slightly away from me. As we threaded through the broken lines of cars and groups of people crossing the streets, our conversation echoed and amplified the beat of the night.

I remained relatively quiet: sober enough to embrace the mood, but not yet drunk enough to make a spectacle of myself. That would come later.

"Where are we going, Mark?" I asked.

He broke away from his conversation with the girls.

"A little place called Shakespeare's first," he said.

"Really," I said, surprised. "That's crazy! I picked up this kid in New Mexico and this morning he went off to find some friends of his. He left me a note at the hotel telling me he would be at Shakespeare's tonight!"

"Well, you know what that means," said Mark. "That means we're gonna have a good night!"

"That's exactly what I was thinking!" I said.

"What hotel are you staying at?" asked Lacy.

"The Plaza on 5th Street," I replied.

"That's a cool hotel," she said. "We should have an after-bar there."

"I lost my virginity there," said Nicki, snapping her gum and cocking her head to the side.

"That's great," I said, turning to the window to hide my laughter.

When I'd met Nicki and Lacy, they had exuded a subtle air of sophistication. There was never any doubt as to their intelligence, yet they seemed to have a certain amount of social grace. As the night drew on, however, and their true personalities became ever more obvious, it was clear what they were really like-not the kind of girls you took home to Mom.

The cab stopped behind a long line of cars, at the front of which a police car was blocking the street.

"They're closing the street, guys," said the driver. "You want me to take you around?"

"No," said Mark. "We'll walk from here."

As we stepped out of the taxi, the traffic began to move around us. Mark and the girls stumbled through the lines of impatient cars, and I followed behind them. The four of us stood on the sidewalk as the taxi turned under the yellow glow of a streetlight and disappeared in a long river of red lights. Mark pulled out a cigarette, and the girls leaned against the light pole and whispered to each other.

I could imagine that they were quietly talking about Mark's mysterious friend, and how he was good-looking in his rugged appearance and sexy in his complicated inwardness. Then one of them turned and let loose a snort and a long, piercing laugh. I found this display and their general behavior to be in conflict with their earlier poise and attitude. It was difficult to sort through my attraction to their beauty and my disgust at their personalities. I used to be happy to spend time with women like this, but something had happened when I met Naomi. A voice in my mind was telling me not to fall prey to frivolous sexual desire.

'Wait for something worthwhile,' it said. 'Don't sell your soul to the sexual devil!'

Mark turned to me. "What's up with you?" he asked.

"Nothing, man," I replied. "You know—new town, new people. I'm just takin' it all in."

We turned and walked a few steps down the street while the girls talked.

"You don't like those girls, do you?" he asked.

"That's not it," I said. "It's just that I don't know them and they seem a little snotty. I don't have patience for that."

He turned to look at the girls, who were laughing again.

"I know what you need," he said, putting his firm hand on my shoulder. "Let's go to the bar."

He began to walk and the girls caught up and interlocked their arms with his. I walked slightly to the right of the group and when Nicki reached out her arm, I took it. We walked, the four of us coupled together, through the bulky crowds of the 6th Street bar district.

26

On weekend nights the streets were closed to cars, and people wandered freely around the cobblestones and sidewalks, searching for the best places to drink or otherwise enjoy the complexities of the social hierarchy. The sharp effect of the summer weather brought large crowds mingling around, capturing and creating the grand illusions of a night in the city.

The muffled roar of the throngs of people and shrill sounds of the street vendors and bar callers echoed over the buildings and the hills beyond. The carnival atmosphere reached into the night to the west, all the way to the great valleys of the Gore Range, where the little lodge and the quiet riffling river held Naomi, D and the rest of my old friends in their divine serenity. I walked with my group, but I wished I were there.

Shakespeare's Pub sat in the heart of the bar district. It was a squat, one-story building that looked like an alley someone had built a roof across, with a front door at the end. We passed the bouncer, who nodded at Mark, and went through the front room toward a small courtyard in the back.

I pushed through the tightly-packed crowd, holding Nicki's hand behind me and leading the group. Within the narrow room was an ocean of young college kids, bunched in small circles, drinking, or compactly dancing in front of a small DJ booth. The air was a mixture of sweat and smoke and perfume, chewing gum and liquor. It was the smell of social tension and the inebriated, youthful pursuit of sexual compatibility.

In the open courtyard, around the back bar, casual laughter and conversation shadowed the synthetic, thumping beat. A tattooed man sat playing the guitar on a small stage. The music was slightly off-key, but the tables around him were full and everyone was enjoying the night in relaxed comfort. It was a scene vastly different from the one on the street, and its atmosphere suited my sensibilities.

We walked to the bar, and Mark ordered vodka drinks for the girls, and beer and shots of whiskey for us. We toasted to the women we loved best, tapped our glasses against the bar and drank.

The whiskey was warm and strong. It breathed life into me, and the prospect of a wild night began to rise in my inner recesses.

"We should go to a club tonight!" said Lacy.

"Yeah," said Nicki, "I want to dance!"

The girls began to grind against each other to the distant beat of the dance music from the front bar.

"Have patience, my darlings," said Mark. "We just ordered drinks. We'll go in a little bit."

"Promise?" said Lacy.

I turned out of the conversation to see Randy leaning against the bar with a small group of people. I approached him and laid my hand on his shoulder.

"Mr. Randy," I said as he looked up. "Did you get things turned around for yourself?"

"Hey, bro," he said as he stood and gave me a firm hug. "I did. Hey, these are my friends."

He introduced me to the group—a tall, well-dressed guy who reminded me very much of Naomi's friends in Buena Vista, and two others. I started to shake hands but the tall guy, whose name was Jason, grabbed me and pulled me into a tight embrace.

"We don't shake hands around here, friend," he said with a laugh.

Randy then introduced me to the two girls behind the bar. Their names were Elizabeth, or Lizzie, as she was called, and Catherine. They were twin sisters and the managers of the bar.

Over my shoulder, I could see Mark and the girls. They were standing near a table, and had been joined by a group of guys who were fans of Mark's music. Mark yelled at me to come over to them.

"I'll be right back, Randy," I said.

"Hey," said Mark, when I got back to him. "These guys bought us shots."

I bounced back and forth between Mark and Randy for a while, taking shots and drinking beer with both. Gradually I began to define my role in both groups as the new guy in town with strange stories from the road. Eventually, the two clumps of people merged, and I was finally able to introduce Mark and Randy. Evidently they had experienced similar adventures in California, and bonded through the memories of their respective tragedies.

Nicki and Lacy pulled Mark away from the bar and I talked to Randy, Lizzie and Catherine. The twins asked me questions about where I had come from and what my story was, and I thought I detected an air of suspicion in their tone. It was as if they didn't know what to make of me, and were trying to find out my underlying purpose.

The two women were both small and beautiful, with an elegance that was different from anyone else in the bar. They exuded a compelling and confident air that was pleasing, and a solid sophistication that I hadn't experienced with anyone I'd met on the road. It was satisfying to know that there were still women like that in the world, and I talked to them with a distant admiration.

"Hey," said Mark, "we're going to run down to this club for a minute. Do you want to come?"

"No, man," I said, "I'm going to hang out here."

"Cool," he said. "We'll be back in a while." He turned toward the bar. "Hey, Lizzie," he yelled, "I'm going to Soho. Leave my tab open, I'm coming back in a minute."

"All right," she said. "Are you actually coming back this time?"

"Yeah," he said, "you have my credit card."

"Okay, but if you don't, I'm going shopping tomorrow on you."

———

I stayed at Shakespeare's with Randy and his friends, and soon we were all very drunk. We stood in a group around the bar all night, breaking away only to order drinks. I tried to talk to the twins and tell them all my ideas about life and the road, but I was too far gone and it all came out badly.

Mark and the girls came back from the club toward the end of the night. Lacy and Mark stood by the bar flirting, and Nicki grabbed my hand.

"You should have come with us," she said.

"Oh," I replied, "I'm not much of a dancer."

She was looking at me strangely, and she grabbed my hand and leaned up to my ear. "I want to play tonight," she said.

"Oh yeah?" I asked.

This was a crossroads for me. I didn't like her, but evidently, she liked me-either that, or it was getting close to the end of the night and she wanted something to show for it. Lacy pulled Nicki away before I had time to more fully respond, and they went to the restrooms.

"Well," Mark said, "it looks like you're doin' all right now."

"Yeah," I said. "I don't think I want to hook up with her. She's an idiot."

"So?" he said. "Who cares? You're not going to marry the girl."

"That's true. By the way, man, I've been thinking about it and I can't take the job. I have to get out of here soon, you know? I'm thinking about looking Bryan up in New York. I just can't stick around here very long. I gotta bird-dog on down the road."

"Really? Well, that's okay. If you change your mind, though, we'd love to have you. No worries, though."

"Thanks for being cool about it," I said.

When the bar closed, we went out to the street to make plans for the rest of the night. Ultimately, Lacy's prediction came true and we went back to my hotel for the after-bar party. Randy and Justin came along with the four of us and we struggled through the crowd toward the less-populated end of the street, near the hotel.

Everyone on the street was intoxicated, and there were fights breaking out all around us. We treaded our way toward the hotel through the masses of whiskey-drunk college kids, avoiding the brawls and trying to stay together. Cops rushed around, picking apart brawling groups of drunks, and the whole thing was on the verge of collapsing in on itself.

We walked quickly and closely together, throwing out whatever conversation that would connect us and keep us apart from the strange atmosphere that surrounded us. When the group entered the hotel the lobby clerk looked at me with suspicion, as if he were already certain that our party was going to be a problem. Mark approached the desk, whispered something to the clerk, and slid a thin roll of money across the counter. The clerk's countenance changed dramatically at the sight of the payoff, and Mark winked at me as he rejoined the group.

"You should shit-can this hotel tomorrow," he said as he walked down the hall to my room, "and stay with me. I have a spare bedroom and you're welcome to crash there for a while."

"Thanks, Mark," I said, "that would be great. I've been in one hotel or another for so long, I can't remember what it's like not to have to check out of a room when I wake up."

"I feel like that on the road sometimes," he said. "How long are you going to stay in town?"

"I don't know," I said. "A week or so. I need to call Naomi and straighten some things out with her. Oh, I was thinking, you should call Lance and see if he wants to come work for you. I think he would be pretty good at it. He just needs a little encouragement to get him here."

This plan would have the added benefit of ensuring the return of my motorcycle.

"Hmm," Mark said. "I'll give it a try."

I opened the door, and we all filed in. I called the front desk to ask about getting some liquor, and the attendant told me that the hotel's policy was to charge by the shot, even for a whole bottle.

"Also," he added, "because of the liquor law, we can only take cash."

It was likely that he was scamming me and pocketing the difference, but I was drunk enough not to care. I ordered a bottle of whiskey, a bottle of vodka, some beer and some other drinks for mixers. I collected the cash from my bags and paid nearly three hundred dollars for all of it. There was a sharp stab of guilt at such a waste of my dwindling cash, but I wanted to make an impression. I graciously paid and tipped the man, but no one in the room noticed. The twins joined us, along with a few other people from the bar and the party swelled inside the narrow walls of my room.

All was in chaos, and the shrill run of the booze through my veins had reached its zenith. I felt like I was twirling through the crowd, listening to the crash of music from the TV, and the laughter of the group that stood around drinking *my* liquor. I wasn't into any of it, and I could neither listen nor participate.

"Are you okay, honey?" asked Nicki.

"Yeah," I replied. "I'm fine. Are you?"

"Yeah," she said, "I'm fine. I wish all of these people would leave."

"Why? Is there something you'd like to try to discuss with me?"

I was trying to make fun of myself for being so drunk, but it came out wrong and she took offense. She turned and rejoined the group, and I went to the window and looked out over the dying night. In the reflection of the glass, I could see Randy break away from the group and approach me.

"Dude, who the hell are those girls?" he asked.

"I don't know," I replied. "I didn't fucking bring 'em."

I was contemptuous of the fact that these two girls felt like they could release all social constraints and rely solely on their beauty to achieve their own version of prosperity. Unfortunately, Nicki and Lacy heard what I had said to Randy and Nicki immediately turned and stormed out the door. Lacy looked at me and said something to Mark that I couldn't make out, then followed her friend into the hall. The room became quiet, and everyone looked at me.

"What the fuck did you say to them, man?" Mark said.

The whole night was coming to a crashing end.

"Dude," I replied, "we had a little misunderstanding and then…"

"No kidding," said Mark. "Nicki was going to stay here with you and I was going to take Lacy home with me."

I held on the back of a chair for support, as my legs were beginning to grow weak.

"Shit, man," I replied, shaking my head. "I'm sorry."

Mark stopped as an idea crept slowly across his face.

"Unless," he began slowly, "I can get them both to come home with me. Yeah…thanks man, I'll call you tomorrow. You come to my house tomorrow and you can stay there. I'll call Lance, too."

He finished his drink and ran out the door after the girls. Mark's night was still open to possibility. Mine was over. Randy took the remainder of the group to his room, and I went to bed. My last thought was that maybe Naomi wasn't in State Bridge anymore. Maybe she was back in Denver with her husband, and I was stuck in love with her. Maybe I had no business being in love. Sometimes it feels natural, when you find yourself at your worst, to think about something that will take you all the way to the bottom.

27

The next day when I woke up, I drank a large glass of water and took two Vicodin, which Randy had given me at the bar. I made one phone call to Naomi, and one to Bryan Hillary. Neither of them answered, but I left messages for each to call me at the hotel.

I took the liberty of assuming that Mark's receptionist could take a few messages for me, then called the front desk and told the attendant that I would be checking out, and asked him to direct all calls for me to Mark's office. After I left him the number, I lay back on the bed and closed my eyes, hiding from the intense sunlight that filtered through the crack in the curtain.

As I drifted back to sleep, I was haunted by the memory of Naomi and broken reflections of the previous night. My hangover made the embarrassment of it even more painful, and in the end all I could do was laugh and pray that it didn't happen again. If I had any more nights like that, I probably wouldn't be welcome in Austin much longer.

Mark called in the late morning, and I knew that my opportunity to sleep was gone and I would simply have to work through the rest of the day as best I could.

"Hey, man," he said cheerfully, "wakey wakey!"

"Oh, Christ," I said. "What the hell are you so happy about?"

"Well, you can only guess," he said. "All I can say is that your loss was most definitely my gain."

"How do you live with yourself?" I asked, falling back into the bed.

"Well, pack your shit and meet me at La Colina and I'll tell you all about it."

"Where? Don't forget that I don't know this town at all."

He gave me directions and hung up. I was almost angry at his cheeriness. Meanwhile, all I had to look forward to was sitting in hung over agony, hearing about his triumphs of the night. So goes it, though—the only thing that builds more character than feeling bad is knowing that you are about to feel much worse.

I gathered my loose collection of belongings and walked through the deserted marble lobby to the desk. Randy was already gone, off to stay with the twins, so I checked out of both rooms. The attendant thanked me and I went to the parking garage for the Land Rover.

Outside of the parking lot ramp, I nearly decided to turn left toward the interstate. At the last moment I thought better of it and decided not to admit defeat. After a long sigh and a determined resolution to cleanse mind, body and soul after I left Austin, I turned right toward the river and my lunch with Mark.

It is always difficult trying to negotiate traffic in a new city, but doubly so after a night of heavy drinking. Yet, in the midst of my worried confusion, I found the restaurant and began an afternoon of margaritas and queso with Mark, and the faint desire to rediscover my own obscurity.

═════

The first half of the week was relatively quiet. In theory Mark's house was a good place to relax. He lived in a secluded cabin in a remote section of the Texas Hill Country south of Austin, and it was pleasant to be away from the city. In reality, though, there was a constant stream of visitors coming and going, mostly at night. Musicians would come to write songs in the evening, and during the day, Mark and his friends would spend time shooting guns or whatever other activity they could invent.

Nicki was also a frequent fixture in the evenings, which I was less than pleased about. She herself was not hugely distasteful, outside of her normal unpleasant personality. The fact was in my mind, she had become the embodiment of the fractiousness of the human spirit, and I looked upon her with contempt and disgust. Still, I tried to make the best of it.

During my time at Mark's, I tended to spend the day exploring the Hill Country on Mark's Harley, and at night I would quietly observe the process of writing songs. Mark and his friends, along with Nicki and I, would fill his living room and experience the music in an almost spiritual environment.

On Tuesday morning, Mark's receptionist called with a list of messages for me from Bryan, Naomi and Lance, who said that he was definitely coming to Austin and would be there by Friday. I passed the message on to Mark, and he was pleased to hear it. Bryan called to say that he wasn't going to make it to Austin at all, and to call him.

I hoped that Naomi's message might make some reference to her coming to Austin, though I had never gotten a chance to invite her, or something else that would give me an idea about her intentions. The only thing she said, though, was that she wanted me to call her.

When the house was finally empty, late in the afternoon, I picked up the phone and called Naomi at the lodge. The phone rang several times before it was picked up.

"State Bridge Lodge," said an unfamiliar female voice, "now home of the famous Wild Turkey Wednesday, Christi speaking, may I help you?"

"Is Naomi there?" I asked.

"Yeah, just a sec."

There was a long pause, and then the sweetest voice in the world.

"This is Naomi."

"Hi."

"Oh my God! Hi! How are you? Hold on one sec."

The phone clicked, paused, then picked up again.

"I'm sorry," she said, "I went to get the cordless. How are you, love?"

"Oh," I said, "I'm all right."

"Good," she replied. "Where are you?"

"I'm in Austin with Mark right now. Lance is coming down here this week. Bryan was supposed to come, but something came up. I haven't talked to him yet, but he's not going to make it."

"Well, that's good that you'll get to see Lance at least. I was able to spend some time with him after you left. He's so funny."

"Yeah," I said. "He's one of a kind, for sure."

"I'm sure you guys won't have *any* fun," she joked. "We've been so busy here. This is our busiest time of the year."

The small talk was beginning to frustrate me, but I didn't want to change the subject too abruptly. As it turned out, I didn't need to because she did it for me.

"So," she said gently, "you got my note?"

"Yes, I did. I'm sorry I haven't called sooner, but I just needed a little time."

"I know. I am so sorry about all that. Everything is just so messed up right now. I hate that we had to leave each other like that."

"Look, Naomi," I said. "I don't want to make anything more complicated for you than it already is. I just need to know how to feel about all this. I need to know how you feel about it."

"Ever since you left, I haven't been able to stop thinking about you, and about us, and about everything else in my life. I met you, and I almost can't even talk to him. He's just so far away from anything I want or need. I need to end it, but I don't know how."

"Don't end it because of me, Naomi. You have to do it for yourself. I mean, who knows what will happen with us. I'm out here wandering, and you're there with your daughter. I want to be with you, but I also want you to do what's right for you. I'll still love you no matter what you do."

"I know," she said. "I have a lot to figure out. Just be patient with me, please."

"You know I will," I said. "I'm not going anywhere, darlin'. I'll always be there for you."

"When will I get to see you?" she asked.

I wanted to see Naomi, but I didn't want to go back to Colorado. My last memories of it were unpleasant, and I wanted to see her in a place far away from our troubles, unfamiliar to both of us. In earlier conversations Mark had mentioned that he would be going to a songwriters' weekend in Key West later in the summer, and the notion of visiting a tropical climate had stuck with me.

"Would you be able to take a little trip?" I asked.

"Maybe," she answered. "What did you have in mind?"

"Well," I said, "I've been thinking about taking a trip down south, maybe to the Keys. Would you maybe want to meet me down there in a few days?"

"Sweetie, I'd love to, but I can't afford it. I can't take the time off to drive, and I could never afford the plane ticket."

"What if I got you a ticket?"

"I don't know," she said with hesitation in her voice. "I don't know if I can get off."

I was resolved, however, to see her again.

"Look," I said, "here's what I'll do. I will get you a ticket for next Wednesday. If you can make it, great. If not, then I'll understand. I don't want to make a big deal of it or make you feel pressured. I just want to see you again."

"You don't have to do that," she said. "It would be wonderful to see you, especially in a place like that, but—"

"It's not a problem," I said. "I'll book the ticket and you can decide if you want to come. No pressure at all."

"Thank you," she said. "I will make it happen. That would be a beautiful experience."

We talked for a long time, and the unpleasant aftertaste of our last meeting had been flushed away. We laughed and talked just like we had in State Bridge. When I hung up the phone, I felt as though we were back on track, and I was ready to leave Austin that very minute and get back on the road. Lance was coming, though, and I would have to stick around for one more weekend with him and Mark. I didn't know when I would see either of them again, and we had been planning this last weekend together since State Bridge. I only wished that Bryan were able to meet us in Austin.

Throughout the week, I kept trying to connect with him, but it never happened. In the end, he left a message on my voicemail, telling me that his legal problem in New York had been taken care of and he needed to get back as soon as possible. His voice sounded frail and distant, as if he were regretting going back. I felt for him, and wished he had another option. He had a strong desire to return to his family, though, and as much as I disagreed with it, I respected it. I would be there to catch him if he fell.

The middle of the week passed as the beginning had, and I weathered all of it. I had begun to feel deeply guilty about the lifestyle in which I had become involved. Due to the backlash from meeting Naomi's husband, I had violated almost all of the cardinal rules I had set for myself after leaving Kansas City.

When I'd left, my intention had been to spend my time actively seeking the pieces of my life that I had gone without. Now, the whole thing was one long experience of surviving day-to-day and town-to-town, in unrevealing environments with strange girls, bad situations and endless nights. This was supposed to be a journey of self-discovery, but in the end, I was left with more questions and very few answers.

28

On Friday, Mark and I were to meet Lance and Randy around 4:00, on the patio of La Colina. On the way to the bar, we talked about the night and the rest of the weekend to follow.

"When are you going to blow town?" asked Mark.

He was as ready for me to leave as I was to get back on the road. To some extent, I think my sour mood had dampened the experience, but it was true too that he was not-used to having long-term house guests and would be grateful to have the place to himself again.

"Probably Monday," I said. "Then I'm going to drive down to Key West and meet Naomi for a couple of days."

I didn't tell him that there was a chance that she wouldn't come, but I didn't want to complicate the conversation. Nor did I want to jinx the possibility that she would come.

"Good for you, man," he said. "You two should have a pretty good time down there. I'm actually going down in a couple of months for a songwriters' deal."

"Yeah," I said, "I know. We talked about it a couple of days ago. That's where I got the idea."

We sat on the patio of the bar as the happy hour crowd began to collect. The day was warm and humid, but I was used to it by then. The wind carried the faint and distant smell of salt air from the Gulf of Mexico. I wanted to be on the road again. I wanted to be in Key West, wrapped up in Naomi, smelling the same salty air.

A bubbly blonde waitress approached us from out of the shadow of the thatched bar. "Like, what would *you* boys like?" she said in her thick, high-pitched, Texas drawl.

"Like," Mark said mockingly, "two margaritas."

She didn't get it. "Frozen or on the rocks?"

"I'll have mine on the rocks with no salt," I said.

"My man," she replied.

"Like, frozen, no salt," said Mark.

"K, I'll get those right out for y'all." She spun around and skipped off to the bar.

"She's hot," Mark said, "but almost too stupid, even for me."

"Hey, man," I said, "aren't you the one who always says, 'You're not sleeping with their intellect?'"

"Good point, my friend," he said. "Good point."

"You watch. She's probably working on a PhD or something. She's probably doing that on purpose because one, she doesn't want to deal with talking to people, or two, she gets better tips when she does it."

"It's a good theory," said Mark. "We'll get Lance to test it out. If he actually comes here, that is."

In typical Lance fashion, he showed up an hour and a half late. He swaggered up to the table with his usual air of over-confidence.

"What is up, my bitches?" he said.

He was wearing torn-up jeans, a black Harley shirt and a red bandana. It had been just over a week since I'd left the bike with him, and he already looked more like a biker than I ever had. That pissed me off.

"How's my bike?" I asked.

"Well," he said, "It's running great, but…"

Mark laughed loudly, and I stared at Lance with a mixture of anger, confusion, laughter and hatred.

"Tell me you're kidding," I said. "It's only been a week!"

Lance clicked his cheek and looked away.

"You asshole!" I said, jumping up and darting out the door to the parking lot.

My old Harley was sitting by the door, parked in a handicapped spot, and I knelt down to survey the damage. The right side of the gas tank, the mufflers, the forks and the engine covers were all scratched and dented. The right brake handle was broken in half and most of the front spokes were all scratched as well. I stood up and looked at Lance, who was standing in the doorway and well out of reach.

"Don't forget the other side," he said.

I leaned over and looked down the opposite side of the bike. The damage was less, but still very noticeable.

"What the hell happened?" I asked.

"Well, I was riding at night and this deer jumped out—"

"No," I said, cutting him off, "don't feed me that 'I swerved to miss a deer' bullshit. What really happened?"

He sighed. "Okay," he said, looking at the ground. "I was cruising down this road out in the middle of nowhere, and I was doing like thirty-five or so when I saw this—"

"How fast?"

"Fifty-five. Are you going to let me tell the story? Anyway, I turned to look at something on the side of the road and when I looked forward, I realized I was at a stop sign."

"If you were in the middle of nowhere, why didn't you just blow through the intersection?"

"Well," he said, "it was a T intersection. There wasn't a road on the other side, so I laid it down."

"Okay, I'll give you the benefit of the doubt on that one, but why are *both* sides messed up?"

"I picked back up, but after I got it straight, I lost my footing and it fell over on the other side."

"You're a goddamn idiot!" I said, scratching my head.

"Yeah," he said, "but you already knew that."

He had me—I couldn't argue with that. Mark had told me that giving Lance a motorcycle was a bad idea. I'd even known it myself deep inside, but I'd done it anyway.

"So what do you want to do about this?" I asked.

"I was just thinking that you could keep the Rover until I can get this thing fixed, and then we can swap back whenever we see each other again."

"Done," I said. "Now you go on in and get a drink, and I'm going to take a quick spin around the block."

"Excellent," said Lance, "and thanks for being such a good sport about all of this."

I took off out of the parking lot and down the street. The sun warmed my face, and it felt good to be back on the motorcycle-the wind lifting my hair and the loud popping of the engine. I rode for about 10 minutes down a long road running along the lake, then turned around.

When I got back to the bar, Lance and Mark were sitting around the table, along with Randy, who had arrived during my absence. As I approached them, they stopped talking and turned to look at me.

"What?" I asked.

"Have a seat," said Lance. "We have a plan."

"Oh, great," I said. "Am I going to like it?"

"So we've been thinking," said Mark. "You've been kind of moping around about this whole Naomi thing, and Randy here is about partied out in Austin for now and Lance, well, you know Lance, he's the adventurous type."

"Go on," I said.

"Well," said Randy, "we were thinking about taking a little trip to New Orleans."

I had known that whatever they had planned was going to be a bad idea, but when they said New Orleans, I knew that things were about to take a turn for the surreal. It would be against my new plan to agree to such a voyage, so I gave them the only response that a person in my state of mind could honorably give.

"All right, let's do it. When do we leave?" I asked.

"Tomorrow morning," said Mark. "We can catch the French Quarter on a Saturday night, maybe hit the casinos, who knows?"

"I told Naomi I would meet her in Florida on Wednesday," I said. "I won't be able to get to New Orleans and back and then make it to Key West in time."

"No worries," said Lance. "If you drive to New Orleans, then Mark and I can hop a plane back to Austin."

"What are we going to do about the bike?" I asked.

"I told you I'd get it fixed for you," he said. "Just leave it with me and we can trade up somewhere down the road."

I wanted the bike back, but it was pretty badly damaged and Lance looked as though he really wanted to make good on his promise to deliver it in good condition. I agreed to let him keep it, and I would drive us all to New Orleans the following day.

"What about you?" I asked Randy. "How are you going to get back?"

"I need to get up and see the folks," he said. "The twins offered me a job at Shakespeare's, so I'll just hitch back whenever I need to."

"Okay, guys," I said, against my better judgment. "I'm in!"

"Here's the thing, though," said Lance. "I volunteered to call Mandy and ask her if we could stay at her place. She lives pretty close to the Quarter and I guarantee you it's going to be impossible to find a hotel room this weekend."

"Mandy?" I asked. "My Mandy?"

"Well, our Mandy, actually," he said.

Mandy and I had history. The last time I'd seen her I had been in college. She and I had dated for over a year, but it was a college kind of love, steeped in the exploration of each other as lovers and companions. After graduation, she'd moved to Colorado and fallen in with Lance. She and Lance had lived close to each other and they came together romantically for the same reasons that she and I had. In the back of my mind, I wondered which one of us she was going to sleep with on this trip. Given her past record, it would probably be one of us.

We stayed at La Colina through dinner, and then took off to the downtown bar district once again for one last appointment with the city. The prospect of seeing Mandy again distracted me, which kept me from furtively taking part in the evening. I thought that I should be thinking about Naomi, as she was the only one who had ever truly captured my heart. Instead, I mostly thought about my old college love, and the simple innocence of the experience. The evening passed around me without really taking part.

Shakespeare's was our only destination for the remainder of the night, and we crowded around the bar, telling impressive stories to whomever was near enough to us to listen, and friendly enough to care. The twins quickly became tired of our antics as the night went on and made our drinks progressively more potent, hoping that the strong mixes would drive us away. In fact, they had the opposite effect, and though we had agreed to take it easy that night, the group found itself as impaired as it had been the entire week.

I was beginning to look forward to going to New Orleans. I watched the unfolding and falling of the evening with intense interest. We were joined by Nicki just before the bar closed, and after it finally did we left Lance's car downtown, and the five of us took a taxi all the way back to Mark's house in the country.

When we got there, Mark made us whiskey drinks and we sat around his table, playing a new card game called 31. Nicki sat on Mark's lap, and though I tried to hold on to the idea that she might still have some interest in me, it was clear that she wanted him. That fact made me dislike her, so I bowed out of the game and went to bed.

I was in love with Naomi, and I disliked Nicki. Still, the idea that she once had a romantic interest in me, and no longer did, was of some concern to me. I didn't like her, but it would have been better for my ego if she still showed an interest in me.

29

"Let's go, let's go," said Mark, bursting into my room in the early hours of Saturday morning.

It wasn't actually early at all, but my schedule had changed since leaving home. In the corporate world, I was at work before 8:00. On the road, I was lucky to get to bed by then. The schedule was very similar to the one I'd kept in college, which I'd found felt moderately embarrassing. Then, I realized that everyone I was with, except for Randy, was as old as or older than I was, and didn't feel bad about it at all.

"We need to get on down the road, ol' boy!" said Mark as be began to jump up and down on my bed.

Nicki walked into the room behind him, wearing a short t-shirt and thin cotton underwear. I hated the sight of her, but held back comment regarding her presence out of respect for my host.

"We made you some coffee," she said in her sweetest voice.

"Thank you," I said, taking the cup from her.

"Lance and Randy are on their way over here in my car, and then we'll be ready to go," said Mark.

"Oh, can you guys wait?" said Nicki. "I have to go home and pack!"

She ran out of the room and I frowned at Mark. He shrugged his shoulders.

"Better get going," he yelled on his way out the door. "I'd hate to leave your ass here!"

The time I'd spent in Austin had begun to fall apart almost immediately, but I'd stayed through the week to watch the destruction complete itself. When the five of us left that afternoon for New Orleans, it occurred to me that I was leaving Austin for the last time.

The city itself was beautiful and majestic, yet something was not quite to my expectation. It was a wonderful place, in the same way that the mountains had been when I'd seen them for the first time, despite the vast differences between them. Coming out of the mountains and through the desert, I had an expectation of the release that time in the city would allow—especially the distraction it would give in the wake of my experience in Buena Vista.

In the end, though, I left Austin with more questions than when I had arrived. It was anxiety that had ultimately defined my time there, and I was happy to be on the road again. These had been the lowest days of the journey, and I felt more lost than I ever had. I looked forward to a night or two in the Big Easy and a long, relaxing trip along the coast…perhaps even time alone with Naomi in Key West.

I desperately wanted her to meet me there. It would have been paradise within paradise to see her and be with her for a few lovely days on the soft beaches of the Florida Keys, but I wasn't going to raise my hopes too high. There was a very real possibility that she wouldn't be able to get away, and I didn't want to feverishly wait for something that would never come.

═══════

These were the last thoughts that occupied my mind as we cleared the tangled traffic of Austin and turned east toward Louisiana. The original plan had been for the four of us to go to New Orleans for our last few nights of exuberance before we all split up. Nicki had decided to come along to try to land Mark, which changed things somewhat. Even though we hated each other, we did our best to be civil.

Mark sat in the front with me and Randy; Nicki and Lance sat in the back. Lance was quiet as we left Austin, and Nicki was soon asleep. Randy sat watching the green lines of trees go by, and Mark chatted away on his cell phone to some friends he was planning to meet in New Orleans.

Mark, Lance and Nicki were to stay in New Orleans for as long as it took to create their worthwhile memories, and then they would fly back to Austin. Randy was going to hitch north to see his parents in Baton Rouge, and then return to Austin to take the job that the twins had offered him. I would continue east to Florida, then south to the Keys. I had grandparents in Sarasota, and planned on stopping for a night with them. Beyond that, I could only imagine where the road would take me.

I had romantic notions in my mind of driving north along the coast to New York to save my friend Bryan from his sad life in corporate America. Together, perhaps, we could cross the ocean in the old way, on a great ship and then traverse the roads of Europe, as we had planned. We could keep going, eluding that great shadow forever, continually going east into parts of the world unknown to us. I knew that, in a distant time, all of those things were possible, and the world was able to unfold easily in front of me because I had the distinct advantage of having no goals in life.

We flew along the concrete road, out of Hill Country into the tree-lined flatlands of east Texas; passing through Brenham and Chappell Hill, and stopping for gas near Hempstead. Nicki slid out of the car onto the pavement with a yawn, and she stretched, reaching her arms high in the air, showing the outline of her young body. Mark grabbed her around the waist and threw her over his shoulder, running and screaming, across the parking lot. She giggled with delight and Randy laughed.

I watched her and I couldn't understand why my friends didn't see her the way I did. They saw a pretty young thing with questionable morals and a fun-loving nature. I saw a scheming shrew who was trying to hook up with a semi-famous singer. Yet, I knew that time would reveal everything, as it does. People can never hide the less attractive parts of their personalities for long.

The numbers on the pump clicked as the tank filled, and I leaned against the car, inhaling the sugary smell of the gasoline. Lance ran into the store to pee and I stayed by the car, disgusted with Nicki, and her fruitless high hopes for Mark's lasting attention.

The cars passed on the highway in front of the corner station, and I closed my eyes. The wind had carried me from Kansas City to the west, and then down to the Gulf Coast, all these towns across America sewn together in my memory by the experiences they embodied. I daydreamed about the channels of time, old friends and the string of past events that kept dragging me along.

I imagined still being in the company of Bryan Hillary, and we were still on the road together. The world seemed more real when he was around, as if there were some purpose to it all way off in the distance. He brought some connection to the adventure, and that unity of events had since evaporated. When we were riding together, it felt as if we were running perfectly between that pursuing shadow and the elusive truth.

That old anticipation about the road was gone, and I was only passing the time from one party, one cheap night, to the next. I had only to look forward to the long drive to Key West, and the thought that I might get to see the woman I loved. Far in the distance I even dreamed of seeing Bryan again, and continuing the noble pursuits of the journey.

Mark had let Nicki go, and he now walked over to the pump and leaned against the car next to me. Nicki went inside the store and we were left alone to talk candidly for the first time in days.

"Don't go through Houston," he said. "I-10 will be a parking lot this early in the week."

"Which way do we go then?" I asked.

"I'll drive," he said, "and we'll miss the whole thing."

"Fine with me."

"Got something on your mind?" he asked.

"What's the deal with that girl, man?" I said, not being able to resist the temptation to ask.

He smiled. "Don't worry, man," he said. "I know you think she's an evil bitch, but she's only along for the ride, like the rest of us."

"I don't like her," I said. "There's something about her that just bugs the hell out of me."

"Well, you're probably right, but I'm not going to marry the girl, for Christ's sake. I just wanna have a little fun."

I went inside to pay for the gas and buy cigarettes. Randy caught me as I walked out of the store and gave me a handful of Vicodin.

"For tonight," he said.

"Thanks, man," I replied.

I took one and shoved the rest in my pocket, and then Randy gave some to everyone in the car. "Y'all save those till you really need 'em," he warned. "I only have a few left."

Everyone took their full allotment immediately and soon we were back on the road. I sat in the front and Mark drove. He shot out of the parking lot with the determined rage of a madman on a quest. He darted in and out of the slow, in-town traffic, laughing maniacally at the screeches of protest from everyone in the car, until we reached the highway.

We turned north to Navasota, Texas, and then east through Conroe and Cleveland. Mark pushed the pedal to the floor on the wide open, two-lane stretches over the Trinity River, toward Beaumont.

We were pushing ninety miles per hour when we heard the short pop of a siren, and the flutter of strobe lights appeared behind us. Mark pulled the car to the shoulder and shut off the engine.

"Shit!" he said, searching through his wallet for his license.

"Well," said Lance, "we've made pretty good time until now. Nice drivin' Earnhardt!"

"Shut up, asshole," said Mark. "I think I have some warrants out around here."

"Afternoon, fellas," said the officer, as he approached the window.

He was a state trooper, and the feeling in the car turned from excitement to nervousness. He looked in the backseat and saw Nicki, surrounded on all sides by a carload of dubious-looking males.

"Are you ok, ma'am?" he asked.

"I'm fine," she said.

Randy looked straight ahead, frozen like a statue. Mark handed the trooper his license. He looked at it, then at Mark.

"No shit!" said the trooper, then turned and walked back to his car.

Fuck," said Mark. "I know I have a warrant out in Beaumont for some unpaid tickets. You assholes better bail me out. Lance, if you leave my ass here, you are so fired."

"No way, dude," said Lance. "I don't think they can arrest you for something like that."

"No," said Mark. "I'm pretty sure they can."

"It's no problem," I said, turning to Lance. "If they take him, we'll just follow the cop to the jail and bail him out. We'll be back on the road in an hour."

Randy continued to stare straight ahead motionless and, after a few minutes, the trooper returned and handed Mark his license.

"Mr. McDaniel, I'm not going to write you a ticket, but could you sign my notebook? My wife's a big fan, and she'll never believe this."

"Sure," said Mark, instantly relaxing. "What's her name?"

"Ellen," the trooper said.

Mark reached over and signed the book: "To Ellen, Hugs and kisses you hot mama, Love, M. McDaniel."

"Oh, that's great," laughed the trooper as his round belly jiggled with delight. "That's just great. She'll love it. Thank you!"

He turned back to his car, then turned back again toward us. As he stuck his head back in the window, Mark jumped in his seat.

"Oh, and try to keep it under 80. Thanks again,"

"No problem, man," said Mark.

The trooper drove away, leaving the five of us in amazed fits of hysterical laughter. Randy, most of all, was relieved, but Mark acted as if he expected the SWAT team to show up and take him away. He signaled, merged back onto the highway, and accelerated to 80, then back to sixty-five.

"Well," I said, "now I know why we brought you along."

━━━━━

We passed through Beaumont, the big oil town east of Houston. The air hung hot with humidity and the dank smell of oil. The refineries pointed out from behind the screen of trees, belching streaks of orange flame into the afternoon sky. We stopped in town to eat, then turned east onto I-10. A half hour later, we crossed the Sabine River into the bayou-filled parishes of southern Louisiana.

Randy watched the world pass quietly by his window while Lance, Mark and I traded road stories. Nicki leaned against Lance in the backseat and laughed at Mark's quips. She was flirting with Randy now, and his arm was draped around her chest. She would constantly interrupt my stories with questions for him.

For me she had only contempt, which helped me to solidify all the reasons I thought she was little more than a tramp, vying for attention from whomever she could get it. However, the trip ahead would afford no time for me to dwell on that, and she wasn't worth the time, anyway. Soon, she would be gone and I would never have to see her again.

30

Just inside the Louisiana state border, we passed a sign that read, "Louisiana State Police Drug Enforcement Checkpoint: 2 miles."

"We have trouble, boys," said Mark. "Anyone have anything on 'em?"

"Why?" asked Randy, snapping to attention and sticking his head between the front seats. "What's going on?"

"We just passed a sign that said there's a drug checkpoint ahead."

"Oh, fuck!" said Randy. "I have some pot on me."

I began to understand why he had acted so nervous during our previous scrape with the law.

"Awesome," said Mark. "You better start eating it or something."

"No way," he said. "Pull off at the next exit and I'll dump it."

"No," said Lance. "Fuck that! As long as you don't have a lot, then they won't find it. All they'll do is run a dog around the car."

"How much do you have?" I asked.

"Just a little bag, no more than a quarter," said Randy.

239

"You'll be fine," I said.

Randy was nervous and sat straight and motionless, just as he had during our last traffic stop. We kept going along the interstate and passed the two-mile mark, then the three-mile mark, and then the four-mile mark. We never came to a checkpoint, and the excited air in the car slowly dissipated.

A little while later we stopped for gas again and Lance asked the cashier at the store about it. He told Lance that the state troopers sometimes put that sign up and then waited at the next exit for people to pull off and dump their drugs. Lance's practical instinct had saved us, and no one even thought to thank him for it.

Soon we were back on the road to New Orleans, with the boisterous air of a group of young people on a road-trip. Lake Charles, Mermentau and Lafayette rose up, then fell away. Outside of Lafayette, we crossed the 10-mile long bridge spanning the Atchafalaya River and its surrounding bayous. Then came the Mississippi River itself: the old man running from the top of the country all the way to the bottom and into the sea.

The sun was setting behind us, and the broad gulf of the newborn night opened her jaws ahead. The great, black bridge arched tall and wide over its dark neighbor below and I thought of an obscure poem by Whitman:

How Solemn! Sweeping this dense black tide!
No friendly lights I' the heaven o'er us;
A murky darkness on either side,
And kindred darkness all before us.

As we crossed the dark, swollen river, it came to me that the waters of every river and stream I had crossed on the road that summer would eventually pass under this cold, steel bridge. The circular motion of everything within the experience forced me to remember that this journey, as all journeys, would eventually come to an end, and only I had the power to ensure the nature of its conclusion. It was increasingly apparent that the fulfillment I was seeking from the adventure had not yet been discovered, and I should either return to the search, or abandon the attempt. The fact that I had spent so long in idle self-gratification nearly brought me to tears, as I might have already missed whatever it was that I was looking for. The only option was to re-commit to the noble pursuit after this debauchery in New Orleans was completed.

I could think only of Bryan Hillary. He would have offered something to this thought—a piece of wisdom, a smile, a nod of agreement. But, he wasn't there. He was in New York by then, probably, and back into the ocean whence he came.

I turned my hot face to the window to try to see down the river to the Gulf of Mexico. The meandering channel offered no straight line of sight, so I returned my thoughts to the events in the car. The mindless chatter, my hate for Nicki, the prospect of a night in New Orleans, and the thought of seeing Naomi again: all of these kept my mind away from the pressing questions, and I gladly accepted their distraction.

———

The interstate turned south at Baton Rouge and began its long dip to New Orleans. Along the highway clung the lines of candescent factories and refineries, the dim lights of run-down gas stations and small, white homes propped on concrete blocks. Finally, New Orleans itself appeared on the horizon, and the mood in the car began to lift.

Lance called Mandy, our host in New Orleans, to get directions, and hung up the phone without writing anything down. We passed close in toward the city center, and the great shadow of the Super-dome came into view. The city was beautiful under its flickering bonnet of light, and her colors felt inviting.

This was just before Hurricane Katrina, when New Orleans was in its rustic, elegant glory, long before her name became synonymous with political fallibility. Past the city to the south was the long, dark shadow of the delta, reaching into the great gulf beyond, drifting currents of blue water sweeping past the city to the Texas Gulf Coast and to Mexico.

"So, Lance," said Mark. "You didn't write down any directions?"

"No way, man," replied Lance, sounding irritated that someone would even suggest that he didn't know where he was going. "She said it was easy to find, right by Tulane. Take the Canal Street exit."

"Okay," said Mark, exiting the highway and pulling up to the stoplight. "Where to now?"

"All right," replied Lance. "Take a left and then go six or seven blocks, then take another left."

"Well, which is it?" asked Mark. "Is it six or seven blocks?"

"We'll say six," said Lance.

"We're going to get lost, and we're going to get shot," I predicted.

"You guys are such guys," Nicki said flirtatiously.

"Now, darlin," said Mark, "this isn't us being guys. This is just a classic example of Lance having his head up his ass!"

"Nonsense," said Lance. "I know exactly where I'm at."

Less than 10 minutes later, we stopped at an intersection far from the festive revelry of the French Quarter.

Several shadowy people lined the streets looking at us, and Lance put his baseball cap on Nicki's head so they wouldn't see that she was a girl. I would have preferred to kick her out of the car and then make our getaway. I started laughing at the idea, and Mark turned toward me angrily.

"What the fuck are you laughing at?" he whispered.

"Nothing," I said.

"Can we get out of here now?" asked Nicki.

"I'm going to try to call Mandy again," said Lance.

"Anyone want to get high?" asked Randy.

We all turned to look at him.

"What?" he asked.

A loud hand slapped the passenger window next to my head and a crazy old white man in overalls stood there cursing and yelling at us with a thick, French accent.

"What zee ell are yoo doing ere, yoo stupid Yankees? Get back to zee quarter before yoo geet killed!" he said, and pointed behind us. "Zat way," he said, "go zat way right now!"

That was all the invitation Mark needed, and he put the car in drive and made a U-turn in the middle of the deserted intersection.

"Nice fuckin' work, Lance!" he said as he accelerated toward the French Quarter. "Now call her and write down the goddamn directions this time."

Lance called Mandy and jotted down a few vague notes on the palm of his hand, nodding into the phone. He told her the turns we had made and where we had ended up, then paused, listening.

"Ohhhhh," he said, "that explains a lot. Okay, thanks, baby. We'll see you in a sec. Bye."

I turned to look at him.

"Okay," he said, slapping his hands together, "we were supposed to take a right on Canal Street, not a left. Wow, I am sorry, I am sorry, I am sorry. That could have worked out badly for us."

═══════════

We found Mandy's place easily this time. It was an old brick tenement on a shady lot, and we shuffled up the stairs to her second-floor apartment. Counting the stops and scrapes with the law, the trip had taken us nearly nine hours, but coffee and Vicodin had done their jobs and we were all ready for a night in New Orleans.

Mandy lived in a small college get-up in an old neighborhood near campus. We were all sharing what amounted to two medium-sized rooms, plus a kitchen and a bathroom. Mandy was happy to see us, and Lance ran in and picked her up in his arms. Then I approached her and we hugged. It was an awkward hug and she patted my back in a distantly friendly way. Our relationship had ended badly and I hadn't seen her since we'd all left school. She and Lance had evidently parted on better terms, and he was the one who excitedly introduced her to the rest of the group.

We all showered in turn, spreading our bags and street clothes in various corners of the apartment. None of us was modest about changing, and we all paraded about the apartment with single-minded determination to get ready and get back to the Quarter.

I showered under the hot water, letting it embrace me. It smelled slightly of sulfur, a characteristic smell coming from old pipes, and bad water. It was an odor that reminded me of my college days in my ancient fraternity house.

By the time I emerged from the bathroom, a towel around my waist, Lance had already discovered Mandy's liquor stash, and everyone had begun taking shots from the bottle as they dressed.

"You better get in there and take your medicine, baby," said Mandy, as she walked past me and into the bathroom. She locked the door behind her, and by her tone of voice, I guessed that she was growing more comfortable with me being there, and possibly even was flirting a bit.

Mark and Lance were talking on the couch, while Randy and Nicki stood in the narrow kitchen. Randy leaned against the counter with a bottle in his hand, talking loudly and waving his free hand around.

"You see, you pretty young thing, we are in New Orleans," he was saying. "Do you know what that means? This is my town, sugar. I grew up just up the river from here and I know how this town works! What we have to do is, we have to eat a late dinner and drink lots of wine, and then descend on the Quarter all with single-purpose determination."

He took a long drink from the bottle, and Nicki's eyes began to glaze.

"Once we are released from the tight requirements of solid consumption," Randy went on, "then we will be free to seek out the darkest corners of the city and, my dear, that is where you will see things that you haven't even imagined."

He turned to look about the room.

"Yes," he said with a satisfied sigh, "this will be a night. This will be a *night*, and we shall remember it always."

He turned to me, wiping his nose and sniffing hard. The area around the base of his nose was red, and I knew that his habits stretched beyond the Vicodin and pot that he had already been sharing.

"This friend of mine here, for example," he said, resting his hand on my shoulder. "After we leave this city, I can't say if I will ever see him again, so we have to make this night count in every possible way! Here, my friend, take this for later, you might need it."

Randy stuck a joint in my shirt pocket and then turned to finish his barrage on Nicki.

On the outer wall of the room, the window sat open and hot ocean air floated into the apartment on a smooth breeze. On the other side of the bubbled frames, beyond the reach of the yellow glow around the building, the distant lights of the French Quarter were calling. The thick smell of salt and the city, the distant sound of music and the bustling crowd of the Quarter screamed high and clear into the black night of the deep, deep South.

31

Weekend nights in the French Quarter were born late in the evening. The six of us left Mandy's apartment around 10:00 and drove to a long parking lot next to the railroad tracks. Beyond them, the tall levees held back the Mississippi, which ran its restricted course high above the Quarter. Occasionally, a ship or a barge would pass and we would look up to see its lights. We started across the lot and waves of people were crossing the sidewalks ahead of us. I felt submerged in the beautiful heat of old New Orleans, and the excitement of the air floating around my bizarre collection of friends.

Going past the Café Du Monde, and across Decatur Street, I felt the breath of the dirty streets and looked down the long rows of buildings with their covered balconies hanging over the tops of the crowds. In long lines, groups of people walked the gray concrete through Jackson Square. We followed them to the statue of the conqueror of New Orleans, under the godly gaze of St. Louis Cathedral. The city held the low clamor of the growing night and music, and blinking neon in the windows. Costumes, billowing jazz from the open doors of the clubs and the bright, blessed crowds; swarming in endless lines and circles through the humid streets, and moving in the timed rhythm of the mystical New Orleans night.

"Yes, my friends," said Randy. "This is what we should have been doing from the start. *This* is were we are supposed to be!"

The expectations that I had of Austin were finally met in New Orleans, and I couldn't agree with him more. The old street exuded a spiritual air and it coursed through the crowds and buildings. I embraced it, and my fears about home and about Naomi, and the lonely and endless ribbons of road, began to drift out of my imagination. I drank in the sweet poetry of the evening, and the machine expanded around and through me.

"Where are we heading?" asked Mark.

"We could eat at Muriel's," said Mandy, "They have a great view from the balcony. It's a little pricey, though."

"Let's go," said Mark. "I'll buy dinner if you all promise I won't have to pay for a drink all night."

"Done," said Lance.

We crossed the square to Muriel's and sat at a long table on the balcony, overlooking Jackson's Square. Beyond the levees, the lights of a barge passing above the Quarter reflected on the rippling waters of the river. Mandy and Nicki excused themselves to the restroom, and the four of us stayed behind.

"Lance," said Mark. "What the hell have you been so quiet about?"

"I'm just waiting for the right time to spring my trap," he replied.

"No," I said, "you *have* been rather quiet."

"Well," he said, "I kind of feel like a jackass for almost getting us killed."

"Ha! Ha!" Randy said loudly. "You *are* a jackass!"

"Don't sweat it, man," I said. "We're here and we're going to have a blast tonight."

"I know, but I just hate looking like an ass in front of females. It throws off my game."

The girls returned, and we ordered and ate as the crowds passed toward Bourbon Street on the sidewalk below. Randy ate very little, and we all drank wine-nearly a bottle each. We were loud and bubbling with the undiluted pulse of the street. It struck me that I was looking at one of the only places in America that still held its old identity, unchanged by the politics of the day. The atmosphere of the restaurant and the city beyond, even in the midst of modern revelers, still bled an archaic elegance that was deeply romantic, yet has all but disappeared from American cities.

We were loud and obnoxious under the hard gazes of the restaurant staff and they tried to hurry us out, but we resisted. After dinner, it was back down to the crowded sidewalks and the pounding rhythms of the night and back amongst the writhing crowds. On the way to Bourbon Street, we stopped in and out of every good bar we could find: Deril's, the Maison, Yo Mama's and others. It took us two hours to get to Bourbon Street, which was only a few blocks from the restaurant.

When we finally found the legendary red-cobblestone road, we went straight into Pat O'Brien's for Hurricanes, the signature drink. This drink marked the beginning of the collapse of the evening-when our fragile collection of personalities began to come apart.

I stood at the bar, talking to Lance, laughing loudly at the crowd and taking shots of warm well whiskey. Mandy, Lance, Nicki and Randy stood around a table in the crowded front room, near the corner of the bar. I glanced over at the group, and Mandy looked back at me. I recognized the look; it was a look that she had given me a long time ago, whenever she'd wanted to disappear into some dark room together, and I smiled at her. She turned away again, and I held the possibilities implicit in that look in my mind. I imagined having an affair with her, and the thought made me smile. Sometimes, even knowing that you have the opportunity for lust with another person is just as fulfilling as taking advantage of it.

Lance elbowed my arm and motioned toward the far end of the room, where a delicate-looking blonde girl stood, talking to her friends near the bare, brick wall.

"Check out that beautiful little honey," he said. "Now *that* is a woman. I wonder how she likes her eggs. Scrambled or fertilized? *Ha! Ha! Haa!*"

Mark had been on his cell phone, but closed it abruptly, swallowed the last of his drink in one forlorn gulp, and called out to the group.

"Let's go!" he yelled.

"Where are we going?" I yelled back.

"We have to meet some people," he said. "It'll be worth it, I promise!"

We collected outside the bar, waiting for Lance, who was trying to talk to the blonde he had been watching.

"How'd it go?" I asked when he finally came outside.

"Oh, she has a boyfriend," he said. "Or a husband or something. I don't know. She didn't like me, so she's probably gay."

"We have to go to the Parish, above House of Blues, and see some friends of mine who are playing tonight," said Mark. "Can you get us there, Mandy?"

"I can get us there," Lance said with a laugh. He was quite drunk by then.

"No way in hell, man," said Mark, turning toward Mandy.

"Yeah," she said, "it's this way."

We all followed behind her. Lance and Nicki walked arm in arm, and Randy and Mark continued a loud conversation about the sad state of the country, which they had evidently started in earnest before leaving the bar.

The House of Blues was at the other end of the Quarter, so we walked to Toulouse Street to hail a cab. An old, black man sat on a folding chair at the corner playing a steel guitar with an intense, concentrated look on his face. Mark reached out and dumped a few wadded-up dollar bills into his guitar case. We all piled into the taxi under the orange glow of a gas streetlight, with the strains of thick delta blues echoing across the street. We threaded through the crowds and pedicabs, and the horse-drawn carriages that tourists could ride for five dollars.

The smells of cigarette smoke and horses, mixed with the sound and smell of the crowds and the street, hung in the air. The entire bouquet of the city drifted through the open window of the taxi.

Large numbers of uniformed servicemen filled the crowded streets: sailors in their tall, white, dress uniforms, Marines in their brilliant black and gold, and soldiers in green. They walked in small groups, in and out of the bars, and collecting in the drunken orgy of the street. I thought that it must have looked like the New Orleans of the 1940s, filled with young men on their way to war, looking to experience one last night of revelry. Indeed, that is the experience that New Orleans always gives to the traveler—a feeling of the past and the present colliding.

The Parish was a small room above the House of Blues and we walked up the long stairs, past a brightly painted bust of the great Satchmo, Louis Armstrong. Mark knew the band playing, and had gotten us all on the guest list. We walked past the ticket booth and the short line of patrons without having to pay.

By that time, Nicki had moved on to Randy full time, and she held his arm as we went into the club, and she smiled excitedly.

Mark's friends were onstage, playing a rocked-out rendition of Bryan Adams' "Summer of '69," complete with an electronic synthesizer. We stood in a line along the far wall, amid the packed crowds of native Texas college kids. The band was good, and the crowd was excited.

Randy disappeared to the bathroom, but none of us followed him. Mandy and Mark began to dance, and Lance and I went to the bar for drinks. I ordered a beer and swallowed two more Vicodin.

"You better go easy on that stuff, man," said Lance.

"What are you? My mother?"

"I should be your mother, you fuckin' drunk," he said, and punched me in the arm.

We laughed and continued to drink. The whole night and indeed the whole trip descended steadily downward in one long spiral. Randy returned and shoved his way past a guy sitting next to us, and pounded on the bar for a beer. The situation was getting bad, and we were on a fast road into the darkness.

At the end of the set, Mark wanted to go backstage to see his friends. He motioned for us to follow him, and we all started toward the back corner of the room.

Randy turned to whisper something to me about the state of the crowd and we fell behind the rest of the group. Ahead, I watched Mark, Lance and Nicki disappear through the stage door. I approached the security guard, a tall man with rippling muscles and no negotiating skills, and told him we were with the group that had just gone back.

He wasn't having any of it, though, and to him, we looked like trouble. He turned us away and we traced the side wall back to the bar. As we walked, I noticed, for the first time, seven elaborate, wood-framed murals lining the wall, depicting the seven deadly sins. I ran my fingers over the carved nameplates: Lust, Gluttony, Avarice, Sloth, Wrath, Envy and Pride. I had touched them all in my adventure, and was oblivious to it the entire time. Randy turned and pointed at the murals.

"That about describes my last two years," he yelled over the noise of the crowd.

We waited for Mark and the others for a while, then gave up and went out to the street to find a good bar. I had Mark's cell number and would catch up with him later. We decided to return to Bourbon Street and paraded ourselves in the colors of the night.

As we passed by the opening of a narrow alley, a shadowy figure stepped out of the darkness and offered me $20 for my pants. I was considering the offer when Randy grabbed the guy by the back of the collar and brought his elbow onto the top of his head, then kicked him in the face with his knee. The man dropped backwards like a wet towel back into the alley. He didn't move, and we ran into the crowd and down the street.

"What the fuck is your problem, man?" I yelled.

"You don't let these guys get away with that shit," he bellowed back. "I grew up here, you don't let them get away with that."

We stopped in the middle of the street and we looked around to make sure no one had seen us. I turned back to Randy. "You're an asshole," I said. "I'm going to find Mark and Lance."

"Don't be such a fag!" he yelled as I walked away.

After a moment I glanced back discreetly and I watched him turn and disappear into the crowd. It was the last time I would see him, and I would have been glad, but I'd been optimistic for the lost young man. I'd had high hopes that I could help him find the right track, but I'd failed in that, too. I'd failed him as I had failed all the others in my life by a lack of dependability. The road began to call to me again. The group was beginning to break apart, and the old shadow from the early road had caught up. I wanted to fly far away from it, and so I would leave New Orleans as soon as I could.

It was about three in the morning and the crowds were beginning to thin. I walked the street alone, the famous Bourbon Street, which was beginning to lose its peculiar innocence to me, and stopped at Pat O'Brien's again. Inside the main bar, standing at the counter, was Lance Hamilton. He was unmistakable with his long hair and six-foot four-inch frame. Next to him was a dark man in leather, and my heart leaped, but it wasn't Bryan.

"Hey there, chief," I said to Lance.

He looked up surprised. "What the hell happened to you guys?"

"Well," I said, "that big mother at the backstage door wouldn't let us in, so we went out to look for another bar. Where's everyone else?"

"Well, Nicki stayed with the guys from that other band, and I lost Mandy and Mark in the crowd. I didn't know where you guys went so I came back here, figuring you might show up. *Voila*! You're here."

I told Lance about Randy's behavior and the incident near the alley, but he didn't seem surprised. The conversation soon moved on to Lance's area of expertise, and we talked about girls and drank until the final toll of last call echoed across the crowded room.

We left the bar with little ceremony, and wandered through the Quarter until pink and orange light began to glow in the east. We sat in the park, under the statue of Andrew Jackson, and talked of times past. It was a calm sort of conversation, the kind that two old friends have before they part ways indefinitely, one of those pure conversations in which we quietly laughed at the strange journey. When the bell of the cathedral tolled five times, we finally stood up and started back to the car.

Lance and I walked quietly through the nearly empty parking lot, amid the blowing trash. We sat in the front seats and I pulled out the joint that Randy had given me at the beginning of the night. I held it up and looked at Lance.

"Might as well," he said.

I lit it, and we leaned our seats back flat so no one could see us. I passed it to Lance, and he passed it back to me. I took a puff and a blur ran past my window, stopped at the hood of the car and ran back toward me. For a split second, a crazy, wild-eyed man stuck his tongue out at me, gave me a thumbs-up, and took off running again. Three cops on foot followed right behind him and they disappeared across the parking lot. Lance looked at me.

"There's no *way* that just happened!" he said, and we laughed together.

We drove slowly back to the apartment, through the dead Sunday traffic, to finally get some rest. Randy's bag was gone, and Nicki was asleep on the couch. Empty bottles and cigarette ash covered the table, and a stack of blankets and pillows sat folded on the kitchen table.

The bright light of day filtered through the thin curtains, and Lance took a blanket and sprawled out in the recliner. I went to the bathroom, and through Mandy's open door, I heard the sound of rustling sheets and the soft moaning of her and Mark in bed together. I grabbed a blanket, found a spot on the floor and went to sleep in disgust.

32

Lance woke me up in the afternoon and I took him and Mark to the airport for their short flight back to Austin. On the way there, we talked about the strange night we had all experienced. I never brought up the fact that I had heard Mark and Mandy in bed together, and Mark had no idea that he had twice interfered with my advances toward women on the trip. The truth was that none of it was his fault at all, and any thought otherwise would have been me trying to push blame away from my own inadequacies. There's no reason that I should care, given that I had made a commitment in my own mind to Naomi. Yet, I was feeling territorial and the facts weighed on me. I felt so low that I just wanted to turn back to Kansas City and go home, and forget the whole adventure ever happened.

The drive to the airport felt like an eternity. Finally, the two men disappeared through the electric doors and into the New Orleans airport. They were off to whatever adventure waited for them down the road. As before, I didn't know when I would see Lance again. I did know that when we crossed paths, somewhere along the way, we would pick up exactly where we'd left off.

I went back to Mandy's apartment with the radio on and the thick, soupy Louisiana wind in my hair. When I got there, Nicki was gone, off with the band that had played at the Parish the night before. It was probable that Naomi wouldn't make it to Key West, and I knew that my recent behavior didn't warrant such a magical prospect. As such, I had almost been tempted to ask Nicki to come east with me, but thankfully, I never had the chance. She passed on in the way Randy had, disappearing back into the world with her own memory of the time we had spent together.

Mandy began to clean the apartment, which showed the wear that our night had inflicted upon it, and I helped her. She told me that I could stay the night if I wanted and I graciously accepted. The uneasy feeling that had run between us when I'd first seen her had vanished completely; now we spent the evening together quietly and diplomatically.

We took a cab back to the Quarter and ate at the Café du Monde, and walked together in the quiet evening streets as the sun set over the top of the levee.

"I liked your friends," she said.

"I know you did, one in particular," I said with a laugh.

She elbowed me in the stomach. "That's not what I meant, smartass!" she said. "I mean I think they all had a good time last night."

"Yeah, but it was kind of a strange night."

"I know, but we had fun, didn't we?" She paused. "So, what are you doing these days? I mean, what are you *doing*? I figured you would have a job and kids and a wife and all that."

"I almost did," I said.

It occurred to me that I had no earthly idea what I was doing out there. My adventure, which had started with such noble expectations, had lost its purpose and I was floating around in an endless void. It was all experience and no meaning now, and the greater glory of the journey had dried up back in Colorado.

Mandy and I walked, and talked about old times and the passionate experiences we had shared in college. We'd raced around our shapeless lives back then, with no real idea about the future, enjoying the freedom that such ignorance could give a young couple.

She wasn't angry with me about the way our relationship had ended, even though it had been my immaturity that had caused its collapse. The relationship had ended the way most passionate relationships end-with long, volatile arguments. My inability to decide if I wanted such a serious relationship had been the spark that ignited the powder, but the relationship had been on feeble ground from the beginning.

In the end, I believed we both understood that our love, if you could call it that, had always been temporary. What we'd loved about each other was the idea of loving each other, for we were too young to know anything else. *I'd* loved her for the most selfish reason of all: I had loved her because I was young.

We slept in the same bed that night, holding one another closely in the dark. We were two lonely souls who found each other again for one night, and we comforted each other the only way we knew how. For a short time, we were able to forget, and to forgive, and to lay in the quiet calm as the world passed us by. The world continued, but without us in it for one sweet, solitary night. Yet, the sounds of the city, trickling in from the thin, glass windows, were continual reminder that reality was just outside.

It was calming to feel the soft heat of another human, that glorious and maternal feminine touch that quells a person's fears and makes all things tolerable. We lay in the bed awake, and talked.

"I'm so bored here," she said.

"But it's such a beautiful city."

She was in graduate school, and just beginning her last summer before her last year, before she would be turned out into the world.

"It's great if a person is visiting, and it's not even the city I'm bored with. I just feel so lonely sometimes," she said.

"I know how you feel," I replied. "Sometimes I think that life is really only about being alone. You never know anyone, no matter how long you've been around them. I mean, you get comfortable with people, but you never *know* them. In the end, they'll all disappear and then nothing will be left. It won't even matter."

Immediately after I said that, I knew that I was wrong—that it did matter. I knew what made Naomi so special to me. I didn't know a lot about her, but I *knew* her. It had never hit me until right then, when I was at the bottom of the well. Too often, the things that I said and the things that I felt were vastly different.

Naomi and I belonged to each other in the same way that we all belong to life, and I had only been kidding myself to think it was anything other than that. I decided that there was only one place I belonged, and it was with her. I would go to Key West, and if she came I would be with her and commit my heart to her. That would be the end of the road for me.

———

I slept well that night and woke before dawn. Mandy did not wake up, but turned slightly as I rolled out of the bed. My few belongings were in a corner of her living room, and I collected them silently. I didn't want to leave without saying goodbye, yet the perfection of our evening together warranted no complication and I was satisfied that we would separate as better people. She had healed an old wound, and I had closed a recent one, and now it was time for me to return to the road alone.

There was a little over 700 miles to go before Sarasota, where I would spend the night with my grandparents, then another 300 miles to Key West. If all went as planned, I would see Naomi on Wednesday night. Her flight was due to get to the island at 8:30 in the evening, and she would take a taxi and meet me at the Weatherstation Inn on Front Street. We had planned it well, and I knew that something profound would happen on that island if she came.

I stopped for fuel on I-10, just outside of New Orleans, where the tall, metal skyline traded itself for the budding tops of the towering cypress trees. At the station, I called my grandparents to let them know I was coming.

"Oh, dear," my grandmother said, "my dear. Don't you know how worried your father is about you? He hasn't heard anything from you in weeks. My God, we all thought you were dead on the side of the highway."

This was the first conversation I'd had with anyone in my family since leaving Kansas City. I had left a couple of cryptic messages with my father, but was never able to get in touch with him. I was anticipating that I would have to deal with a certain amount of backlash from it eventually.

"Your father will be so happy to know you're okay," she continued. "And I'll have to call your Aunt Dorothy, she'll be so happy, too, and my God! Did you say you're coming here today? When? The house looks just terrible. I'm going to have to put your grandfather to work, and oh, he's not going to like that, dear! I'm so glad you called."

It was good to hear my Grandmother's voice again, despite her worry. For one night I would be in a familiar place with familiar people, and it would be a welcome thing after so many weeks in so many strange places.

I got back on the interstate, the great highway across the South. I-10 ran all the way from Los Angeles in the west to Jacksonville, Florida, in the east. It connected the two divergent halves of the country in one long, proud stretch of concrete culture.

Turning east on the highway, I looked in my rearview mirror. Behind me, the highway unrolled to Houston, El Paso and L.A., where the Pacific Ocean unleashed its foaming voice onto the wide beaches of California. In front of me, it crossed the great Gulf Coast through Mobile, Tallahassee, and Jacksonville, to the cold, majestic Atlantic.

From L.A. to Jacksonville, I-10 stretched 2,313 miles. Within the length of every one of those miles is the soul of America, from past to present, and even beyond. Travel the length of it one day, and you will understand.

I followed one part of it, and it took me along the Gulf Coast, through the swamps and bayous and the great open mouth of Mobile

Bay in the hot, humid Gulf Coast sun. The air was alive with a strong, southern breeze, and gray and purple clouds hung in the sky to the south. I smelled rain and salt, and the unbelievable sensations of life once again burned through my body.

I was on the road, and I was on my way into the future, rather than away from it. If Bryan Hillary could have seen me, he would have been proud. I was like a kid going off on my own for the first time. Bryan had done all that he could for me and I was finally able to *live* on my own.

At noon, I passed a sign at the turnoff to Panama City, that wondrous concentration of unfettered adolescent lechery. I had spent many spring breaks there during college, and had drunk in its errant legacy. In Panama City there were no days—only long, endless nights full of bad decisions and fastidious regret. It was the Gomorrah of the South.

In the afternoon I turned south on I-75 toward Tampa, then the city of Tampa Bay came into view and finally over Tampa Bay itself, the long Sunshine Skyway Bridge crouching over the dark blue water. At 7:00, I arrived at my grandparents' house in Osprey, 12 hours and 700 miles after leaving New Orleans. My grandfather answered the door when I knocked.

"Well, look at you," he said. "Back from the dead."

33

He was a tall man, thickly built, with a quiet countenance and deliberate features. When I looked at him, it was easy to tell that he was and always had been a very good-looking man. He had grown up in the 30s, and came with all of the stoic determination that everyone in that generation held in such high regard.

I looked forward to talking to him, and my grandmother, and feeling their simple and stable energy. I hoped that there would be the opportunity to learn something from him, but I resigned myself to, if anything, enjoying a brief stop with familiar people. I was seeking perspective, but I would accept peace of mind as a worthwhile substitute.

I followed the old man into the house, and I heard my grandma's voice from the kitchen. There was something soothing in the sound, something that connected my distant, youthful past to my turbulent present.

"Is he here?" she yelled.

"Yeah," said Granddad. "He looks skinny, too."

She came out of the kitchen, grabbed my hands and kissed me on the cheek with grandmotherly intensity.

"Oh, dear," she said, "have you been feeding yourself at all? What have you been into? I have to finish dinner and you need to rest, so go sit down and we'll talk at dinner."

She led me to a large, comfortable chair, and then disappeared as quickly as she'd arrived. I sat next to Granddad in the living room, and there was a still, familiar quiet between the echoing ticks of a clock from the hall. He folded his newspaper and looked at me.

"So, what's on your mind?" he asked.

"What makes you think something's on my mind?" I replied.

"Well," he said, "when a guy like you just up and disappears like that, there has to be something. I wandered around a bit when I was a boy, but hell, at least I told somebody what I was doing."

In my youth, my granddad had always looked like a man of gigantic stature and worth. He had a thunderous voice and a fearful countenance. Yet, there was a quiet, gentlemanly air about him. He was easy to talk to, and had the innate ability to give advice simply and directly.

"I know," I said, smiling and shaking my head. "I just felt trapped, you know?"

"No, I know all about that," he said.

I told him about the road, and all the reasons I'd left, and as I spoke he smiled and nodded occasionally-as if he had experienced similar situations. I told him the slightly censored version of the story, though, knowing that what I said would all trickle back to my father. At the end, I told him the sordid details about my affair with Naomi: about our promises, how we were in love, the fact that she was married and that I didn't know what to do about it—everything. Mostly, I talked about the future, and how I wished, more than anything, that I knew what was going to happen.

"Do you remember the shaggy dog story I told you a long time ago?" he asked when I was done.

"Of course," I said.

═══════

When I was a kid I'd spent a summer with my grandparents, back when they still lived in Missouri. It had been a perfect summer, beautiful, warm and peaceful. It was then that he had told me that story.

My grandparents had lived at the edge of a lake, in a forest of towering oak trees and great, statuesque pines. Some of my first memories were of that lake, and of my grandparents when they were still young and active. We passed the time together on the trails in the woods, and swimming in the lake. It was there that I'd found my first group of real friends, a group of kids from the neighborhood, and we'd bonded in the shared experiences of catching frogs and playing games in the seemingly endless forests. I had my first kiss on the edge of the lake, and my first experience with heartache.

One day, I went to play baseball with my friends. The day had been beautiful and it had been a great game. There had been a guy on first and a guy on third. The game had been tied and it was late in the afternoon. I had just stepped up to bat and I'd felt the urge to swing with everything I had. The pitch came in low and to the left. I'd dug in with the ball of my foot, swung and connected with a loud crack.

It was a high fly ball to the left, and it had arced and begun to fall toward the house. It had landed on the roof, sailed perfectly through the middle of the glass kitchen skylight, and landed on a vase of flowers. My friends had taken off running, and I was left to explain the damage. When my granddad got home, I'd met him at the door.

"Granddad," I'd said solemnly, "I broke Grandma's vase in the kitchen."

"What happened?" he'd thundered.

"Okay," I began, taking a deep breath. "I broke a vase. I was playing baseball and"

"Wait," he'd said. "This isn't going to be a shaggy dog story, is it?"

"What's that?" I'd asked.

"Here, sit down," he'd said, "and I'll tell you."

We'd sat on the couch in his office, and he'd begun to tell me the story.

"There was an English gentleman who left his estate to travel, on business, to London. When he returned, his manservant met him at the train station. The gentleman asked the manservant if anything notable had happened in his absence.

"'Well, sir,' said the manservant, 'I'm sorry to say that your dog died.'"

"'Oh,' said the gentleman, 'that's not too surprising. Old Rover was getting on in years and—'"

"'No, my lord, he didn't die from old age. He died from eating burnt horse flesh.'"

"'Burnt horse flesh?' asked the gentleman. 'How in the hell did he get a hold of burnt horse flesh?'"

"'Well, it was when the stables burned. We tried to get all the horses out, but—'"

"'The stables burned? How did the stables burn? That was a brand new building. There wasn't anything in it that could catch fire!'"

"'Well,' said the manservant, with a pause, 'It was sparks from the house. They landed on the roof and—'"

"'Wait,' said the gentleman. 'The house burned down? How did the house burn down?'"

"'There was a window open,' said the servant, 'and it blew the curtains into the candles, and they caught fire.'"

"'Candles? What candles? Why were there candles lit in the house?'"

"'Well, sir, they were the candles by the coffin.'"

"'Coffin? What coffin?'"

"'Sir, it was your mother-in-law's coffin. She had a heart attack when she found out that your wife had run away with the gardener.'"

There had been a long pause, and my grandfather had looked at me, waiting for the story to click.

"So you see, my boy," he'd said, "there are two points to remember from this story. Number one, any time someone tells you something, you should always expect that there is more to the story.

Number two, there is no way that you can ever predict how a story, or a situation, is going to turn out. You just have to listen, and see where you are at the end of it."

═══════════

"Yes," I said, "I remember the story. That was a good summer."

The old man looked at me expectantly, and I saw the subtle wisdom of a long life of experience.

"I can't tell you how many times I've almost gone back home." I said.

"No," he said, "you can't do that. You're too far into it now. You go back now and it will haunt you for the rest of your life."

"So what do I do now?" I asked.

"Well," he replied, "for starters, you need to quit trying to plan everything out in your head. It'll all happen the way it's supposed to. The only thing you can do is relax, be a part of the world, be good to the people around you, and let the situation unfold. You can't predict what will happen tomorrow, or in two weeks, or a year from now."

"So I should just sit around and wait for Naomi to figure her life out?"

"No," he said, "I didn't say that. You just have to let life run its course. It'll happen no matter how you try to steer it, but in the end, you have to just let it go."

"I don't mean to be disrespectful, Granddad," I said, "but this is a little more complicated than you're making it."

"Trust me, boy," he said. "One thing I know about life is that it's far less complicated than people would like to believe. Everyone assumes that what they're going through is new, and much more complex and difficult than anyone can know, but the truth is that you're not experiencing anything that hasn't happened before. Look at literature, history… The whole human record is filled with stories like this. You can't possibly think that your problem is the exception. You just need some perspective, that's all—some kind of jolt to pull it all back into place."

There was a long pause. "You remind me a lot of me when I was your age," he said.

"Oh yeah?" I asked. "How's that?"

"Well," he said, "when I wasn't much younger than you, I went through a similar time in my life. After the war, I was about to ship back to the States, but something caught me just before I was supposed to leave. Something told me to stay, so I did. I wandered around Europe, as best as you could in those days anyway. There was just something in my head that wouldn't let me go home—kind of like what you're doing, it sounds. So I did that for a number of months and then I met your grandmother. She was doing some work for the Red Cross in Germany, but she was engaged. Long story short, we fell in love and spent a little time together, but she was honorable about the guy she was with, and I respected that. The night before I was to catch a train back to France, I gave her a letter and told her I loved her and to look me up any time she wanted to when she got back home. After that, I left."

"So I assume she looked you up later?" I asked.

"Oh, yeah," he said. "It turned out she wasn't the only fiancée the guy had. He wasn't even in the Army. He just went around Europe, trying to scam these Red Cross girls."

"What an asshole," I said.

"Yup," he replied, "but I think I got the better end of the deal. Let's see…that was in '46, we got married in '49, and I haven't loved another woman since."

"Okay," I said. "I think I know what you mean."

"No, I'm pretty sure you don't," he said with a laugh, "not yet. But I bet it'll come to you soon."

═══════

After a full dinner and a long chat with my grandmother while I washed dishes, I sat in the quiet reserve of the house. I read old *National Geographic* magazines, trying to imagine the lives behind all of the faces. My grandparents went to bed early, and I sat on the back porch and listened to the wind drift through the rustling palm trees.

The old man had been right about everything. I had struggled the entire trip thinking that I was in a unique situation, but the reality was that I had millennia of human experience to draw upon. There was nothing I could do about what was going on, but allow the future to happen on its own. Since leaving Buena Vista, I had been backsliding down the road to ruin. The time for expectation and careful planning had gone, and I had to face the fact that I had no control over these events at all.

In leaving Kansas City, I had proven to myself that I had the will to leave the socially-accepted mechanics of life behind. Now all I could do was wait and see where I would fit naturally into the world. This, I decided, is how I *would* live from then on.

The next day, Tuesday, I said farewell to my family and returned to the road. Grandma cried when I left, heaped a box full of groceries into the car, and forcefully reminded me to take care of myself. Granddad shook my hand and gave me a long, powerful embrace.

"Good luck to you, my boy," he said. "I know you'll need it, where you're going."

34

As I drove away, they stood on the edge of the driveway, watching until I turned the corner at the end of their street, and then they disappeared behind me. My grandparents were sweet people, and represented the last of a generation that was slowly disappearing. The older I became, the fewer of them remained, and I remember, even as a young man, worrying, even when I was very young, that we had not listened to them as much as we should have. Their story was unique and proud, but there were lessons that we had failed to learn, and it would have been hard to believe that hearing them wouldn't have made us a better people. For they lived, as a generation, in a time that redefined and amplified that great American spirit.

Highway 41 dipped south out of Osprey, and I followed its straight, flat, inland course along the intercoastal waterway. South of Naples, the road turned east through the Everglades and parallel along the Tamiami Canal. Tourist traps and rundown gas stations sat spotted along the road, amongst the tall cypress trees dripping with Spanish moss. At one point, the traffic slowed to a trickle to watch a fat alligator, who sat in the grass on the side of the road, staring back at the cars as they cruised slowly by.

Four hours after leaving my grandparents' house, the skyline of Miami appeared on the horizon, tall and broad against the deep-hued sky.

I made a brief stop in South Beach, then drove along Collins Avenue between the brightly-colored stucco buildings and the rolling khaki dunes of the beach. A small parking lot bordered one of the access points, and I stopped and walked down the boardwalk.

The sun was high above, in the middle of the sky, and its heat dropped down onto the sparkling sand in waves. Tall palm trees lined the border between the art deco world of the city, and the bright sand of the beach and the ocean beyond. The water heaved and reached in swells, then rolled over on itself, falling into foaming breakers on the sand.

I sat near the shore, under the shade of a patch of sea oats, and watched small clumps of people walk by. The tourist season was over, and it was the beginning of the rainy one. The city and the beach were more sparsely populated than I remembered, but the lack of a crowd in the bright heat was a relief.

I went back to the car and turned inland, to the Florida Turnpike and the final turn south to the Keys. Highway 1, near Homestead, ran southwest from the Turnpike, and began its long traverse across the long bridges and the narrow fingers of land jutting out from the southern tip of the peninsula. To the left of the highway bridge, near Bahia Honda, were the abandoned remains of the old Highway 1, built in the fifties, rotting in the light blue water of the shallows. As I lurched closer, I began to feel nervous about the next few days. Would Naomi come? What would I do if the unthinkable happened? What would I do if she didn't come?

By mid-afternoon, I reached the end of Highway 1, at Fleming Street in Key West, then drove to The Weatherstation Inn, near the Mallory Pier, the place where the enormous cruise ships docked. There were no ships in the harbor, but a clump of gathering rain clouds far beyond the pier obscured the sun. In Miami, the sky had been clear, but these menacing clouds began to gather as I descended south, and the threat of distant rain was no longer distant.

The hotel was an elegant, two-story stucco building in Old Town. I checked in with the concierge and went to my room—one of eight in the hotel. My room was on a corner, and there were two windows on each of the outer walls. One set looked out over a tiled piazza, surrounded by a dense garden. It was a serenely beautiful place, the best I had been in during the entire voyage.

The setting in and around the hotel was one of grand, tropical decadence, and I was eager for Naomi to join me. I settled into the room, and outside a light rain began to fall. The windows were open, and the wafting heat and the smell of salt and wet concrete filled the room. The fan circulated above, bringing the heavy air around in great, floating circles.

I lay on the bed with the third and final of the books that I had packed. It was *Narcissus and Goldman* by Herman Hesse, and as I read I listened to the rainfall tap against the wooden shutters. The story was about a passionate and wayward youth, and a scholarly, fatherly figure, and about the journey of life and the often uneasy friendship they shared. The writing style was strange, but I couldn't help smiling at its parallels with my own journey. I paused to think of Bryan, unaware of the terrible series of events that were about to unfold a thousand miles to the north.

When the rain stopped, I put on my shorts and blue button-down, and walked a few blocks to Duval Street, the lively bar and restaurant district of Key West. It was evening, and the street was coming alive with music and gathering crowds of people. Beautiful, tanned Americans and dark-skinned islanders filled the district in an impromptu kind of festival meant to welcome the beginning of hurricane season.

I turned east and followed Duval to Fleming Street, then back to the quiet reserves of Old Town, and through the old naval station. The concrete pier jutted out and around the harbor, past an earthen parapet and the tall, brick walls of Fort Zachary Taylor. I stopped at an elbow of the pier where it turned to the west, and sat on the lip, with my feet hanging over the water, to watch the sunset.

There were sparse groups of people on the walk and the beach just to the east, and the remains of the storm clouds passed overhead. As the sun sank into the water and the last breaths of dying oranges and reds glowed on the horizon, I was struck by the notion that I was sitting on the southernmost point of the United States, and that I had traveled over 4,300 miles since leaving home.

The road on which I had passed spread in one great traverse through swamps, deserts, mountains and plains. I had passed over rivers, valleys and great peaks of gray stone. In those geographical confines, I had experienced the great immensity of the journey, and the promises and disappointments found cradled in its arms. It was a sweet, sweet evening, and I held my breath at its magnificence.

As I sat on the pier I looked west and saw promises yet unfulfilled, and memories of my triumphs and falls, but for that brief time on the edge of the world, I was at peace just knowing how far I had come. The distance had been great, but the experience had been greater. In the setting sun I saw the faces of everyone I'd met along the way, all the memories of friends who had come and gone, and the belief in love that I had come to rediscover.

There is a sense of accomplishment and character that comes to a person after climbing mountains, crossing continents and beholding the great ocean of a life finally lived. All of the sunsets and all of the sunrises came as one grand adventure in the remembering. A life lived is difficult, a life less lived is forgotten, and on that pier, there was no doubt in my mind which was better.

When the sun was gone, I walked along the quiet side of Fleming Street, past the courthouse, to the Blue Heaven on Thomas Street, for dinner. As I ate, I watched the crowd and read the *Key West Citizen*, the city's daily newspaper. I sat outside and read by the light of a string of globe bulbs between a pole and the corner of the building. A tan and dignified older woman, who proclaimed herself as a life-time resident of the island, served me my dinner. We chatted briefly during a lull, and she told me about all the people who came to Key West to find their souls.

"They think they can come down here, hop off a plane, and plant their toes in the sand and cure all their troubles," she said.

"No," I agreed. "It isn't that easy. You spend your whole life getting everything lost and confused, and then expect that a couple of days of vacation a year will solve it all? That's just not the way it goes."

"Hell no, babe," she said, "and I guarantee, we're the only ones here who understand that."

She cleared off the table, and I sat in the comfort of the dark, moonless night. Within the still air the sweltering heat of the day had begun to ebb and chased the sun over the edge of the horizon. The waitress, Karen, brought me a cup of thick, black coffee and a slice Key Lime pie with ice cream. They were both delicious, and I ate them vigorously. For a short time the tart, sweet pie and the cold cream wrenched the exhausting memory of the voyage from my mind for a short time. The beautiful tastes, and the smell of the sea on the edge of the world— this was the perfect serenity. The breeze was fanning across the open courtyard from the south and a dark-colored chicken clucked and strutted across the gray cobblestones of the square.

When I left the Blue Heaven I wandered back down the sandy streets near the naval station, back past the fort again, and I came to a long beach. The white sand was still warm from the day, and I lay down and rested the back of my head on my hands. In the gathering black of night I listened to the waves rolling onto the land and lapping at the barrier islands just off shore.

The lights of a tall ship, as she rode at anchor, reflected off the bobbing water, and I knew that I was witnessing perfection. The winds stretched northward from Cuba and from the great, dark waters of the Gulf and the Isthmus of Panama beyond. I wrote a poem in my head:

How many sights the wind must see
across the gulf of time,
how many days do I lay back and
wish its memory were mine.

I walked back to the hotel under a fast-moving sky, and fell asleep in the cradling heat of the dense, tropical air.

⸻

Early in the morning, the sun poured through the open window, and I walked to the sill and admired the brilliance of the day. I took my book and a large hotel towel to the beach on the other side of the fort.

Because it was early still, there were few people on the beach, though the heat had already permeated every crevice. I left my towel and the book on the sand and waded into the salt water, past the low-breaking waves. The turquoise water rolled past, and when the next decent-sized wave came along, I dove into it, broke its base with my arms and shot out of the water on the other side. I swam with the rolling tops far out into the water and the water turned to a deep blue. As the earth sank from beneath me and the water was deeper I had the sensation that I was flying.

This was not the dirty Gulf of Mexico I had seen in New Orleans. This was the Atlantic, in her ancient and mysterious power. The water was cool, and the salt stung in my eyes, but I felt its baptismal immersion as it both enveloped me and glided past. My arms and shoulders flexed, free from the constraints of the dry land, and I pushed against the water until I had reached the small barrier island, then turned and pushed again back to the shore.

When I came to the beach, I stumbled awkwardly through the surf to the soft sand and once again onto dry land. I lay on my towel and let the sun dry me. That was a Wednesday morning, the day that Naomi was due to arrive—or not arrive, depending on the will of fate.

When I left the beach for the hotel, I walked along the pier. A cruise ship had docked during the night and the eastern sun reflected across its towering, white hull. It was held to the pier with long docking lines, which looked small in comparison to the mammoth liner. From my vantage point, the thick ropes looked like a web, tying the great ship to the land. The deck was alive with people in motion on the deck, and crewmembers tending to their duties. Tiny strings of passengers streamed across the gangway and onto the pier for their day of exploration on the island.

There was a small coffee shop just down the street from the hotel, and I changed clothes and walked to it. On the way I passed by the Little White House—the vacation home of President Truman, with its sweeping white porches, and three squat chimneys pointing skyward from the ridgeline of the roof.

I sat in the coffee shop and ate breakfast, and drank a thick cup of South American coffee, and continued to read Hesse. Naomi's plane was scheduled to land in Key West that evening, and she was to meet me at the hotel. I had the whole day to wait in mounting anticipation. As I sat, soaked in the inanimate air, a young girl cleared dishes from a nearby table. She was small and dark, the color of earth, with a sweet smile.

"Are you enjoying the morning?" she asked.

"Yes," I said. "I've already had a swim in the ocean. It's a great day so far."

"It's going to rain later, though," she said.

"Really?" I asked. "It doesn't look like it right now."

"It's the rainy season," she said. "It rains almost every day now."

The air was still, and we were alone on the patio, accompanied only by the screech of gulls on the pier, and the rustle of ceramic in her small, brown hands.

"Where are you from?" I asked.

"I grew up in Miami," she replied, "but I was born in Nuevitas. It's in Cuba."

"What's Cuba like?"

"I don't remember," she said. "I left when I was very young. My family is still in Miami."

She turned away with her dishes and walked toward the door. She stopped, and then turned back and smiled at me. She was a beautiful young woman, with an unforgettable grace. She had the image of an American, a soul from a distant land, surviving as best she could.

The entire day had yet to pass and I was already counting the minutes. The rains came again in the afternoon, but this time they stayed into the night. I spent the rest of the day in the hotel, reading until I could stand waiting no more. I would go to the airport and meet her, that way, at least, I would be able to fill the time. The concierge called me a taxi and I went to the airport to meet Naomi. I said a little prayer on my way out the door that she would be on the plane when it got there.

I asked the driver to stop at a store along the way and I bought her a flower, a single red rose, and continued north. We arrived at the airport at 5:00, and her plane was to get in at 7:00. I went to the airline desk to check on the flight, and it was on time—in fact, it was already in the air. I found a row of seats outside the security entrance and waited for what felt like an eternity.

When the time came for her plane to land, I stood up and walked to the middle of the terminal hall, near the security checkpoint, and watched the tired faces streaming through the high, glass doors. My heart thumped wildly in my chest. A long line of people came through, and I watched expectantly. Soon the flow began to trickle, and then stopped. The TSA official at the exit door looked at me knowingly, as if she understood that the person I was waiting for wasn't coming.

Naomi had not come. I had been so excited, so expectant, and for nothing. I felt my heart grow weak. I turned away quietly. All around me, people were returning to the arms of the ones they loved, but I was empty-handed. I dropped the rose onto the cold, marble floor, and walked outside to the curb to hail a cab back to the hotel.

On the ride back, I held my face out the open window of the taxi and let the damp air surround me. I tried to remember the words of my granddad, tried to remember that I should let life happen and not read into it. Fate would intervene if Naomi and I were supposed to be together. Just because I didn't get what I wanted didn't mean it wasn't going to happen at all.

In the end, though, the pain was overwhelming and I could think only the worst thoughts of Naomi, and had only fears about my abilities as a lover. It was impossible to avoid, and unthinkable to accept.

I rode the distance back to the hotel with the window down, in dejected silence. The rain was falling again, and far offshore, a yellow flash of lightning reverberated in the puffing clouds. The air smelled wet and dead, and all things closed around me.

When I got back to the hotel, I went straight to the room. As I walked through the lobby, the concierge smiled. He was being polite, but to me, he looked like he was laughing at my misfortune. There was no way he could have known what had occurred, but the pain was affecting every bit of me. I wanted to hit him, but instead, I nodded and walked away.

In the room, I sat on the bed and listened to the rain. The memory of the last half of the journey washed over me and I remembered that I had behaved so badly over the last weeks. If karma had any part to play then I definitely did not deserve to see Naomi. If it were true that all things worked in their own way, and that people do indeed reap what they sow, then the fact that Naomi wasn't with me in Key West was entirely my own fault. Somehow, this made me begin to feel better about the situation, and even a bit relieved that our feelings for each other would not be strained by another illicit affair.

I picked up the phone and called Kansas City to check my voicemail. I hadn't listened to my messages in some time and I wanted to see if there were perhaps a message from Naomi, explaining why she didn't come. I scrolled through the list of old messages, listening to that long sequence of forgotten names and missed appointments.

It was in that string of unheard voices that I learned that Bryan Hillary was dead.

35

A person's life can change in a heartbeat, in a single solitary second. As in the moment when I'd looked at Beth for the last time, after overhearing her conversation in Kansas City, or perhaps the instant when I'd decided to turn left in that little town in Kansas and begin my journey instead of going back home. Or the decision to stop in State Bridge, or the first second when I discovered my deep feelings for Naomi.

Then, there was the long string of bad decisions that I had made between Buena Vista and Key West-the drinking, drugs and the careless lifestyle. All of those moments, those small decisions, changed the course of my journey and the outcome of my life on the road. Yet, none of those situations had changed my manner of thinking quite like hearing of the death of Bryan Hillary.

I had received a call from Bryan's brother, whose name Bryan had mentioned only once. He'd left me two messages. In the first one, he'd told me that Bryan had talked about me and that he'd found my number in Bryan's wallet, and asked me to call him immediately when I got his message. On the second, he'd told me that Bryan was gone.

Late on Tuesday night, Bryan and a young woman had been leaving his parents' house in Bridgehampton when they were hit head-on by a drunken tourist who had wandered into their lane, going around a curve. Bryan had died immediately, the girl a few hours later. The driver of the other car had lived, walking away from the accident with minor injuries. He was alive, and Bryan Hillary was dead. Such is life.

The phone receiver clicked and the dial tone buzzed intermittently in my ear. I hung up, and walked downstairs and into the piazza next to the hotel. The rain was gone, and only the soft drops of water falling from the leaves of the mangroves echoed against the gray stucco walls. The courtyard was dark, and the light from the hotel windows reflected off the small pools of water on the red-tiled floor.

Bryan was a friend, a brother, and we had shared exciting times together. He was behind every beautiful discovery and every terrible experience that I had come to find on the long road. Because of his enthusiasm and intense adoration for all the joys of life and of the journey, he had persuaded me to continue. His mind had been resilient, and he had been a survivor in all the ways I was not. The idea that he was no longer alive seemed foreign to me—unbelievable, unthinkable. A world without Bryan seemed like a terrible place to have to live. Bryan was dead, and I remained in the world to suffer.

There was a small trail through the thick vegetation, and I followed it, crossing Front Street to the wet, sandy roads and the pier. The cruise liner was gone, and I was alone. Slowly, I made my way to the very end of the pier, then turned to face the town.

Across the quiet mouth of the harbor, life continued as it always had. The people in Key West continued in their day-to-day pursuits with no idea of what had happened. Beyond the city, far across the Gulf to New Orleans, Austin, Pueblo, State Bridge, Cody and McCook, the world continued in mechanical revolutions with no pause and no sympathy for the memory of my friend.

As I stood on the pier, separated from the world, I tried to see whether there was still good left in it. In the end, I didn't know how to feel. I had no perspective. I was neither sad nor angry. I simply existed in an otherwise uncaring world.

I walked back to the hotel and called Mark in Austin, to tell him what had happened. It's hard for two people to know what to say to each other in that kind of situation, so I cut the call short and asked him to tell Lance, and we planned to meet at JFK Airport the following afternoon, then drive to Southampton to help bury our friend.

The line clicked and went dead. I called the airline and bought a ticket on a flight leaving at 9:00 the next morning for Miami, then one that would get me to JFK in New York at two. Mark called back to tell me that he and Lance would be in at three, and to meet him at the American Airlines counter, at the gate.

I put the phone on the cradle, turned off the lamp and lay back on the bed. Only a few hours before, I had assumed that my friend was alive. Now, I had a plane ticket to New York and a schedule to follow. It all seemed to happen so quickly, and in the absence of any freedom of thought, I had forgotten about my missed appointment with Naomi. The night passed sleeplessly, and I lay in the dark room as the minutes ticked away.

The next morning was a Thursday. According to Bryan's brother, there would be a wake on that night and a funeral mass and burial on Friday afternoon. I woke with the sun, packed my few possessions in the quiet of the morning and left the hotel for the last time.

The coffee shop down the street was open—I could smell its earthy aromas in the glare of the morning—and I walked to it for breakfast. The young girl was not there, and I ordered coffee and a muffin from the older man behind the counter, then asked him to call a cab for me.

On the long flight from Miami to New York, I sat by the window and watched the ocean pass underneath, the east coast in the distance. As we flew over the country at 30,000 feet, I thought about my travels, with and without Bryan, across the West. Several times, in the vast, open skies of Wyoming, Colorado and New Mexico, I had seen the long contrails of jets crisscrossing through the air, high above.

I remembered thinking of the people onboard those planes, zooming from all points on the map, from west to east and back again, and wondered if they ever gave any thought to everything going on below them. Traveling over the country at 500 miles per hour is an efficient way to travel, but not one that allows a person to see the country in the same way as a car or a train. Traveling along the ground allows for time to engage the mind in thoughts of life and the world. Each town, each house and each mountain contains stories of humankind. In each building or patch of land, there are stories, either from the past or the present, that involves a life, or many lives.

Every minute of time is duplicated in a unique way by every person in the world. Each life has its own use of time, and it is impossible to imagine them all. Yet, you can watch the fixtures on the land, and imagine the lives that dwell, and have dwelled, within them. We read and write stories to capture as much of that humanity as we can, but how many worthwhile events happen every day whose stories will never be told?

Too often, for me, the experience of life was only what I would see close around me, and I would mostly ignore the fact that there were lives beginning and lives ending, lives surviving and lives flourishing, all over the world. Life is the present, and the present happens to everyone at the same time. Each breathing soul on the planet has a different set of experiences, thoughts, emotions and memories, and they change with every singular heartbeat. It would be difficult to look at the world as it *truly* is and see anything but naked equality. From 30,000 feet, though, the view became obscured.

———————

The plane landed at JFK, and I disembarked into the massing throngs of traveling humanity. There was a bank of monitors near the gate, and I scanned the arrivals screen as people streamed past, and found Lance's and Mark's flight, on time and due to arrive in an hour. I walked to their gate, detached from the world around me, and sat down to wait in the terrible confusion of the terminal. I hadn't slept well the night before, and the white noise of the crowds lulled me into a light sleep.

"Hey, man," said a voice out of the darkness.

I felt a heavy hand on my shoulder, and shuttered and opened my eyes to see Mark and Lance standing over me. I stood up and the three of us embraced, then left the airport by a long parkway east, to Southampton, where our dead friend waited.

There were nearly a hundred miles between the airport and Southampton, and we drove through the descending sprawl of the city in silence. After the death of a friend it is difficult for survivors to convey emotion to one another. The three of us had known a man who had always been alive, and alive with an intense passion, but in the car that day there was no way to describe how we felt about his death. The words simply did not come.

I think that we looked on death, in general, as only a formality. A wake and a funeral weren't ways to remember or memorialize a person. Funerals exist to comfort those who remain alive, giving them closure and a chance to say goodbye to someone else's life. They are the ritual wherein the living can mourn their loss, and the historical record provides the world with a date from whence that dead person exists no more.

The unspoken truth in the car that day was that we didn't want to forget, and we didn't want closure. We wanted to remember our friend as a living, breathing memory in all of us, not a cold body stuck in a metal box. However, we were all present for his funeral because tradition dictated that we should be. I wasn't going to his funeral to say goodbye; I was going so that what remained of his life in my own memory would be present at his death.

After the funeral mass the next day, Lance, Mark and I followed the hearse to the cemetery. I was glad to have them with me, even though they'd only known Bryan through their short experience with him in State Bridge, and my stories of him. We filed silently around the open vault and waited for the pallbearers to carry the box to the grave.

The priest began to speak, talking about grief and loss, and reciting the biblical references that assured everyone present that Bryan Hillary was in a better place. As he spoke, my thoughts turned to the road and the beautiful memory of him.

It felt wrong to bury our friend in the salty air of the outland leg of Long Island, so far away from the Western beauty in which we'd known him. Yet, that was where he lay, above the cold ground, with a carpet of false grass around the dark hollow that was his eternal rest. We were strangers at his funeral, standing far away from the groups of people clumped around the grave, muffling sobs or mourning silently. We did not know him as they had, and they did not know him as *we* had.

36

With the death of my friend and the end of the innocence of the adventure, I began the long trip home. I flew back to Key West to get the car and then drove north alone, all the way to Kansas City, in one great stride across the South and back into the Midwest.

As I drove, I gave the landscape little notice. I was held captive in the reality of everything that had happened, and this part of the trip seemed dead to me. I passed through the sprawling cities of Miami and Atlanta, over the tops of the Smoky Mountains and down into Chattanooga, then to Nashville, St. Louis and finally, the long traverse across the Missouri plains to Kansas City.

The circle had been completed, and I turned down the wide, tree-lined street where I had passed Beth on my way out of town, which was now over a month past.

The loop had led me nearly 6,000 miles across the country, only to bring me back to the place where I had started. The strangeness of the road is immeasurable. You can never know where it will lead you, or who you will be when you get there.

Something felt different about my old city when I returned. The streets were smaller, the houses looked older and the possibilities of life seemed strangely different from when I had left.

My house was dark and empty, and I opened the front door and paused. Inside, there was a cavernous gloom and a musty odor, and I walked slowly from room to room, to feel the widening gap between that life and this. All of Beth's personal belongings were gone, and a thin layer of dust covered everything. I went upstairs and slept for almost a full day, then awoke to begin my life—a new life, with all of the beauty and freedom that I had not experienced before.

Yet, as I looked back on my journey across the heart of our country, I couldn't help but think that there was a door that had not been closed. There were certain pieces that I had hoped to find out there, something to tie what had happened before I'd left to what happened after. I sat in the still quiet of my empty house, searching through my vast array of experiences looking for the one thing that would tie it all together. Nothing came to mind.

Then I thumbed through the stacks of bills and magazines piled on a table near my front door, and saw an envelope in a familiar hand. It was from Bryan. The date on the postmark read June third—three days before his death. I opened the envelope and looked at the small collection of pages, and the elegant handwriting of my friend. The letter read:

My dear friend,

If this letter finds you, I hope it finds you well. If you are reading this, then you are home, and probably trying to understand why.

I myself have settled back into the old life, and I have to say that it was everything I expected it to be. Though I am very happy that I have worked things out with my family, and I have resumed the normalcy of the standard life that you always talked about, I have to say that I am not without deep regret.

There are days when I have to remind myself why I am here, and why I chose to return to the life that I never really saw as mine in the first place. I find myself looking out the window and trying to see all the way into the West, where I know you are with Lance and Mark and all of our memories crowded around you in one long, beautiful story. I'm sorry to say, my friend, that I feel as though I let you down by going back to all the things that we promised each other we would never experience again. Believe me, though, that it has all been done in loving loyalty to my family, and to what my heart told me to do.

However, there are a few things that I want to tell you before I disappear back into life. If I may, I would like to tell you what my experience on the road has led me to believe. Perhaps it will help you when you return.

First of all, it took me a long time to realize that there is no magic moment out there that will change your life, or your outlook on the world. When we were riding together, we were always looking for the next thing, the next experience, the next golden cow. However, it wasn't until I came back home that I realized that it isn't one part of the journey that is important; it isn't even the whole thing. It is the memory of the journey that you will carry with you, and the memories you have within the journey, that you will have forever.

Life is a snapshot memory, my friend, and it is strange and beautiful. If you don't remember that, then it will all pass you by and you will never know it was there to miss. When you look back, all you have are snapshot memories—small flashes of past experience. They are the memory of a sight, a smell, the look in a person's eye— anything that reminds you of something pure.

You can never cure the past, and you can never reinvent yourself; all you can do is live so that when you reach the end, you will look back with fondness at all of those snapshots that you carry. What you do becomes the past very quickly, but what you remember, your memories, will always guide your future.

If what you do is beautiful, then your memories will be beautiful, and in turn, your life will be everything you want it to be. You don't have to always walk away from parts of your life that don't work—just always remember that what you do right now will determine who you are forever.

It has been a pleasure to know you and learn with you, my friend. No matter what happens to us, we can always live on in memory. I hope I can see you again soon, and we can take that last trip together across the ocean. Then, we will see where life takes us.

Your friend,
Bryan

I folded the letter, smiled, and went back to the business of living.

———

Through the rest of the summer and into fall, I did my best to mend the rift with my father and the rest of my family, the best way I knew how. He hated the fact that I had left my job the way I had; to him, it was always business.

Everyone else didn't seem to trust me anymore. I'm sure that everything that happened had been good gossip, and I became the black sheep of the family who no one understood. In the end, I knew that time and good will would be all that could heal the wound that I had deliberately inflicted, and that had kept my family and me at bitter odds.

I never went back to corporate America. As summer went on and the employment market began to thin, I took a job as a waiter at a small bar near my house. In the fall, I enrolled in the university to take some English classes, and when winter came, I planned to apply for admission to the graduate program. My father went along with my plan, mostly out of consolation for what he described to others as my "little breakdown."

As summer turned to fall and fall turned to winter, I settled into a routine of sorts. I talked to Naomi from time to time, but our conversations were initially very distant and I think we both were trying to relieve our past expectations of each other. She did tell me that she and Dan had split up for good finally, and that a divorce was underway.

"It wasn't fair to keep lying to myself and to him at the same time," she said. "I told him everything about you and me, and released it all to the universe."

As we continued to talk during those months, our conversations began to unfold, as they had when we were together in Colorado, and in them came the possibility that our time together might be approaching. I was still trying not to hope, or to force the future, and so I never made any real plans to see her. We never talked about getting together, aside from frequent allusions to our lack of physical presence.

Yet, through our conversations, we learned a great deal about each other—our pasts, our beliefs and our best and worst moments. Our love only grew, and the purity and simplicity of it became increasingly evident. Love isn't a feeling, or an experience, or a shared attraction. Love simply exists.

━━━━━━━

Winter came and went, and soon the faint green haze of spring began to appear in the landscape. As the days became longer and warmer, I couldn't help but turn my wandering eye toward the road again. It was that time of the year, when curious, wayward travelers across the country would take to the back-roads of the country. First in the South, and then further north as summer inched its way up the continent, doors would fling open and those young spirits would take to the highways.

While my eye was transfixed on the road, I stayed in the relative comfort of my home, knowing that the time would come again one day, very soon, and I would turn my course once again to the West and leave the safe confines of home, perhaps for the last time, and find my way to Colorado and back to my friend, and my love.

═══════════

Sometimes at night, after coming back from the west, I would lay awake in bed and look at the great, arcing ascent of the moon over the sky, and think of the road. That same moon hangs over the entire world, and in its boundless glow, all events of the past come rushing back like snapshots scattered out over the floor. I would think of my love, I would think of Bryan Hillary, I would think of the limitless roads of the mind, and of life.

I would imagine Naomi looking at the same moon from the boardwalk in State Bridge. I knew that she would think of me, and that someday, I would see her again. Someday, we would have the opportunity to love each other in the way the world intended.

There was an expectation in my heart that I would see *all* of them again, even Bryan, in that great voyage through life, and on to its final stop. We begin and we end in the same way; our eyes open and then they close. As in a river, we begin where we end, and always come back again.

When we take that last breath, all things growing black, it is impossible to know if we've lived perfectly. We can only know that we *did* live, and we know that in our pages of memory, we will see all that made life beautiful, and that will be the afterlife.

We have our snapshots, and we leave them behind however we can to the people in our lives. We travel the great expanses of life, and we all do it together; in it, we find our identity. In the end, after life's simplicities are complicated by our continual search for answers, we must ultimately understand that we all come back to where we begin and we are all connected in our common, mortal humanity. The journey is what defines us, how we live and love, and we all have the same destination, no matter where on the road we begin.

For in the end, all roads are rivers, looping and sweeping across the land, and carrying us on through the corridors of the world. We scatter our snapshot memories along the way for ourselves and for others.

Roads and rivers are life; they begin with us and carry us through our short time on this earth, then back to where the end meets the beginning.

I will always go back to the road in my mind and remember that there had been a time when I'd pretended to live, and a time when I actually did. A sweet, simple moment when I decided to live for life, rather than with it.